IT'S HAPPENED AGAIN

A tale of love, hope, death & disappointment
Arsenal 15-16

IT'S
HAPPENED
AGAIN

Tim Charlesworth

First Published in 2016

Printed by CreateSpace, an Amazon.com Company

© Tim Charlesworth 2016

© Berkshire Trading Ltd. 2016

www.itshappenedagain.com

All mistakes in the book are undoubtedly attributable to me and not to the sources I have used

Every effort has been made to trace copyright owners and seek appropriate permissions. If you have any enquiries, please contact me on

info@itshappenedagain.com

For Julia
I love you more than Arsenal

CONTENTS

BEFORE WE GET STARTED	1
A POTTED HISTORY OF ARSENAL FC	13
THE CUSTODIANS	51
BACK IN THE DOLDRUMS	79
THE CURATE'S EGG	111
HOPE SPRINGS ETERNAL	171
DISAPPOINTMENT & DEATH	243
GRINDING TO A HALT	309
IT'S HAPPENED AGAIN	353

IT'S HAPPENED AGAIN

May 12th 1979
Wembley
England

"A bunch of silken grace and elegance called Liam Brady (think Mesut Ozil in tight shorts with an Irish accent) dribbled effortlessly down the left hand side, evading the Manchester orcs who were trying to scythe him down. Just as the orcs closed in, he cheekily dinked the ball to his left, into the path of pacy Arsenal and England winger, Graham Rix. Rix swept the ball across the penalty area, and just when the chance seemed to have gone, a ball of fuzzy 70s afro hair, called Alan Sunderland, ghosted in from nowhere at the far post and swept the ball into the net, past the despairing United keeper. I was just six years old, but I was smitten, and could never love another football team."

BEFORE WE GET STARTED

IT'S HAPPENED AGAIN

Let's be up front here. This first section is supposed to be an introduction, but really it's the ramblings of a middle aged man, so if you want to skip to the football stuff (very wise if you ask me), just go to The Curate's Egg later in this book. If you think the author is interesting after reading his footballish ramblings, you can always come back and read this bit later. You won't miss anything terribly important by skipping straight to the football stuff anyway.

First of all, let's be clear about the purpose of this book. I am a poor accountant (I can feel your sympathy flowing out to me) with a wife and three children. These dear attachments eat money at an alarming rate, certainly faster than I can earn it. I reckoned that if I could sell a few of these books, I might keep the bailiff from the door a bit longer. It's a bit of a gamble, because I have spent ages writing it, and I might not make any money at all, but who knows.

I appreciate that this is not very high minded of me. Writing is supposed to be an art form after all, but if we are to be friends over the next few hundred pages, I thought I should be straight with you. I do also hope that you enjoy the book and everything, but realistically the endless challenge of paying my children's expenses (swimming, gym, football, dance, Chinese alabaster doll dressing classes etc. etc.) comes first.

Anyway, so this is how I put my plan into action. I have wanted to 'write a book' since my late teens. I am now 43, and at no point have I ever threatened the world of publishing. In fact I have never produced any more than about 10% of a book. In the parlance of management gobbledegook, I am most definitely not a 'completer-finisher'. As you might imagine, over the decades, I have rather lost faith in my ability to 'write a book'. To do so, I have discovered, takes an awful lot of discipline and application, which I don't seem to have. A book is about 80,000 words as a rule, and to write 1,000 words takes me a good four hours. 320 hours is an awful lot of time to find. It's nearly an hour every day for a year. And it's worse than this; you need to also do tricky things like plan your book, do research, have a plot (or subject) and various other tedious things. The research is generally a killer as it needs hundreds of hours and lots of access to libraries etc. So when I have got round to writing a book, one, or more of the following happens

- I get mired in research
- I fail to come up with a good plan
- I lose interest in my original subject or story
- I think of another book that I would rather write and start that

So frankly, if you are reading this, a minor miracle has occurred and I have actually progressed from someone able to write 10% of a book to someone able to write 100% of a book (well done me).

I discussed the problem of my endless failures to write a book ('whinged about it' would be a more accurate description) with my long-suffering wife. "Why don't you try writing about something that you are really interested in dear?" she suggested; "What about Arsenal?" (She suffers a lot from 'hearing about Arsenal' and was perhaps hoping I would talk to my laptop, rather than her). I patiently explained to her that the internet is full of tedious and long-winded writings about Arsenal, and that my semi-informed tuppence worth would be of no value to anyone, commercially or otherwise. My lovely wife is a bit naïve like this and I often have to put her straight on worldly matters[*].

Writing about Arsenal worked for Nick Hornby. His first book was pretty much a book about being an Arsenal fan. If you

---

[*] During our courting years I made a gift to my wife (who has a stunning mane of auburn hair) of a tshirt with a life-sized picture of Freddie Ljungberg's head, complete with scarlet-dyed hair, emblazoned across the chest. The caption read 'We love you Freddie because you've got red hair'. She even had the grace to wear it occasionally (usually whilst painting or doing the gardening). As if this wasn't bad enough, the first dance at our wedding was taken to 'Can't Take My Eyes Off You' by Frankie Valli and the Four Seasons (the tune on which Freddie's famous song is based)

IT'S HAPPENED AGAIN

haven't read Fever Pitch, you really should. It's far better than this book, so stop this now and start that one. If you still want to read another book about Arsenal, come back afterwards.

I had clearly established, through long experience, that I was not capable of writing a book. But maybe, I thought, I am capable of writing a series of short articles for a website. This is becoming an increasingly popular way of writing a book. I have read a number of books that were clearly written in this manner. In fact, this idea is in the finest of literary traditions: Charles Dickens wrote his early books for publication in instalments in a magazine (internet blogs not being available).

Anyway, in the name of getting me to finally finish writing a book, I came up with the following plan:

1. Write a series of articles about Arsenal - I am not going to lose interest in Arsenal. Like many football fans, I am way too obsessed for this to be a realistic risk
2. I am always reading about Arsenal, or watching them play anyway, so I effectively already do the research. I don't need to find any extra time, as I already waste much of my time in this fashion
3. Find a website to publish the articles - this will allow me to get feedback in real time on my writing. I don't want to run a blog myself as this will distract me from the writing. By publishing on an already existing blog, I avoid having to create a readership and administer a website
4. Aim to do one a week. This will neatly give me about 40 articles, averaging about 1,500 words each, so 60,000 words. Add 20,000 words of 'filler' (like you are reading now) and I have an 80,000 word book
5. It is possible, if I can be published by a successful and widely read website, that I will establish a reputation and maybe even a readership following before the book is even published. This would be good for sales

6. Do it for a season - this means I create a book in less than a year. It is a fixed timescale, which even a fickle idiot like me will struggle to worm out of
7. At the end of the season, I can just stick the bits together and self-publish on Amazon for Kindle readers etc. I don't need to find a publisher or even print any books

Hey presto, some sort of blog collection, or Arsenal annual. It will be a sort of record of the season just gone. This will be ideal for the Christmas market. It will be especially good if Arsenal have a good season, as it can be a sort of memento of happy times. Hmm.

It has often struck me that a football season is really a great story. It's an epic, lasting almost ten months. It is full of drama, trials and tribulations, controversy and even tragedy. And, unlike many works of fiction, the outcome is authentic. It's not contrived or dramatized: it is real life. When outrageous things happen, like Gabriel being sent off instead of Costa, or Micky Thomas' last minute goal, we can't complain that the story is far-fetched or outlandish. It really happened. And it's more than that. For supporters, a season is something that we live through, with all its highs and lows. It's not just any story, it's our story. And it's a love story.

And yet, it's so hard to find an example of a football season recorded as a true story. We can find the scores and results on the internet, but these don't tell us about the emotions, the tales behind it all, the hopes, the fears, the unexpected triumphs, the heart dropping failures. And these are the things that we really love football for, not the 2-1 result or the fact that Giroud scored after 24 minutes. So this book is my attempt to record the real story of a football season. Only for one team and only for one season, but at least it's a start.

So I have recorded the scores and the scorers. I also give you the team, and the three most useful (in my opinion) statistics: shots on target, shots and possession. But these facts are just context, a necessary backdrop. The real story of the

IT'S HAPPENED AGAIN

season is in the articles that were originally published on Untold Arsenal.

As I mentioned earlier, Nick Hornby is a far superior writer to me. So I can't do better than to quote his description of the essential nature of 'football-season-as-story':

A MATTER OF LIFE AND DEATH
CRYSTAL PALACE VS. LIVERPOOL
October 1972

I have learned things from the game. Much of my knowledge of locations in Britain and Europe comes not from school, but from away games or the sports pages, and hooliganism has given me both a taste for sociology and a degree of fieldwork experience. I have learned the value of investing time and emotion in things I cannot control, and of belonging to a community whose aspiration I share completely and uncritically. And on my first visit to Selhurst Park with my Friend Frog, I saw a dead body, still my first, and learned a little bit about, well, life itself.

As we walked toward the railway station after the game, we saw the man lying in the road, partially covered by a raincoat, a purple-and-blue Palace scarf around his neck. Another younger man was crouched over him, and the two of us crossed the road and went to have a look.

'Is he all right?' Frog asked.

The man shook his head. 'No. Dead. I was just walking behind him and he keeled over.'

He looked dead. He was grey and, as far as we were concerned, unimaginably motionless. We were impressed. Frog sensed a story that would interest not only the fourth year but much of the fifth as well. 'Who done him? Scousers?'

At this point the man lost patience. 'No. He's had a heart attack, you little prats. Now fuck off.'

TIM CHARLESWORTH

And we did, and that was the end of the incident. But it has never been very far away from me since then, my one and only image of death; it is an image which instructs. The Palace scarf, a banal and homely detail; the timing (after the game, but mid-season), the stranger paying distressed but ultimately detached attention. And, of course, the two idiotic teenagers gawping at a tiny tragedy with unembarrassed fascination, even glee.

It worries me, the prospect of dying mid-season like that, but of course, in all probability I will die sometime between August and May. We have the naïve expectation that when we go, we won't be leaving any loose ends lying around: we will have made our peace with our children, left them happy and stable, and we will have achieved more or less everything that we wanted to with our lives. It's all nonsense, of course, and football fans contemplating their own mortality know that it is all nonsense. There will be hundreds of loose ends. Maybe we will die the night before our team appears at Wembley, or the day after a European Cup first-leg match, or in the middle of a promotion campaign or a relegation battle, and there is every prospect, according to many theories about the afterlife, that we will not be able to discover the eventual outcome. The whole point about death, metaphorically speaking, is that it is almost bound to occur before the major trophies have been awarded. The man lying on the pavement would not, as Frog observed on the way home, discover whether Palace stayed up or not that season; nor that they would continue to bob up and down between the divisions over the next twenty years, that they would change their colours half a dozen times, that they would eventually reach their first FA Cup Final, or that they would end up running around with the legend 'VIRGIN' plastered all over their shirts. That's life, though.

Fever Pitch, Nick Hornby, pp62-65

I like this piece of writing for many reasons. It is witty and honest. It wonderfully sums up the silliness of youth -'Who done him? Scousers?' and yet it's also sad, because it recounts the death of someone who, just like me, loved their team. Most of all, it tells us something about the nature of the football

IT'S HAPPENED AGAIN

supporter. Hornby worries about dying in the middle of a season. Notice he doesn't give a moment's consideration for the man's wife or children. His real interest in the incident is what it reveals about the issues that might surround his own death.

The instructive point, however, is that it never occurs to Hornby that he might have lost interest in football by the time of his own death, or that he might not support Arsenal any more. Neither of these ideas merit the slightest consideration, despite the fact that the teenage Hornby might expect to live another 60 years or so at the time of this incident.

And this reminds us of the true nature of football supporters. Endless studies have shown that a man is more likely to change just about anything in life (including his wife) than his football team. This is quite extraordinary when you think of some of the terrible things that football teams can do - and do - to their fans. The owners of Glasgow Rangers, the leading team in Scottish football, recently bankrupted their club by pursuing irresponsible financial policies, including playing fast and loose with tax law. Rangers were relegated four divisions following administration and liquidation, but I haven't heard of a single fan that gave up on them as a result of this debacle. Not one!

When I was first living with my wife, unencumbered by offspring, we used to leave each other affectionate little post-it notes around the house, as young couples do. My wife, who understands more about football than perhaps she cares to, kept one of these notes by her bedside table for many years. It simply read: "I love you more than Arsenal", and she understood what it meant. The, now lost, note is commemorated in the dedication of this book.

In recent decades, marketing people have started to recognise this for the perfect opportunity that it is, and that's one of the reasons why there is suddenly so much money in football. Football fans have what marketing people think of as perfect 'brand loyalty'. And I know that this is true of me. I might occasionally admire another football team, perhaps appreciate the style that they play in, live next to their ground, or even conceivably be employed by them. But the truth is that Arsenal will always be my first love[*].

Over the next 20 years, Arsenal will probably change every single player, coaching employee and director, yet I know I will still be loyal. They don't even play in the same stadium that I used to visit as a child. They wear different shirts, with a different badge on their chests. The only thing that has stayed constant is the name, and even that commemorates a closed down munitions factory south of the Thames in Woolwich!

My loyalty is absurd, and yet somehow it isn't. My loyalty is in the tradition of generations, legions, of working men, who unswervingly supported 'The Arsenal' throughout the twentieth century, man's most terrible, and yet wonderful epoch. They stood and cheered their team through thick and thin, in wind, rain and hail. My loyalty recalls their steadfastness. It recalls their quiet dignity. In tough times, the football was their outlet, their little pleasure, the escape that made life liveable. And I rather like that thought.

In front of the North Bank stand at the Emirates is a life size bronze statue of Tony Adams, Mr Arsenal, arms aloft in celebration. The statue, which will undoubtedly outlive 49 year old Adams, lovingly records the moment that he sealed the league title with a goal against Everton in 1998. Adams, a centre half, scored the goal from a through ball from fellow centre half Steve Bould. Both men were veterans, but rejuvenated by the arrival of new Manager Arsène Wenger. They were part of the legendary but dour back four who had served Arsenal for a decade. The goal, scored on a riotous spring day, symbolised the

---

[*] Interestingly enough, there is one exception to this rule. I have a little boy, who is quite good at football. Like many football-loving dads, I fondly imagine that he might be a professional footballer one day. Should this happen, it is unlikely that he will play for Arsenal. If he ever plays against Arsenal, I am pretty sure that I will hope that Arsenal lose

IT'S HAPPENED AGAIN

revolution that Wenger had brought to Arsenal, making it possible for two 'blockers' to engage in such an expressive and adventurous form of football.

In his celebration, Adams (the statue) overlooks a low stepped wall, known as the North Bank Terrace. The terrace is decorated with thousands of 'stones'. The stones are really a commercial initiative, but they contain personalised messages from Arsenal fans (who have paid for the privilege) deeply engraved in stone for all eternity. The messages are often poignant, memorialising lost grandads and fathers who supported Arsenal all their lives. There is a sense that the terrace contains the spirit of many an Arsenal fan past. Of course, as time passes, this will become more and more true. The authors of the messages will slowly die, until eventually, every single one will be a message from beyond the grave.

The terrace is also littered with messages from fans proclaiming that they are 'Arsenal 'til I die'. I don't really like this phrase, which has become fashionable with fans of many clubs. The internet and social media is littered with such proclamations. Whilst undoubtedly accurate, it seems unnecessarily morbid, even a little crass. It also carries a slightly intimidatory undertone which I don't really care for; suggestive of being prepared to die for the cause. But in the context of the terrace, the message seems strangely appropriate. I look at some of these messages and muse 'well… after writing that, you're going to be Arsenal after you die too'.

I may dislike the phrase, but the truth is that just like Hornby and just like virtually every other Arsenal fan around the world, I am Arsenal 'til I die.

A POTTED HISTORY OF ARSENAL FC

CHAPTER ONE
A GAME CALLED FOOTBALL

It is often said that football was invented by the English. This is, of course, complete and utter tosh.

Football portrayed on an ancient Greek vase

The origin of football is hard to identify. Certainly, the Ancient Greeks and Romans played a similar game. Indeed, games played with air filled balls can be found all over the world, including aboriginal Australia, native North America and ancient China. Various forms of football were played throughout the middle ages with a wide variety of rules in different regions and eras It is not clear whether the name 'football' refers to the fact that the ball is struck with the foot, or the fact that it was played 'on foot' (as opposed to on horseback or sitting down).

Football was a casual leisure activity, so it is not well recorded by historians. However, more than 30 English laws passed between 1314 and 1667 tried to ban the game, suggesting that it was every bit as popular then as now (if it wasn't popular then why so much effort?). The reasons for the bans were various from 'creating a disturbance' to 'endangering national security by distracting men from archery practice'. The game also seems to have been as widely loved across all strata of society as today. Henry VIII was one of the kings to try to ban football, but a pair of football boots is listed in the inventory of his possessions at his death.

The game became formalised thanks to the efforts of public school boys in the early nineteenth century, who started to write down rules and regulations governing things such as size of goals, number of players, goalkeepers etc. The earliest known of these codes is the popular 1815 Eton code. However, each school created its own rules. The growth of the railways in the 1840s made inter-school matches a practical possibility, with the variations in the rules then becoming a problem.

When football playing boys went up to Oxford and Cambridge, they found that they didn't have a common understanding of the rules. This led to the development of the Cambridge rules in 1848, which were widely adopted. However, alternative codes, notably the Sheffield rules, were still widely played.

IT'S HAPPENED AGAIN

Various attempts were made to standardise, but it proved difficult as the men from each school were keen to retain the bits of code unique to them. The main problem was that some codes allowed players to pick the ball up in their hands, and others allowed players only to kick the ball with their feet. This created different styles of 'tackling': in the codes where players held the ball in their hands it was necessary to physically manhandle the player in possession to the ground in order to recover the ball, whereas in codes where 'handling' was not allowed, it was sufficient to dispossess your opponent by just kicking the ball away.

The main division was between schools who played on fields (Rugby, St Pauls, Wellington), and those who played in paved courtyards (Winchester, Harrow, Eton, Charterhouse). In schools that played on paved courtyards or cloisters, manhandling the player to the ground was dangerous and painful, whereas on a nice grassy field, such things were more acceptable[*].

In 1863 twelve clubs got together at the Freemasons Tavern in London to form the 'Football Association' in another attempt to standardise the rules. This code was first known as the 'London rules', but later just the 'Association Rules' after it was merged with other sets, most notably the Sheffield rules, which introduced concepts such as the corner and free kick. 175 years later the 'FA' is still going, although all but one of those original twelve clubs have ceased to exist (Civil Service FC is the sole survivor). The FA is the progenitor of the modern world game, and it is this fact that has led to the claim that Englishmen

---

[*] The traditional story, that there was a game called football, where nobody handled the ball until William Webb Ellis, a Rugby schoolboy, picked it up one day in 1823, is attractive, but entirely apocryphal. In fact, the rugby version of the game may be closer to archaic forms of football than the more popular soccer code that has become the world's most popular game Certainly, 'scrummages' are common to many of the surviving forms of football, as is the handling of the ball in routine play. So it is curious that the Rugby community itself, perpetuates the myth that Rugby is some kind of descendant or variant of true football

invented football. The modern word 'soccer' is a slang contraction of 'association footballer'.

One of the twelve clubs, Blackheath, withdrew from the process of setting up the FA in protest that the rules allowing 'running with the ball in hand' had been repealed. Blackheath, originally formed as an 'old boys' club for former pupils of 'Blackheath Proprietary School', continued as a club, playing matches against other clubs that played the 'Rugby style' game. Eventually, in 1871, 22 clubs (including Blackheath and my alma mater St Pauls School) which played the 'Rugby style game' got together at the Pall Mall restaurant on Regent Street and formed the Rugby Football Union.

Blackheath, which still exists today (unlike the eponymous school which closed in 1907), is the oldest rugby club in the world. It has the distinction of having been present at the founding meetings of both the Rugby Football Union and the Football Association, demonstrating neatly how indistinguishable these early codes of football were[*].

In 1871 the FA introduced its famous 'Challenge Cup'. The FA (Challenge) Cup is still contested annually today, with Arsenal and Manchester United jointly holding the record for the most wins (12 each).

As the nineteenth century wore on various Factory Acts were passed which tried to stop working class children from spending all their waking hours in factories. The idea was to allow some time for them to go to school, but inevitably they also used their new found freedom to play football. The result was that working

---

[*] Francis Campbell, representing Blackheath at the fifth meeting of the FA, argued that: hacking was an essential element of 'football' and that to eliminate hacking would "do away with all the courage and pluck from the game, and I will be bound over to bring over a lot of Frenchmen who would beat you with a week's practice", thus demonstrating both the prevalence of other forms of football in other countries and the disdain of public school boys for foreigners. Blackheath withdrew from the FA at the sixth meeting in protest at this and other issues

IT'S HAPPENED AGAIN

class children and, in time, working class men, started to become as good at football as the public school boys.

The football world changed forever during the 1883 FA Cup final. Defending champions Old Etonians lost 2-1 to Blackburn Olympic after extra time, in front of 8,000 at the Kennington Oval (now exclusively a cricket ground). Blackburn (folded 1889) were the first professional team to win the FA Cup and no amateur team would ever win it again.

We have to remember that at this point in time the English public school boys were a pre-eminent power, not only in England, but the entire world. Britain was the leading superpower of the time and public schools were considered the training grounds of the global elite. There was little doubt that 'God is an Englishman' and even less doubt that public schoolboys were his (he was definitely male) chosen agents on earth.

The 'Corinthian Spirit', the embodiment of the public school values of 'grit', 'pluck' and 'trying jolly hard' were not to be trifled with. Professionalism and training were considered forms of cheating. As the game became ever more popular with the working classes, public school boys struggled to hold on to their monopoly of football administration. In particular they were less numerous in the North of England, where they had lost control of the rugby associations, and soon lost control of the county FAs there. The tide of professionalism became unstoppable. Football is a physical game, in which stamina and strength are huge advantages and working men were naturally better conditioned than gentlemen of leisure.

Both of the main football codes were now at a crossroads. Clubs like Blackburn Olympic were flouting the amateur rules by arranging sham jobs for their players. It became clear that the professional tide was unstoppable; that the amateurs could not compete with the professionals. The Football Association relented in 1885, when 30 northern clubs threatened to pull away and form the professional 'British Football Association'.

The Rugby Football Union didn't want to give in to such threats and as a result split into two in 1895; to form a professional League based in the north (now known as Rugby League) and an amateur game based in the south (Rugby Union). Rugby Union remained an amateur code until 1995.

Twelve of the FA clubs from the north and midlands that had threatened to break away, now formed their own competition. Although the FA had reluctantly allowed professionalism, it would not countenance a professional league so, in 1888, the clubs formed their own organisation known as the 'Football League'. Crucially, unlike the Rugby League, the Football League decided not to form its own rules code, so the Football League clubs remained within the mainstream game. Top flight football would not, however, return to the control of the FA until 1992, when the Premier League was formed.

Even after the formation of the Football League, the London FA still had considerable autonomy and resisted the distasteful Northern fashion for professional players until 1891, when it finally relented and momentously allowed Woolwich Arsenal to become the first professional team in London.

CHAPTER TWO
THE BIRTH OF ARSENAL

Arsenal was born in 1886 into a world with no cars, no antibiotics and no internet. The original kits were borrowed from Nottingham Forest (hence the red colour).

Telephones had just been invented, but you couldn't phone anyone because no-one else had a phone to answer your call, and you most certainly couldn't walk around with one in your pocket! Germany was a new country, just 15 years old, having formed in 1871. Its people had not yet developed any tradition of successful penalty taking. Queen Victoria was queen, not just of Britain, but also a vast and haughty global empire. Global empires need armed forces to govern them, and armed forces need explosives, shells and gunpowder to keep them fed. Such things were manufactured in Woolwich, East London, and such a place is known as an 'arsenal'. The Royal Arsenal in Woolwich was, in fact, the largest site in the world for the production and storage of munitions. You had to be very careful with matches! It was a factory of death and injury, but it also produced something wonderful and still beautiful today when, in 1886, its workers decided to form a football team.

TIM CHARLESWORTH

The club still has a cannon on its badge in memory of its origins and the club's official merchandise shop is known as 'The Armoury'. Supporters themselves, are known as 'Gunners' or, more colloquially, 'Gooners'.

At its peak, during the First World War, the Woolwich Arsenal employed 80,000 people and closed as a factory as recently as 1967, after over 200 years. The Ministry of Defence finally left the site in 1994, and this once secret and secure area is now being redeveloped as housing, with many of the original buildings restored and converted to flats.

In 1893 the mutually owned football club was reformed as a limited company, and became the first club from southern England to join the Football League. It also changed its name to from Royal Arsenal to Woolwich Arsenal. The club was initially very successful: if you lived in London and you wanted to see the amazing professional players from northern England, Arsenal was the only place to go. As the crowds flocked, the club became wealthy and was able to pay for better players, securing promotion to the First Division in 1904, but then things started to go downhill. In 1907 Chelsea were also promoted, and in

IT'S HAPPENED AGAIN

1909 Tottenham Hotspur joined them. Now there were three teams in London where you could go to see the northern superstars. Arsenal were based in Plumstead. Isolated from the rest of London with poor public transport connections, Plumstead's very inaccessibility is the reason it had been chosen to house the secret Royal Arsenal in the first place.

Football fans in the early years of the twentieth century were more fickle than today and many of them chose to go to Tottenham or Chelsea instead. Income at the Manor Ground in Plumstead fell and the club was bankrupt by 1910, subsequently purchased by a businessman called Henry Norris, who was also the owner of Fulham.

Norris' next idea was to merge Fulham and Arsenal, but the Football League blocked him, leaving Norris to possibly regret his purchase. Arsenal drifted, and were relegated at the end of the 1912-13 season. Over 100 years later, this is still the only time that Arsenal have ever suffered that fate. Norris, exasperated, came up with another idea for his ailing club. In 1913 he moved Arsenal to an area called Highbury in Islington, North London, some 20 miles away. This represented a massive risk for Norris, at huge cost, but he was rewarded with average attendance of 23,000 in the first season in Islington (compared to 11,000 the previous year). The club renamed itself 'The Arsenal', and later just 'Arsenal', as the Woolwich prefix was no longer appropriate. The new Arsenal was only three miles from Tottenham, and the Tottenham fans felt that Arsenal had somewhat invaded their 'patch'. This long established rivalry continues to the present day.

Arsenal, now ensconced in Islington, finished fifth in the Second Division in the last season (1914-15) before the League was suspended for World War One. For the reopening of the League in the 1919-20 season, it was decided to expand from 20 to 22 teams. One of the extra places was awarded to Chelsea, who had been relegated after finishing 19th in the First Division, with the other place awarded by election. Arsenal were joined in the ballot by Tottenham, who had finished 20th in the First Division; and Barnsley and Wolves, who had finished third and fourth respectively in the Second Division. Surprisingly, Arsenal won, with Tottenham in second place. Any chance of good relations between the two clubs was gone forever. Unevidenced accusations have flown ever since that Arsenal owner Norris bought votes, Blatter style, in this election. Arsenal have never been relegated since this incident, and comfortably hold the record for the longest unbroken stint in the top Division (the second longest is Everton: 1954-55 to present). The 100 year anniversary is nearly upon us!

Meanwhile, Arsenal FC meandered along in its mundane trophyless existence, now in Islington, until it hired Herbert Chapman as Manager in 1925. Chapman was a visionary whose influence is still felt in the modern game; concepts such as shirt numbers, European club competitions and floodlights were all pioneered by him. He even introduced white sleeves to the Arsenal strip to improve the ability of his players to pick out team mates. Before his time the strip was a darker shade of red, much more in keeping with the original kit borrowed from Nottingham Forest. The original colour (known as the blackcurrant strip) was revived as a one-off for the 2005-6 season (the last at the old Highbury stadium).

CHAPTER THREE
HERBERT CHAPMAN & THE BANK OF ENGLAND CLUB

Herbert Chapman was born in Kiveton Park, near Rotherham, Yorkshire, in 1878, as one of eleven children in a remarkable coal mining family. The Chapman boys were determined to escape the insularity of the mining community. Being a professional footballer was quite a novel concept in 1900, but two of Chapman's brothers played professionally, including Harry, who won two League Championships with Sheffield Wednesday. Another brother, Matthew, became a director of Grimsby Town. Herbert was a bright child and his chosen method of escape route was through education. He won a place at Sheffield Technical College (now Sheffield University) to study mining engineering.

But Herbert could never quite get football out of his blood. He played most of his career as an amateur, holding down a job besides his football. All in all, he played for 11 clubs (including Tottenham for whom he played professionally and scored 14 times).

After his retirement as a player at the end of a two year spell at Tottenham, his commitment to football seemed rather half hearted, and he never seemed quite convinced that it was a better career option than engineering. He recommended one of his Tottenham team mates as a Manager to his former team Northampton, but the player in question, Walter Bull, changed his mind and turned down the Northampton job, recommending to the club that they hire Chapman instead. Chapman transformed Northampton and was offered a job as Manager of Second Division Leeds City, who were improving under Chapman when the war intervened. Football was suspended and Chapman took a job managing a munitions factory.

He returned to Leeds briefly after the war, but abruptly resigned in December 1918 to take a job as a superintendent at an oil and coke factory. Shortly after he left, Leeds City was embroiled in a corruption scandal. The players were sold off and their ground, Elland Road, was taken over by the newly formed Leeds United. Five club officials, including Chapman, were banned from football for life. And so it seemed that Chapman's long 'on-off' relationship with football was at an end.

Fate intervened in late 1920, when the factory he worked at was sold and he was laid off. Chapman was now unemployed. Huddersfield Town's Manager, the deliciously named Ambrose Langley, was a former team mate of Herbert's brother Harry in the all-conquering Sheffield Wednesday teams of a decade earlier and persuaded his board to support Chapman in an appeal against his ban. Chapman was cleared, on the grounds that he had been the Manager of a munitions factory - and not even in Leeds - at the time of the foul play. Chapman was employed as Langley's assistant, replacing him as Manager just one month later.

This time, Chapman never looked back. He won the FA Cup (Huddersfield's first major trophy) in his first full season, the League in his third season, and retained it the following year (including a 5-0 win over Arsenal). Chapman was then lured to Arsenal and thus denied the opportunity to become the first Manager ever to win three League titles in a row. Without him, Chapman's team did go on to win a third title, becoming the first team ever to do so, in 1925-26. Even today, only three other teams: Arsenal, Liverpool and Manchester United have repeated the feat. No team has ever completed four consecutive titles; Huddersfield never won it again after the 1925-26 season.

Success was slow to come for Chapman at Arsenal by modern standards. Arsenal won its first real trophy, the FA Cup, in 1930, and then the floodgates opened. Arsenal won the First Division in 1930-31, 1932-33, 1933-34, 1934-35 and 1937-38. This was an era of swashbuckling heroes such as Denis

IT'S HAPPENED AGAIN

Compton, who played for the 1937-38 Arsenal title winning team. He also played 78 cricket test matches for England. By the outbreak of World War II, the club was widely recognised as the best in the world.

This bronze bust of Herbert Chapman is probably the club's most celebrated treasure. It was created by pioneering sculptor Sir Jacob Epstein and commissioned just before Chapman's death in 1934. It was displayed for many years in the famous Marble Halls of Highbury and now resides at the Directors' Club Entrance in the Emirates. A bronze bust of Arsène Wenger is displayed nearby.

The money poured into Arsenal and the club became known as the Bank of England because of its wealth. The Arsenal Stadium (known universally as Highbury) became a modern super-stadium during the 1930s; with a 73,000 capacity. Its iconic East and West Stands, complete with their legendary marble halls, were built in the art deco style fashionable in the 1930s and are now listed buildings in which you can buy a flat if you have enough money. The nearby tube station, Gillespie Road, was renamed 'Arsenal'.

The 1930s were truly Arsenal's golden age. Sadly this period is receding from living memory now and few supporters remain from this time. Only the history books, the black and white photos and the silverware remain.

Arsenal became the second team (after Huddersfield) to win three consecutive titles: in 1932-33, 33-34 and 34-35. But Chapman was again denied the opportunity to become the first Manager to achieve this feat. Death took him in January 1934, with Arsenal top of the League. The achievement of three consecutive titles by a Manager would not be completed in the twentieth century. Sir Alex Ferguson finally achieved it with Manchester United in 2000-01.

Chapman died of pneumonia, probably brought on by overwork. Like many of the best Managers (including Arsène Wenger), he loved his job and pursued it to the exclusion of everything else. He celebrated New Year 1934 at home in London before travelling on a scouting trip to watch Bury play Notts. County on 1st January 1934. On the 2nd he travelled to Sheffield to watch Arsenal's next opponents, Sheffield Wednesday, spending that night in his home town of Kiveton Park. He returned to London with a cold, but still watched Arsenal's third team play Guildford City on the 3rd. His cold developed into pneumonia and he died at home in the early hours of 6th January 1934; revered to this day both by Arsenal, and the wider football community around the world, as one of the all-time greats.

CHAPTER FOUR
POST WAR ARSENAL

Arsenal failed to recover from the wartime break. In 1947-48, the old team, including Denis Compton and his brother Leslie, had one last hurrah, winning the First Division. An FA Cup followed the next season, and a final First Division title in 1952-53, but Arsenal were living on past glories and went into a long decline.

The light emerged again in 1970 when Arsenal won the Inter-City Fairs Cup, the forerunner of today's UEFA Cup/Europa League. It was a second tier European trophy, but the team were inspired and won the legendary 'double' in 1970-71, becoming only the second team (after Tottenham) in the twentieth century to do so. The 'double' meant winning the First Division and the FA Cup in the same year, an honour which had eluded even the great 1930's Arsenal teams.

But the double was a false dawn. The team broke up and returned to mediocrity. Three FA Cup finals were reached in the late 70s, but only the middle one was won in 1979. It was only one, but what a glorious win it was; back in the days when the FA Cup final was the single biggest match in the world, rivalling even the World Cup final for global coverage. Arsenal gloriously dominated Manchester United throughout and led 2-0 with only five minutes to go. But United scored two quick goals and despair gripped my six year old heart, watching on TV with my Dad and his Arsenal supporting best friend. But with 89 minutes on the clock, a moment I would never forget:

A bunch of silken grace and elegance called Liam Brady (think of Mesut Ozil in tight shorts with an Irish accent) dribbled effortlessly down the left hand side, evading the Manchester orcs who were trying to scythe him down. Just as the orcs closed in, he cheekily dinked the ball to his left, into the path of pacy Arsenal and England winger, Graham Rix. Rix swept the ball across the penalty area, and just when the chance seemed to have gone, a ball of fuzzy 70s afro hair called Alan Sunderland, ghosted in from nowhere at the far post and swept the ball into the net, past the despairing United keeper. Joy had turned to tragedy and, in a second, back to joy unbounded. I was smitten, and could never love another football team.

This was probably the most dramatic FA Cup final played in the old Wembley stadium. If you have never seen the goal, look on YouTube; it was a truly magical moment just eight days after Margaret Thatcher had become Prime Minister of Britain. The world would never be the same again.

Losing faith in my Willie

I was irretrievably in love, but Arsenal was set to disappoint for a while yet. More mediocrity followed, including losing the 1980 FA Cup final to Second Division West Ham. Arsenal, the overwhelming favourites, had reached the final by defeating Liverpool, the leading team of the day, in an epic semi-final that concluded with a *third* replay (the previous three matches all having been drawn).

To add to my woes, I was invited to a school buddy's birthday party that clashed with the match and my mother, to my eternal disgust, made me go. This was a disaster, but actually the party was quite good and I found out later that Arsenal had lost 1-0. It was the first (and not last) time I was glad to have missed an Arsenal game. I knew what it felt like when Manchester United had equalised the previous year and I realised that an entire game of defeat would be ten times worse. The whole thing was too awful. The winner was a header scored by Trevor Brooking, a player with magical feet, but not known to have scored before or since with a header. I'm not sure why, but this made it worse.

The 1980 final is famous for one of Arsenal's less glorious moments, which also made a great impression on me. Seventeen

IT'S HAPPENED AGAIN

year old West Ham midfielder Paul Allen became the youngest player to play in a Wembley Cup final that day. He received a lot of media attention before the match. Three minutes from the end of the game, as Arsenal desperately chased the equaliser, space opened up for Allen and he was through on goal. The defenders were hopelessly beaten and Allen had only the goalkeeper to defeat. One of the beaten defenders was Arsenal's legendary flame-haired centre-half Willie Young, a legend for a number of reasons which don't really include being good at football: his wonderful red hair, the general propensity of Arsenal fans to idolise 'honest' centre-halves and the wonderful 'chantability' of his name - chants along the lines of "we have a Willie and you don't" particularly appealed to my seven year old sense of humour.

On this occasion Young was hopelessly beaten. He launched himself through the air and just managed to clip the back of Allen's ankles. The ball was a good four feet away from the point of Young's tackle, leaving nobody in any doubt that he was going for the man and not the ball. Allen was brought down and so denied a golden opportunity to wrap up the match with a famous goal. West Ham got a free kick just outside the box and Young got a yellow card. I loved Willie, but this was a moment that told me that the world might be a little more complicated than I had first thought. Clearly this was wrong, and everyone was upset. Even Willie himself looked a little unsure about the wisdom of his actions. Allen reinforced the injustice of it all by howling, tears running down his face, as he collected his winner's medal. As a seven year old who would respond to injustice in a similar manner, those tears were all too easy to relate to. The general outcry at this incident led directly to the rule change allowing referees to dismiss a player for a professional foul that denies a goal scoring opportunity. It also led directly to a realisation on my part; that Arsenal players were not infallible.

1979-80 was in fact a great tale of woe. Arsenal were simply out on their feet by the end of the season. As well as the FA Cup semi-final epic, the season was further lengthened by a run to the final of the UEFA Cup Winners Cup. Four days after the West Ham debacle, Arsenal faced Valencia in the crumbling Heysel Stadium in Belgium. The Arsenal fans returned with complaints that the stadium was unfit to host a major European final which sadly fell on deaf ears. There were 39 Cup Winners Cup finals between 1961 and 1999, when the competition was abolished. No team ever retained the trophy, despite the winners getting an automatic entry, and only one final (this one) was decided on penalties. The only other occasion that the game nearly ended in penalties was in 1995 when defending champions Arsenal got within seconds of a penalty shootout, only for former Tottenham player Nayim to score by lobbing the goalkeeper from just past the half way line (it's not all Alan Sunderland moments!).

In 1980, Arsenal scored the same number of goals as they had in the FA Cup final four days earlier (none). But they made it to penalties after a dour 0-0 match. The wonderful Liam Brady missed his penalty, but it was four-all after the first five penalties. This meant 'sudden death' - my first introduction as a seven year old to this rather startling phrase. I soon discovered the true meaning of it as Graham Rix missed the sixth penalty and we lost. He literally looked too tired to hit it hard. Liam Brady was sold to Juventus in the summer and a little bit of Arsenal magic was gone forever.

The second coming of Gorgeous George
Another six years of mediocrity ended in 1986, when the Arsenal Board brought back one of the 71 double winning team, George Graham, as Manager.

Gorgeous George was the youngest of seven children. Born in November 1944 in a small village just outside Glasgow, George's father died on Christmas Day 1944 from heart failure and tuberculosis, when George was just a month old. A war weary Britain had little spare sympathy for his mother, left in

IT'S HAPPENED AGAIN

poverty with seven children. One of George's sisters also died of tuberculosis, aged just 19, when George was seven years old. Life was no bed of roses for little George. He was, however, a talented footballer and came to Arsenal via Chelsea. He was the star of the 71 double winning team, known as 'the stroller' for his languid style.

Graham was a borderline psychotic, but this rather suited the football world of the late 80s. The game was at its lowest ebb, with English teams banned from European competition following the Heysel disaster. This was the same Heysel stadium which Arsenal fans had complained about after the 1980 Cup Winners' Cup final. Heysel had been the venue for the 1985 European Cup final of Liverpool vs. Juventus; by this time it had had another five years to crumble. Before the game, Liverpool fans attacked the Juventus fans. The escaping Juventus fans pressed up against a wall which collapsed, killing 39 and injuring 600. English hooliganism could no longer be dismissed as high spirits. It had finally led to tragedy, and English teams were not to return to the European stage until 1990.

The English game became insular and fell behind the rest of Europe during the exile. A shocking, heavy drinking culture developed amongst the players. Crowds dwindled and violence escalated to the point that it could be witnessed at almost every match. Back on the pitch, the Arsenal team was full of celebrated players, but never looked like winning anything.

Graham proceeded to get rid of Arsenal's unsuccessful pampered stars and replace them with hungry young players, many of them developed by the Arsenal youth system. It paid dividends pretty quickly. Arsenal went on some good runs and even led the League for a while during his first season.

They fell away in the League, but went on a glorious run in the League Cup, vanquishing local rivals Tottenham in a barnstorming comeback victory in the semi-final and progressing to play the near invincible Liverpool in the final. There was a bizarre but often quoted statistic that, in several years, and 144 games, Liverpool had never lost when their striker, Ian Rush, scored a goal. It was a silly statistic, but was repeated so often that it became part of Liverpool's aura. When Rush scored in the final, it looked like curtains for Arsenal. But Arsenal replied with two goals from the unlikely source of Charlie Nicholas, one of Arsenal's greatest flop signings and someone who never fitted in with Graham's teams. Nicholas never did much for Arsenal before or after, but for that one day he was an Arsenal hero.

The League Cup may have been the most minor of the prizes available to Arsenal, but the effect was galvanizing. Belief returned to the club. By late 1988 Arsenal were unstoppable, racing into a big lead in the League with England's best team, Liverpool, trailing in their wake. It finally seemed that the 18 year wait for a League title since the double year was coming to an end. It looked like Arsenal might finally become champions for the first time in my lifetime.

The North Bank and other terraces

This was the period of my life when I had the most opportunity to attend matches in person. Although I was only a schoolboy, it was laughably cheap to get into the ground (£3 for the big games if I recall). Unlike today, when tickets are like gold dust, you could just turn up from the tube half an hour before kick-off and still be certain of getting in. The downside was that you had to stand on the terraces.

The terraces were something magical and yet something terrible. I'm glad I experienced them before they disappeared forever, but I'm also glad that my children will never stand on them. The terraces were standing areas, where everyone (mostly men) stood packed like sardines, especially at the popular matches. They were big stands at either end of the pitch which gently descended to pitch side via a series of shallow steps or 'terraces'. The 'home' terrace at Arsenal was called the North Bank. The density of people meant that the noise, singing and

IT'S HAPPENED AGAIN

atmosphere were like nothing you can experience in football today. It was a jungle out there.

When the crowd surged forward, we went forward, whether we liked it or not. We were acutely conscious that if we lost our footing (on the poorly surfaced concrete, complete with the occasional steps that gave the terraces their name), we were dead. The people behind us were as helpless as we were, and couldn't stop surging forward any more than we could. If we fell to the floor we would have been mercilessly trampled. Of course, most of the time, falling was not an option even if we wanted to, because we were too tightly packed. But every now and then fleeting holes would open up in the swirling crowd, a bit like an eddy in swollen river. If we were on the edge of such a gap, falling suddenly became a real possibility, so we needed to keep your wits about us. Such anomalies prevented us from simply relaxing and 'surfing the crowd'.

The overall effect was a thrilling one for teenage boys such as me and my friends. The excitement of football was combined with the raw masculinity of the terrace community with its inherent dangers. Add to that the thrill of trying to get in and out of the ground and its environs in the days when football was routinely an excuse for neo-fascists to engage in organised 'leisure violence' (how is this fun?). Many a time, we dodged down side streets to evade charging opposition fans screaming hate and viciousness, or colossal iron hoofed police horses. It was a heady cocktail, and it felt like being initiated into a man's world.

CHAPTER FIVE
TERROR & CHANGE

Ironically enough, just as George Graham was saving Arsenal, English football itself was being saved by a series of terrible tragedies. The first two; Heysel (described above) and Bradford, both occurred in May 1985.

At Bradford's Valley Parade ground, an old wooden stand caught fire during an end of season match at which Bradford City were celebrating promotion. Due to combined failures of management and fire enforcement action, the stand became an inferno in just four minutes. 56 people died, some of them incinerated in their seats. Live TV cameras were rolling. If you ever want to understand how dangerous fire can be, watch that video but be warned, it is truly harrowing. Fifty people received Police awards or commendations for bravery. Without their actions the outcome would have been even worse.

The worst tragedy in English football history took place in 1989 at Hillsborough, the home of Sheffield Wednesday, the venue for the FA Cup semi-final between Liverpool and Nottingham Forest. A series of unfortunate circumstances combined with Police mismanagement of crowd safety led to tragedy. Too many Liverpool fans were shepherded onto one of the terraces. Some grounds, including Hillsborough but not Highbury, had added fences to the front of their terraces to prevent hooligans from invading the pitch. For this very reason, the FA had stopped using Highbury as an FA Cup semi-final venue. Now the fences became prisons at Hillsborough. Fans were crushed against them and couldn't escape onto the pitch. 96 people were crushed to death. The Police made matters worse by tampering with evidence after the event, and trying to deflect blame from themselves. The attempted cover up was one of the most shocking examples of Police malpractice in British history,

IT'S HAPPENED AGAIN

finally eliciting an official apology from the British Prime Minister in 2013.

Everyone was so shocked that it was agreed, even by politicians, something had to be done. The tragic, innocent deaths reminded everyone that football fans were human beings with a right to be protected, not just hooligans. It was no longer acceptable for people to go to football games and never come home. Legislation followed as day follows night: the terraces and the unsafe old stands were condemned in law, with all future attendees at a football stadium allocated a seat in a safe environment, and alcohol banned from sale at all matches. It looked like a hammer blow to football. Stadiums like Highbury instantly lost 20,000 in capacity because seats take up a lot more room than men standing up. The atmosphere at games was doubly destroyed by the reduced capacity and the loss of the vibrant terrace atmospheres.

The disaster, violence and death of the 80s meant that football was shunned by the middle classes, who dismissed it as a game for working class yobs. This was not great for a football lover like me. I was being educated at one of England's oldest public schools, and football was decidedly off the curriculum. I was forced to play rugby (a beastly game for gentlemen with odd shaped balls) and football could only be engaged in, in an illicit manner, 'after prep' or games organised by boys at lunchtimes on the sports fields.

The greatest goal ever

Despite being a sports lover, I've always rather disliked sports-based fiction. It usually involves rather farfetched and improbable storylines of defeat snatched from the jaws of victory and vice-versa. Actually, real sport is dramatic enough, and it always seems a shame to embellish the purity of it. Nothing could ever be as improbable and far-fetched as the conclusion to the

1988-89 season, which had everything: drama, coincidence, tragedy, joy, despair and unbelievable tension.

As the season drew to a close, things were deteriorating for George Graham's young Arsenal team. They were wilting in sight of the finishing line and the experienced Liverpool team were closing in, breathing down their necks. The Liverpool players had been deeply affected by the Hillsborough tragedy, and seemed to be inspired by the memory of their fallen supporters. Now the true Liverpool, managed by the legendary Kenny Dalglish, was reasserting itself. It was men against boys as Liverpool slowly reeled the upstarts in. By a strange twist of fate, the Liverpool vs. Arsenal game had been due to take place shortly after the Hillsborough disaster. The Liverpool players were in no fit state to play and the match was postponed as Liverpool took a 21 day break from football. With Liverpool still in the FA Cup, there was no opportunity to reschedule the match until after the season had finished. So the season was extended and the final match of the season was the rescheduled Liverpool vs. Arsenal game.

By some miracle, Arsenal clung on to their League lead, but only because of Liverpool's backlog of matches. As Liverpool played the missed fixtures, they inexorably caught and then overtook Arsenal. On Saturday 20th May Liverpool won an emotional Cup final against city rivals Everton 3-2 after extra time, amidst touching scenes of solidarity from the vanquished Everton fans. Now all they had to do was to finish off the League. In so doing, they could achieve the feat which had so narrowly escaped them the previous season and become the first team ever to win two doubles (the double double).

Liverpool were level on points with Arsenal, but had a game in hand. On the Tuesday, they played the game in hand, thrashing West Ham 5-1. And this score line was more than just a psychological blow: Liverpool were now three points ahead of Arsenal. If Arsenal could win the final game, they would tie on points and the title would be decided on goal difference. Before the West Ham match the two teams had identical goal difference,

IT'S HAPPENED AGAIN

but because Liverpool had won by four goals they now had a goal difference of four more than Arsenal. To win the title Arsenal wouldn't just have to beat Liverpool, they would have to win by two clear goals. Such a result would make the teams level on goal difference, and Arsenal would win by virtue of having scored more goals (which was the second tie-break in the case of teams having an identical goal difference). Of course, no title had ever been won on such a slender margin.

Since the start of March Liverpool had played 17 games. They had drawn one, and that was 0-0 with Everton on the day that Liverpool returned to football after their 21 day post-Hillsborough mourning. Liverpool were clearly rusty and unfit after taking time out from football to attend the funerals of the victims. Of the other sixteen matches, they had won every one.

It is difficult now to understand what an impregnable fortress Anfield stadium was in 1989. In the last four League games at home, Liverpool scored thirteen goals, conceding just two. Liverpool had lost only two matches at home all season, both by a single goal. The previous season, they had lost none at all. The season before that, they had lost only three home games (all by a single goal). The season before that (1985-86) they had only lost one home game, albeit by 2-0 to Everton. That was the last time that Liverpool had lost at home by two goals, and it was over three years ago. Arsenal hadn't won there by any margin for 15 years. It wasn't just incredibly unlikely that Arsenal could beat the Mighty Red Machine at home, but the idea that they could do so against this inspired team, by two clear goals, was preposterous.

Or was it? There is always hope in a two horse race. And this Arsenal team had spirit. They had shown that during their gutsy League Cup win, slaying the Liverpool legend of Ian Rush's goals. If anyone could do it...

It had been obvious for some time the season would hinge on this final game. Of course it is usually highly improbable that the top two teams would play each other in the final game with the League title still undecided: such a thing has not happened before or since. With an eye for a historical moment my friends and I had planned to go to Liverpool to watch the match. But now we changed our minds. Liverpool seemed like a dark, distant and dangerous place to visit on a late Friday night. Although it was still theoretically possible, there seemed to be no realistic prospect that Arsenal might win the title. We watched it at home.

The match itself was unbelievably tense. Arsenal (Alan Smith) scored just before half-time to go one nil up. Despite this, as time ticked away it seemed that Arsenal would fail gloriously. A win at Anfield was an achievement in its own right, and not one that Arsenal had achieved in recent memory. This team had failed bravely trying, in the finest tradition of English pluck. As the match slipped into injury time, Liverpool supporters began to celebrate the historic 'double', and I resigned myself to my fate. A season of hope and excitement dashed at the very last hurdle. No team had ever come closer to victory and finished second.

And then it happened.

If you are an Arsenal fan, I don't need to describe what happened next. For the benefit of other readers, the ball was lumped forward by Lee Dixon as Arsenal made one last desperate attempt to get the goal they needed. Alan Smith turned the ball forward towards the onrushing Michael Thomas. Thomas, a product of the Arsenal youth system, controlled the ball via a fortunate ricochet off the defender (the wonderful Steve Nicol) and poked the ball past the Liverpool goalkeeper. The impossible had just happened. Arsenal had done it with seconds to spare. No goal can ever match that. I have watched literally hundreds of replays of this goal and I still don't expect him to score.

This was the final table:

	Team	P	W	D	L	GF	GA	GD	PTS
1	Arsenal	38	22	10	6	73	36	37	76
2	Liverpool	38	22	10	6	65	28	37	76

IT'S HAPPENED AGAIN

In hindsight, this was a clash of two great teams. The Liverpool team was coming to the end of their time. They won the title back the following season (1989-90), but they have not triumphed in the League since. A little more of their legend was slain that night and other teams were never quite as scared of them again.

George Graham's Arsenal took the League title back from Liverpool in the following season (1990-91), losing only one match in the process. It was a less dramatic but far more impressive win. As I headed off to University with the world at my feet it looked like Arsenal were the coming team and they would battle with Liverpool for the next few titles. But actually, both teams fell away. Liverpool entered an improbably terminal decline from which they are still struggling to escape 25 years later. Arsenal fared better, winning an FA Cup, a League Cup and a Cup Winners' Cup in the next few years, but only relatively so. A combination of injuries and George Graham's clumsy management meant that Arsenal's great young team of the early 90s fell apart. The defence stayed together and the Arsenal back four became a national treasure. But the midfield was decimated. In an act of pure irony, Michael Thomas was sold to Liverpool. The saddest demise was that of David 'Rocky' Rocastle, and his story is the ultimate metaphor for the lost promise of that team.

Rocky

Rocky was an exciting, dynamic, wide midfielder or winger. Another product of the Arsenal youth system, he was a beautifully muscular specimen, with mesmeric dribbling skills. As quiet and shy off the pitch as he was stunning on it, he was the darling of the North Bank. The mere mention of his name today will still bring a smile to the face of any Arsenal fan who saw him play. Rocky had deep black skin at a time of open racism in English football: it was difficult for anyone to watch him play without realising how deeply absurd it was to dislike a man for the colour of his skin.

The son of immigrants, Rocky's father died in 1972 when he was just five. He was an unassuming chap, and joined Arsenal as a schoolboy. According to his team mate Martin Keown "They couldn't work out why Rocastle was running around dribbling with his head down. So they took him to the halfway line and said: 'Can you see the goal?' and he couldn't. His eyesight was terrible. They sorted him out with contact lenses and his career took off". He was part of the League Cup winning side, and played every game of the glorious 1988-89 season.

In 1992 Graham inexplicably sold 25 year old Rocky to Leeds. Hindsight suggests that Graham may have been bribed to do so, but this has never been proven. I couldn't believe it. Neither Rocky, nor Graham's team were ever the same again. Rocky moved on several times, taking in Manchester City and Chelsea before moving abroad. He retired in 1999 amidst chronic knee injuries, ending up with only 14 England caps (all gained during his time at Arsenal), a sorry total for a player of his immense talent. He died in 2001 aged just 33, from non-Hodgkins Lymphoma, a form of cancer.

Rocky has never been forgotten by Arsenal fans. His widow and children are treated royally by the club and the fans often remember him in songs and tributes. Age will never weary him.

A new age dawns

It turned out that the post-Hillsborough reforms weren't a hammer blow to football at all. Instead they brought the game back to life. Modern all-seater stadia were much less suited to people who wanted to organise communal violence, and so it slowly leached away, leading to a great revival in English football. It turned out that (despite aspirational bourgeois claims to the contrary) people did love the beautiful game. The middle

IT'S HAPPENED AGAIN

classes came back, as did women and children. Money flooded into the game as it reorganised itself and sold ever more tickets.

George Graham, with his 'hard man' management style and dour defensive teams, looked increasingly anachronistic. Arsenal finished tenth in 1992-93 and the Graham era seemed to be petering out. The Cup successes were a sticking plaster on a team that was in decline. In 1994 Graham was sacked for accepting a bribe to buy a player. It was a sad and ignominious end to a long and glorious association with Arsenal; George never received the farewell from the fans that he had earned. It was rumoured that Graham was the fall guy and lots of other Managers had taken similar 'bungs'. Perhaps the Board was all too glad of a reason to sack him without appearing ungrateful for all that he had done. Nonetheless, the size of the bribe - £425,000 - suggests that Graham was now making decisions with priorities other than the best interests of the club in his mind. I will always be suspicious about the sale of Rocky.

CHAPTER SIX
THE SECOND GOLDEN AGE

In 1996 Arsenal appointed Arsène Wenger as its new Manager and its second golden age began. Perhaps not quite as glorious as the 1930s, but not far off.

The first hint of promise came in 1997-98; Arsène Wenger's first full season in charge, having joined in November of 1996. It wasn't obvious at first that anything much had changed. Our new superstar signing from a year ago, Dennis Bergkamp, started to settle in and score some goals. We had a new midfielder called Patrick Vieira who looked like he might be a bit special and a few players like Anelka, Overmars and Petit who looked like they could have potential. However, we weren't really challenging for the title. We were sixth at the turn of the year, 12 points behind Manchester United. Then something clicked (we discuss later what that might have been). Suffice to say, for two wonderful months we looked unbeatable and indeed we were. We won ten consecutive League games, starting with four one-nils, but blossoming into 3-1s, 4-1s and 5-0s. This run of form also coincided with the crucial stages of the FA Cup and before anyone could say 'What the fu.....' we had won the double.

This magical new team had repeated Arsenal's most legendary feat. Memories of 71 flooded back to North London. All the talk was of which team was better, 71 or 98, with the players from each team compared, position by position. There was dancing (and not a little drinking) in the streets of the Islington. I must here apologise to the residents of Highbury for my own slightly over exuberant contribution to this memorable evening. The next day, there was a wonderful open bus tour. All the little children came out to watch, the black boys in their 'Ian Wright' shirts and the white boys favouring 'Dennis Bergkamp'. I felt as if I was in the middle of a football dream.

IT'S HAPPENED AGAIN

The lull before the storm

The joy of the double was followed by a rather turgid period. We failed to defend the League title, losing by a single point to Manchester United on the final day. They also knocked us out of the FA Cup in the semi-final that year and went on to win the treble (adding the Champions League to the Double). Man U's treble put our double a little in the shade.

We managed to finish second to them in the following two seasons as well, so they added a hat-trick of titles to their treble. When we lost the FA Cup final to two late goals from Michael Owen in 2001, we looked like we were doomed to be forever runners-up.

Big bad Sol

Sol Campbell was born the youngest of twelve children in Newham, to Jamaican immigrants. His strict upbringing kept him on the straight and narrow despite living in a deprived part of London. In his own words:

"I became a recluse within my own house. I became insular because at home there was no space to grow or to evolve, everything was tight and there was no room to breathe. People don't realise how that affects you as a kid. I wasn't allowed to speak, so my expression was football."[*]

Campbell was an obviously talented footballer and played for West Ham as a youth, but left after one of the coaches racially insulted him. He was reluctant to join another club program, but Spurs were persistent and eventually signed him up. By the turn of the Millennium, Spurs were heavily reliant on him as club captain, star player and even - as a defender - one of their

---

[*] *Jason Burt "Inside the mind of Sol Campbell" 2006, The Independent*

principal attacking threats. He was carrying the team and clearly became frustrated with Tottenham's lack of success; allowing his contract to run down.

By the summer of 2001 he was a free agent who could go to any club in the world. A little bit of me hoped that he might like living in London and would sign for Arsenal so he didn't have to move. The rational part of me said 'forget it'. When he actually signed for Arsenal, I was in seventh heaven. It reminded me of when Charlie Nicholas signed for Arsenal in 1983, when he had the pick of all the top teams. I hoped it would work out better than the Nicholas signing.

In my opinion, he is the most complete centre-half I have ever seen play the game. I was frightened of him even watching from the stands. I couldn't imagine how it felt to try to score a goal against him. Arsenal fans love centre-halves and in my opinion Sol is the best we have ever seen. But Sol is curiously hard to love. Quite apart from being a former Spurs captain, he is a very self-contained character, simultaneously confident yet shy, polite yet prickly. He is an elegant looking man, with a powerful physique that makes it a little uncomfortable to be in a room with him. He's a little eccentric and a little unpredictable. There is nothing relaxing about him whatsoever.

Like many centre halves, he was big and strong. He was a powerful header of the ball and it was nearly impossible to get a clean header on the ball if he was anywhere in your vicinity. Occasionally comes a centre half who combines fearsome pace with physical presence; and Campbell had those attributes. Usually such players are prone to errors, or read the game poorly. Sol had none of these drawbacks. He was, in many ways, the perfect centre half. He is certainly the benchmark against which I compare all others.

Surprisingly he didn't age well, so once he started to lose his physical powers, his effectiveness deteriorated rapidly. His 73 England caps don't do justice to his talent. Some players compensate for declining physical powers with improved reading of the game, but Sol always excelled in this respect, so he could hardly improve. We only really had him for three or four seasons at his peak, but he was truly peerless during that period.

In the summer of 2001, Sol joined our team of runners-up and made a world of difference. In 2001-2 we did the double again. Somehow this achievement only served to further overshadow the 97-98 double. Again the League title was won with an irresistible run of consecutive victories. This time however, the team had not come from nowhere, it had always been in contention for the title. And the run of victories at the end of the season was 13 this time, compared to 'only' 10 in 97-8. To make it even more special, the title was sealed with a 1-0 victory at Old Trafford. The stars of the team were Patrick Vieira and Thierry Henry, but I will always think of this as Sol's double.

In the following season, Arsenal defended the FA Cup, but failed to defend the title, as it had in every defending season since the first golden age and 1934-35 (the season after Chapman's death.)

The Invincibles

I won't make any serious attempt to do justice to the Invincibles in this book. They are worthy of a book in their own right (and Amy Lawrence has written an excellent one). Their run of 49 unbeaten games is an English record, surpassing the previous record of 42 held by Nottingham Forest (Nov 77 to Dec 78). Arsenal's run included the entirety of the 2003-4 season, in which they naturally won the League.

Of course they were a little lucky not to lose any of those games, particularly when Ruud van Nistelrooy - one of the world's leading strikers of the day - missed a last minute penalty to give Manchester United victory in game 8. What is undeniable is that this was an exceptional team. It played with pace, verve, style and skill.

From the 1997-98 double winning side only Vieira and Bergkamp survived. The team included some of the greatest Arsenal players of all time at the peak of their powers. Many Arsenal fans will be able to recite the starting line-up of this period. (Other players who made a significant impact included Edu, Reyes, Keown, Wiltord, Parlour, Cygan, Clichy, Kanu and Aliadiere).

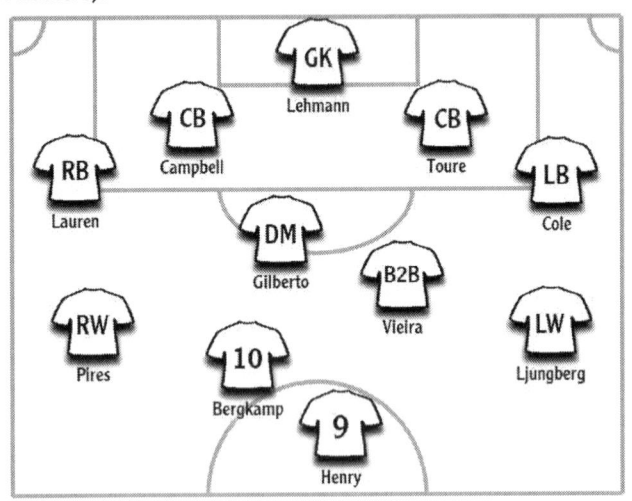

Formation diagram:
- GK: Lehmann
- CB: Campbell, CB: Toure
- RB: Lauren, LB: Cole
- DM: Gilberto, B2B: Vieira
- RW: Pires, LW: Ljungberg
- 10: Bergkamp
- 9: Henry

Game 50, 24th October 2004

After 49 games unbeaten Arsenal came up against Manchester United on 24th October 2004. This was an 'unfortunate' refereeing performance by Mike Riley, who handed Man U a controversial penalty which effectively settled the game. This was the sixth successive time that he had refereed a match at Old Trafford and given a penalty to the home team. His most blatant error was to fail to send off Rio Ferdinand early in the game - Ferdinand's tackle on Ljungberg was pretty similar to Willie Young's effort in the 1980 Cup final. But now this was a red card offence, and Riley seemed to bottle the decision in front of the intimidating Old Trafford crowd. He bewilderingly failed to give

IT'S HAPPENED AGAIN

even a free kick. Even Ferdinand appeared to admit he had been lucky in his post-match interview.

Perhaps more significantly, Manchester United (the second most skilful team of the day) made little attempt to compete with Arsenal's footballing prowess, appearing to adopt a tactic of 'rotational' fouling to break up Arsenal's rhythm. Some feel that this is an 'unsporting' tactic that the referee should have prevented. Others would argue it to be a legitimate way for professional players to play, and a clever choice of approach by Alex Ferguson, although Ferguson has never admitted it was a deliberate tactic. However you look at it, Manchester United were fortunate to finish the game with 11 players that day. Many Arsenal fans still hold a grudge over this match, particularly towards referee Mike Riley, who later became Manager of the referee's organising body (PGMO). If you want to form your own view on this performance, the highlights are available on YouTube.

THE CUSTODIANS

CHAPTER SEVEN
THE PATRIARCHS

No history of Arsenal could be complete without the men who have owned and loved it. And what an extraordinary bunch they are.

Henry Norris

Henry Norris is the first major identifiable, controlling mind at Arsenal. He was a largely self-made man, in an era where such things were frowned upon. He was born into a working class family in Southwark, London, leaving school at the age of 14 to become a clerk in a solicitor's office. Norris prospered, but rather than qualify as a solicitor, he entered into partnership with local housebuilder, WG Allen. This was a big risk for Norris, but both men made their fortunes, and many of the houses built by Norris and Allen can still be seen in the Fulham and Wandsworth areas of London.

Financial success was not sufficient for this ambitious man. In 1903, 37 year-old Norris became the chairman of, and a shareholder in, Fulham FC.

Norris is a curiously central figure in the history of English football. In 1905, a character called Gus Mears purchased an athletics ground, Stamford Bridge. His intention was to persuade Norris to move Fulham to the ground, but the negotiations failed because the two could not agree a price. Mears toyed with the idea of selling the ground to the Great Western Railway to use as a coal yard, but in the end, he decided to start his own football team, Chelsea FC, instead. Norris always seemed to feel a very personal antipathy towards Chelsea FC ever after, something that modern Arsenal fans may relate to.

TIM CHARLESWORTH

In 1910, Arsenal were going out of business in the face of falling attendances and poor performances on the pitch. At this point Norris hove onto the scene. His motivations have been much debated, but it seems most likely that he planned to buy Arsenal as a ruse to gain promotion for his native Fulham. His original plan seems to have been to acquire Arsenal, merge us with Fulham and move the newly merged team to Craven Cottage, ready to play in the First Division.

The FA prevented him from doing this by insisting that the newly merged team would play in the Second Division, not the First. During these negotiations however, the FA seem to have conceded the principle that a club had the right to play wherever it liked and that they could not prevent a club from moving

IT'S HAPPENED AGAIN

grounds. This concession seems to have sown an idea indelibly into Norris's mind.

Norris, by now a major shareholder in Arsenal, gave the people of Woolwich one more chance to support their team, but gate receipts continued to disappoint and when the team was relegated in 1912-13, Norris gambled all, moving to a new ground north of the river, at Highbury. Despite the relegation, attendances were immediately higher and Norris soon bought out the lease and developed the ground further. The modern Arsenal was born.

There can be little doubt that Norris' original interest in Arsenal was ignoble, seeing it as some kind of commercial opportunity, or a chance to boost Fulham into the First Division. But somewhere along the line, these feelings changed. He certainly took a big financial risk in moving the club to Highbury and it seems that he personally scouted London for an appropriate site. He was a wealthy man and would not have been bankrupted if it had all gone wrong, but nonetheless he took a substantial risk for the club. Perhaps that risk and its success was a bonding experience between Arsenal and Norris. By 1919 he had resigned as a director of Fulham and thereafter seems to have been a genuine Arsenal man.

Norris was a truly incredible character. As well as being a successful businessman and football executive, he was also an accomplished Conservative politician. He was a Councillor for the London Borough of Fulham from 1906 to 1931[*], including ten years as Mayor (1909-19). He sat on the London County Council, the Metropolitan Water Board and was Member of Parliament

---

[*] It should be noted that during Norris' time as a Fulham councillor, the Borough gave his firm, Norris and Allen, permission to build hundreds of highly profitable new homes in the Borough. Such a conflict of interests would not be tolerated today.

for Fulham East from 1919 to 1922. He combined all of this with a career as one of the leading Freemasons of his day.

Despite all this activity, Norris is an elusive man. There is no printed biography of him. The best published source is a book called '*Woolwich Arsenal: The club that changed football* ' by Tony Attwood, Andy Kelly and Mark Andrews; but this focuses on what he did at Arsenal rather than the nature of the man. There is a lovingly compiled website at wrightanddavis.co.uk/Norris with a remarkable level of detail on Norris' life, compiled from a vast array of papers and contemporary journalism. This incredible feat of primary research was put together by Arsenal historian Sally Davis. It tells us everything about his daily movements, but little about his innermost thoughts.

The man who had brought Arsenal to Islington and then hired Chapman was not destined to enjoy the fruits of all his hard work and risk. He was banned for life from football following an FA investigation in 1929, shortly before Arsenal won its first ever trophy. His crime was financial irregularities - including pocketing £125 from the sale of the team bus and irregular payments to players (in the days that maximum wages were strictly enforced). The debate about the seriousness of Norris' misdemeanours continues down to the modern day. His conviction is the origin of the rumours that Norris used bribery to secure Arsenal's famous 1919 promotion. To our modern eyes, his sins are trivial in nature and there is a sense that the gentlemen finally got their revenge on the self-made upstart. Whatever the truth of it, his disgrace was certainly considered severe by contemporaries; perhaps this is why so little effort was made (even by Arsenal FC) to record the life of this amazing man.

Arsenal fans really owe everything to Norris. He was the man who saved the club from extinction, took the momentous decision to move Arsenal to Islington and hired Herbert Chapman. Without these happy occurrences, the club would have either ceased to exist, or continued evermore in mediocrity. It is possible that we would never even have even heard of Arsenal

FC. He is sadly uncelebrated. Perhaps it was the ignominy of the end of his career; perhaps later owners of the club preferred to shine the limelight on themselves rather than him. There are no statues or busts of him at the Emirates and his name is largely forgotten.

Norris retired from public life following his disgrace, and died an unlamented death in July 1934, just six months after Chapman. Of all the characters I researched for this book, Norris was the most elusive. I never felt that I got to know him, or understand him. Perhaps this is because he is so historically distant. He was, after all, more a man of the 19th Century than the 20th. There is a surprising shortage of material on him: perhaps he was just a private man and it was as hard to know him in life as it is today, or perhaps it just needs a better researcher than me. Whatever the reason, I felt sad not to be able to get to know him.

It's difficult to know the true extent to which Arsenal was ever ingrained in his heart. I hope it was. I hope he didn't die an embittered man. I hope that Arsenal's extraordinary successes bought joy to him in his final days. The sad truth is: I'm not sure it did. Norris was a fabulously successful man and that kind of success only comes to those who are driven by a constant hunger, an insatiable drive to succeed. The problem with that kind of ambition is that it can never be satisfied and I fear that in his final days, he dwelt more on the sad nature of his departure from Arsenal than on the fact he had laid the foundations of the greatest football club the world had yet seen. In his final illness, he went to Craven Cottage, not Highbury to watch his football. Maybe it was just too painful for him to set foot in Highbury; maybe Fulham FC really was his true love; or maybe Highbury was just too far from home for a sick, old man to travel. Regardless of his personal regrets at the end, my instinct is that Norris really was 'one of us' in the final reckoning. As such, regardless of how he may have felt personally, he must be ranked as the greatest of all Arsenal men.

TIM CHARLESWORTH

Samuel Hill-Wood

After Norris' disgrace and resignation, he was succeeded as Arsenal Chairman by a larger than life character; Samuel Hill-Wood. Born Samuel Wood in one of England's most beautiful spots, Glossop in Derbyshire, in the area now known as the Peak District, Samuel was the son of a successful cotton manufacturer (this was pretty much the only way to make pots of cash in North West England in the 19th Century). Samuel was educated at Eton, where he refined his love of cricket.

These were the days of gentlemen (amateurs) and players (professionals) and Samuel was most definitely in the gentlemen's club. Teams were remarkably segregated: the

IT'S HAPPENED AGAIN

gentlemen would never socialise with the players and they even had separate changing rooms. A similar segregation featured in the early days of association football, but soon disappeared, as the concept was too alien for a sport like football that required intimate teamwork.

The captain of a county was always chosen from the gentlemen and Samuel captained Derbyshire for three seasons. He was not a great player and never scored a first class 100, but did distinguish himself by becoming the only man ever in first class cricket to score ten runs from one shot (some fairly poor fielding was involved!).

Samuel was certainly a man of many talents. He took over his father's cotton business and was the MP for High Peak (Derbyshire) from 1910 to 1929 (where he would have met fellow Conservative MP, Henry Norris). Amongst all this he found the energy to be Chairman of his home town football club, Glossop North End. With Samuel as chairman, and benefactor, they finished the 1898-99 season second in the Second Division behind Manchester City. They were promoted to the First Division for just one season and remain the smallest town ever to have played in the top flight of English football. The club lost its league status after the First World War and today plies its trade in the Northern Premier League Division One with a stadium capacity of 1,350 (209 seated), but retains links to Arsenal to this day.

Samuel changed his name to Hill-Wood in 1910 and became Sir Samuel in 1921 when he was made a Baronet. More importantly, he became a Director of Arsenal in 1922 and, after retiring as an MP in 1929, he succeeded Henry Norris as Chairman. By 1936 Arsenal were the toast of the town and the Chairmanship of Arsenal had become a high social position. Samuel stepped down in favour of three short-lived, aristocratic Chairmen: The Earl of Lonsdale; The Earl of Granard and then the Marquess of Londonderry. It may seem strange to younger fans because this reputation for glamour was firmly killed by the dour Arsenal teams of the 60s and 70s, but in the 1930s Arsenal were the most glamorous club in the world and people from all strata of society wanted to be associated with them. It is during this period that the Duchess of York seems to have become a Gooner, a habit which she passed on to her daughter Queen Elizabeth II and which the Queen has in turn passed on to her grandson, Prince Harry.

As the world moved on and Arsenal's glamour faded, Samuel resumed the Chairmanship during the Second World War. He died in office in 1949, with his Baronetcy passing to his eldest son, Basil. The title is currently held by Sir Samuel Thomas Hill-Wood, the fourth Baronet.

Samuel founded a dynasty

Samuel's four sons, Basil, Wilfred, Denis and Charles all played cricket for Derbyshire, as did his brother in law David Brand. Wilfred even played two games for Arsenal's reserves in 1924-5, scoring three goals. Samuel's third son, Denis, became chairman of Arsenal in 1962. He too died in office, in 1982.

Denis was succeeded by his son, Peter, who was Arsenal's longest serving Chairman (1982-2013). Peter was a remarkable man in many ways. The caricature of a happy go lucky Old Etonian, he always managed to give the impression that he didn't quite 'get' football, an arresting characteristic in a club Chairman. We might reflect that Peter was Arsenal's longest serving Director, with 51 years on the board; the son of a man who was chairman for 20 years and present at most of the games that Arsenal played in that time, so it's a little difficult to imagine he didn't acquire a smattering of knowledge about the beautiful game. If he did, he hid it well.

Peter was never much loved by the Arsenal fans and gradually sold his family's shares during his time in office. Most of them were purchased by David Dein while Peter slowly retreated into a figurehead role. Peter introduced as Arsenal Directors: Sir Roger Gibbs (one of his classmates at Eton) and

IT'S HAPPENED AGAIN

Sir Chips Keswick (a colleague of his at Hambros Bank, where he was Vice Chairman). When he resigned due to ill health in 2013, the magnificently named Sir Chips succeeded him as Chairman. Upon his resignation, there was no Hill-Wood on the Arsenal board for the first time since 1922, a total of 91 years. The 2014 FA Cup was the first trophy ever won by Arsenal without a Hill-Wood in the boardroom.

Sir Bracewell Smith

Arsenal's second great dynasty was the Bracewell-Smiths. The founder of the line was called Bracewell Smith, but his descendants confused matters by adopting the hyphenated 'Bracewell-Smith' as their surname.

Bracewell was born in Keighley in Yorkshire; a successful entrepreneur who made money in the property and hotel businesses. The flagships of his empire were the Park Lane Hotel and The Ritz. He served as the Conservative MP for Dulwich from 1932 to 1945, losing his seat in the Labour landslide of the post-war 1945 General Election.

He was the Lord Mayor of London in 1946 and made Baronet Keighley in 1947. Back in 1938 he purchased shares in Arsenal and joined the Board, becoming Chairman upon the death in office of Samuel Hill-Wood in 1949. His period as Chairman lasted until he retired in 1962 and he was succeeded by Samuel's son, Denis. This was mostly a period of decline from a great height for Arsenal.

An FA Cup was won in 1950 and a solitary League Championship was won in 1952-3 (on 'goal average' from Preston North End - the closest finish until Michael Thomas).

Nonetheless, Smith is generally well loved by the Arsenal community, with his descendants playing a major role in Arsenal's boardroom for the next half a century:

- His son, Sir George Bracewell-Smith (known as Guy), the second Baronet, was an Arsenal director from 1953 to his death in 1976
- His grandsons, Clive and Richard Carr, inherited shares and became Directors in 1981. Clive retired in 2001. Richard

IT'S HAPPENED AGAIN

- retired from Arsenal Holdings in 2008, but is still a Director of Arsenal FC.
- Lady Nina Bracewell-Smith is the wife of the fourth Baronet, Charles Bracewell-Smith. As Charles' health failed, his shares were transferred to her and she joined the Board in 2005. More on her later

CHAPTER EIGHT
HERE COMES THE CAVALRY!

David Dein, the Midas man

Ownership of a football club was not seen as a way to make money for most of the 20th Century. Instead it was seen as a kind of patriarchal duty. Football was the opium of the masses, but it needed the input and organisation of educated men in order to make it all work. This, slightly patronising, approach was very much the motivation of dynasties such as the Bracewell-Smiths and the Hill-Woods. Similar, wealthy families owned and ran many of England's great football clubs. At Liverpool it was the Moores family, while at Manchester United the Edwards family dominated. These families acted more like trustees than directors of a commercial company. They did not pay themselves and never took money out of the clubs. They were mostly competent managers, but not often passionate about their teams (at least not in the way that modern fans understand 'passion'). This sort of arrangement started to become anachronistic in the 1980s. Tottenham and Manchester United became PLCs, listed on the London Stock Exchange, and a new breed of investors began to see football as a possible way of making money.

In 1983 a new animal came on to the scene at Arsenal. David Dein had no connections with the English gentry. He was an entrepreneur who had grown his family's Shepherds Bush food business into an international commodity business specialising in sugar. He was a genuine football lover and lifelong fan. In 1983 he invested £292,000 in Arsenal, in return for which he received 16.6% of the shares of the company. Arsenal Chairman Peter Hill-Wood famously described the transaction as "crazy" adding that "to all intents and purposes it's dead money". Dein sold his shares in various tranches over a period of ten years. He sold his last 14.58% in 2007 for £75m. Not a bad return for 'dead money'!

IT'S HAPPENED AGAIN

Dein steadily increased his shareholding to 42% by 1991, and became Executive Vice-Chairman of the club. This title was a little misleading as he begun to adopt more and more of the functions of a Chief Executive or a Director of Football, becoming widely recognized as the dominant executive power at Arsenal. He represented the club on outside bodies and was one of the major architects behind the formation of the Premier League in 1992. He took on the role of chief negotiator and was instrumental in the signings of players like Ian Wright, Denis Bergkamp, Thierry Henry and Sol Campbell.

Dein was a man who made friends comfortably and inspired loyalty amongst his circle, not only at Arsenal, but throughout European football. One such friend was fellow self-made Jewish businessman Irving Scholar. Scholar took over Tottenham Hotspur in 1983, relieving the Wale and Richardson families of their traditional patriarchal roles at White Hart Lane. Dein loved to be around players and the football staff at Arsenal and made it his business get to know the players and their families. Dein's son, Darren, was the best man at Henry's wedding.

As Dein immersed himself into the world of European football, one of the friendships he formed was with the bookish and bespectacled Monaco manager Arsène Wenger. When the Board sacked George Graham, Dein tried to persuade them to hire Wenger, but this exotic Frenchman was a step too far for the conservative Board who decided instead to hire another Scot, Bolton manager Bruce Rioch. When they sacked Rioch after just one season, Dein had another go at persuading them to hire his friend. This time his persistence was rewarded.

TIM CHARLESWORTH

The boardroom drama

It is not often that the machinations of a board of directors are headline news. But for 48 months between April 2007 and April 2011, the Arsenal Boardroom saga resembled a plot from the 1980s TV show Dynasty.

The Arsenal boardroom was a fairly sleepy place in the second half of the 20th Century. Very occasional decisions were made to hire and fire managers, but that was pretty much it (the Arsenal board appointed a new manager 16 times in the 20th Century, two of them dying in post. This required a - not particularly taxing - average of one decision every six and a quarter years). By 2007 however, things were very different. Two factors were responsible for the change:

Firstly, shares in major football clubs were suddenly worth a lot more money. David Dein had purchased 16.2% of the club for £292,000 in 1983 (valuing the company at £1.8m). This was quite a lot of money to most people in 1983, but was fairly small change for well-heeled people like the Arsenal Directors (remember Peter Hill-Wood thought that Dein had paid too much). In 2000, Granada Media bought 9.9% of Arsenal for £47m. This valued the company at £450m and everyone woke up a bit. You have to be very rich indeed to ignore assets with that kind of value.

Secondly, the Board had made probably the second most important decision in Arsenal's history, when it decided, around 2000, to move away from Highbury stadium, Arsenal's home for 90 years. Whatever else we might say about Arsenal's directors at this period, there can be little doubt that they treated their roles as stewards of the club's history and traditions with the utmost seriousness. Dein felt that the club needed to increase its revenue in order to compete with the top clubs in Europe, and that it was effectively leaving 'money on the table' by having a stadium that wasn't able to accommodate all the fans who wanted to watch the team live. The move to the Emirates stadium was a massive risk that could have bankrupted the club. The

IT'S HAPPENED AGAIN

decision was debated at enormous length for many years. The directors did not all agree on the best way forward, and the discussions created the first hints of strain in the previously harmonious marble halls.

David Dein & Danny Fiszman

Danny Fiszman was a quiet and fiercely private man. He was the son of Belgian Jewish parents who had fled before the tide of Nazi Germany during the Second World War. He made his fortune as a diamond dealer, building a company called the Star Diamonds Group, which he sold for £150m in 2007 to concentrate on his role at Arsenal.

The nature of the relationship between Fiszman and David Dein is shrouded in mystery. It is certain that they started out as friends. They were both wealthy men who moved in the upper social echelons of North London's Jewish community. Dein originally started selling his shareholding to Fiszman because he wanted his friend to join the Board. Dein saw Fiszman as a natural ally and believed he could count on his support. He therefore seems to have figured that he could sell some of his shares to Fiszman without losing his dominant position on the Arsenal Board. He sold him 8% of the club in 1991 and Fiszman joined the Board in 1992.

Dein's assumption that he could count on Fiszman's support appears to have been largely correct and Dein continued selling shares to Fiszman until, by 2007, Fiszman was Arsenal's largest shareholder with 24% of the club's shares. It is difficult to know the extent to which Fiszman took over Dein's role as the power behind the throne at Arsenal. Dein remained the 'public face' of Arsenal, concentrating on the football side of the business. He was Vice-Chairman of the FA, the Premier League representative on UEFA's committee for club competitions and the President of the G14, an influential group of the world's 18 largest football clubs. Fizsman, meanwhile, focused on the longer-term strategic issues facing the club, particularly the new stadium. It seems that power and influence in the boardroom was slowly shifting from Dein to Fiszman.

Dein was worried that the building of a new stadium would drain finances away from the first team (as indeed it did). He was concerned about the effects on the team of high levels of debt and the consequent restrictions on the club's spending on playing staff. Certainly, Dein's fears were well founded; Arsenal's financial power was further diluted by the arrival of Russian oil plutocrat Roman Abramovich at Chelsea, in 2003. Dein memorably reflected that Abramovich 'parked his tanks on our lawn and began firing £50 notes at us'. This was a problem that the directors hadn't reckoned on when they decided to mortgage the club to the hilt and move to the Emirates. Chelsea were throwing money around like confetti. They posted a loss of £140m in 2004-5, more than a third of the cost of the Emirates stadium. That year, they also succeeded Arsenal as Premier League champions and successfully defended their title the following year.

Dein seems to have become convinced the only way forward was for Arsenal to find its own wealthy benefactor. The rest of the Board, and Fiszman in particular, disagreed. They believed that it was dangerous for any club to become reliant on one individual, who could whimsically depart the scene as quickly as they came on to it. They favoured a 'self-sustaining' business model, with the club generating all its financial resources from matchday income, rights payments and commercial activities. The advocates of sustainability believed that their model would triumph over the rich benefactor model in the long-term, and this almost became a matter of faith.

Dein's maverick streak now got the better of him and he brokered the sale of ITV/Granada's 9.9% of shares to American sports and property tycoon Stan Kroenke, a man who fitted his model of what a football club owner should look like. The rest

IT'S HAPPENED AGAIN

of the Board, presumably led by Fiszman, were outraged that Dein had acted without their knowledge.

This was almost certainly the final straw for the already strained Dein-Fiszman relationship. Dein's 25 years of loyal service to Arsenal came to a sudden and traumatic end, with Dein leaving the club in April 2007, due to 'irreconcilable differences' with his former colleagues. It is inconceivable that his old friend Danny Fiszman didn't agree with this course of action; he probably instigated it. Both men maintained a quiet dignity on the subject, so we will probably never really know their true feelings. Chairman Peter Hill-Wood was less adept at 'quiet dignity'. In a final dig at Dein, (the man who had bought his shares at a knockdown price and then usurped him as the leading power at Arsenal, all those years ago) he famously commented: *"Call me old-fashioned, but we don't need Kroenke's money and we don't want his sort".*

The Arsenal community was traumatised by Dein's departure. Arsène Wenger offered to resign in protest at Dein's dismissal, but Dein proved himself twice the gentlemen that Hill-Wood was, by urging his friend not to do so. As far as we know, this is the only time in 20 years that Wenger has offered his resignation. Dein's next move (in August 2007) was to sell his remaining shares (14.6%) to another potential sugar daddy, Alisher Usmanov, an Uzbek-Russian mining tycoon with even more money than Roman Abramovich and Stan Kroenke. Now the Board had two hostile 'foreigners' to deal with. They decided their only course of action was to get in bed with one of them. Stan Kroenke was deemed the lesser of two evils and invited to join the board in May 2008 (presumably following a fairly red-faced apology from Hill-Wood for the 'we don't want his sort' remark).

TIM CHARLESWORTH

The lockdown

The situation had now become unstable. Both Kroenke and Usmanov demonstrated ambitions to take the club over. Usmanov aggressively purchased shares from minor shareholders on the open market and soon increased his shareholding to in excess of 25%. Meanwhile Kroenke made use of his new insider status. He bought up the remaining shares of the Carrs (Bracewell Smith's grandsons) and a substantial portion of Danny Fiszman's shares. This left Fiszman with 16% and Kroenke, as the new largest shareholder, with 29%. The second largest shareholder was now Usmanov, who was totally excluded from the Board. Nina Bracewell Smith was the other major player, with 15.9%.

By the exchange rules, no individual could own more than 30% of the shares without making a binding offer to all shareholders to buy all the rest of the shares, paying at least the highest price that they had paid for any shares in the last twelve months. Both men were now approaching the magical 30% figure.

The Board presented a united front and announced a 'lockdown agreement'. This was first agreed in April 2007 after Dein's departure. The terms were that no director could sell their shares without first offering them to the other directors. This was a transparent attempt to keep Usmanov out. It was meant to promote stability, but tensions seemed to remain high.

And there was more blood on the carpet. Lady Nina Bracewell-Smith was sacked as a Director in 2008. She had always seemed a bit peripheral and there is a suspicion that this ethnically Indian woman was never quite accepted as part of the white public-school-boys' club that was the Arsenal Boardroom. To her credit, she has never suggested such a thing in public. The reasons for her dismissal are a bit elusive. It is certainly very odd for a major shareholder to be sacked in this fashion. It seems most likely that the Board feared she was talking to Usmanov,

IT'S HAPPENED AGAIN

which perfectly sums up the atmosphere of fear and suspicion around the Boardroom in this period.

Richard Carr also left the Board in 2008, apparently because he did not wish to play any part in the removal of his cousin's wife, Lady Nina. As a result, there was no representative of the Bracewell-Smith/Carr dynasty on the Arsenal Board for the first time since 1938 (70 years).

Keith Edelman had been brought into the club in 2000 as Managing Director. He was an experienced executive with a particular strength in financing. He had worked round the clock with Ken Friar and Fiszman on the stadium project. In May 2008 he was abruptly sacked in mysterious circumstances. He was awarded a six figure consultancy contract for a year after his dismissal, but the contract appeared to be window dressing, as he was never seen around the club again.

Only Peter Hill-Wood now remained on the board from the old Arsenal dynasties, bolstered by his allies, Lord Harris and Chips Keswick, but with less than 1% of shares between them, their real power was limited.

CHAPTER NINE
A NEW AGE DAWNS

The death of Danny

The logjam was broken by a very personal tragedy. Danny Fiszman was dying of throat cancer, and had to decide what to do with his shares. The only conceivable buyers were Usmanov and Kroenke. Both men had the money and desire to become sole owners. The future ownership of the club was in the hands of a dying man who was being forced into a decision. He decided to sell the shares to Kroenke two days before his death, which triggered a takeover situation as Kroenke now owned more than the magic 30%. Bracewell-Smith decided to sell her shares to Kroenke as well. Peter Hill-Wood also symbolically sold the last few shares (less than 1%) of the Hill-Wood legacy to Kroenke. To general astonishment, Kroenke kept Hill-Wood on as Chairman.

The lockdown period, the drama, the boardroom wrangles, were all over. Arsenal was now effectively a private company owned by an American, who became the first person to ever own more than 50% of Arsenal shares. Usmanov was left peering in from the side-lines, with just under 30%.

Fiszman was little mourned other than by the few who knew him. Due to his private nature, he was not well known by the Arsenal community. One of the bridges at the stadium is dedicated to his memory, but perhaps next time you look at the stadium, you might reflect that almost certainly none of it would be there if it wasn't for Danny. The stadium is the ultimate tribute to his vision, imagination, willingness to sacrifice his friendship with Dein; and above all his gentle determination to create an asset for his beloved football club that would outlive him. It is perhaps unfair to attribute the creation of the stadium to any one man, but if you had to choose an individual, it would almost certainly be Arsenal's quiet man, Danny Fizsman.

IT'S HAPPENED AGAIN

Silent Stan Kroenke

Trying to work out the real motivation of a super-rich individual like Kroenke is not easy. I can hardly relate to the way he thinks, or the problems and issues that he might face in his life. To the extent that he ever says anything (which is rarely), he says that he is a benign owner who wants the club to be successful. He doesn't want to interfere in the running of the club and although he shows no signs of putting money in, he doesn't intend to take any money out either. If this is truly his approach, then he would be from the same mould as virtually all his predecessors. Of all the shareholders, only David Dein and Granada television have ever put money into Arsenal (both by purchasing previously unissued shares). None have taken money out.

The issue of taking money out of the club is the one over which supporters fret the most. Kroenke has implied that he will not do it, but has certainly never given guarantees on this point; not in public at least. He may have given such guarantees to other shareholders when he bought them out, but even if he did so, can a promise to a dead man be relied upon? What makes people particularly suspicious is that he is American. People who own American sports franchises[*] do take dividends and the track record of Americans who have bought up English teams is not good:

- Malcolm Glazer funded the purchase of Man Utd in 2005 by raising debt. He raised £525m against the club, thus suddenly making Man U the most indebted football club in the world and saddling it with a large annual interest bill, draining money from the club that could otherwise be used for football investment. Success on the pitch continued after the acquisition, but most analysts attribute this success to

---

[*] Kroenke owns the Denver Nuggets basketball team, the Colorado Avalanche ice hockey team, the Colorado Mammoth Lacrosse team, the Colorado Rapids of Major League Soccer and the LA Rams of the NFL (American Football).

manager Alex Ferguson, not Glazer. Glazer died in 2014, reportedly never having set foot in Old Trafford. The club is now run by his sons
- In 2007 two American cowboys called George Gillett and Tom Hicks acquired Liverpool FC with promises of investment and a new stadium. The relationship soon soured when the two broke their promise not to raise debt against the club, thus following the Glazer model. It slowly became clear that they were not able to deliver their promise of a new stadium. The low point was reached when Hicks' son, Tom Jr, a director of the club, sent an email to a fan which included the choice phrase: "Blow me fuckface. Go to hell. I'm sick of you". The two men were effectively hounded out of town in 2010 and forced to sell. They then tried to sue the Liverpool Board of Directors for forcing them to sell their shares at below their true value. This was not a happy episode!
- Randy Lerner purchased Aston Villa in 2006. Another 'absentee landlord', Lerner also failed to live up to his promises. After a long period of stagnation and then decline, Aston Villa were relegated in 2016 and Lerner sold the business
- Now in some ways, it is silly to assume that Kroenke will behave like other American owners of English football clubs. People are clearly not the same just because they come from the same country (and no country is as diverse as the USA). Nonetheless, when Stan says so little, it is hardly surprising that fans draw this conclusion. What else are they supposed to think?

Gillett/Hicks and Malcolm Glazer have both found imaginative ways to siphon money away from their clubs through corporate restructuring. The last two annual reports (2013-14 and 2014-15) have shown that Arsenal has paid 'consultancy fees' of £3m to Kroenke enterprises. Many people suspect that these are disguised dividends. It is only because Alisher Usmanov refused to sell his 30% of shares to Kroenke that the company is

IT'S HAPPENED AGAIN

still nominally a public company and has to publish accounts at all. Without this obligation, we probably wouldn't even know about these payments. The club protests that the payment are genuine, but seem unable to convincingly describe what services it receives in return. The payments are fairly trivial, representing less than 1% of the club's revenue, but are they just the start of something else?

So it's difficult to be certain that Kroenke has not invested in Arsenal in the hope of making money. To be fair to him, he hasn't committed any major misdemeanours yet, but the £3m payments do not help his cause. If his motive is not to make money, we need to come up with a convincing alternative explanation. The difficult question to answer is: if Stan didn't have any 'secret' plans for Arsenal, why did he feel the need to own so many shares? If he just had the best interests of the club at heart and wanted to stay in the background, why not carry on as one of a number of shareholders?

It's worth a minor digression here to think about what we mean when we talk about the 'value' of a football club. There are two major ways to value an asset:

1. **Value of the income stream (dividends) that can be expected in the future.** This is the way that companies are usually valued. As a banker, this is how Peter Hill-Wood would be used to valuing a company. By this measure Arsenal is worth nothing, as the company never pays dividends to its shareholders. That's why Hill-Wood described Dein's investment as 'dead money'. It was money on which no return could be earnt. Kroenke could change this if he finds some (presumably subtle) way of paying dividends from the company
2. **Whatever anyone will pay.** This is a much more useful way of thinking about the value of a football club. If Roman Abramovich and his ilk are willing to pay hundreds of millions of pounds for the privilege of owning a football club, then that is what it is worth. This is the kind of thing that

traditional financiers don't really like. However, this form of valuation gives Kroenke a strong incentive to make Arsenal into a trophy-winning club, as that will enhance its value. The downside of this approach is that if owning football clubs suddenly became unfashionable again (as it was in the 1970s), then this value would suddenly disappear. This exposes the nonsense of Real Madrid and Barcelona being valued as the most valuable sports clubs in the world. Both clubs are owned by their members and therefore cannot be sold, so their value is not only difficult to pin down, but also impossible to ever realise

Most European owners of football clubs are just fans who love the club without looking to turn a profit and the pre-2011 Arsenal owners were basically of this type. Supporters are reasonably comfortable in this scenario. Mistakes can still be made, but they can be confident that the owners will not try to asset strip the club. It is difficult for Kroenke to convince anyone that he fits into this category. He grew up in the USA with baseball and basketball. I strongly suspect that a ten year-old Kroenke would not have known who Arsenal were. Of course people can become fans in later life, as seemed to happen with Henry Norris all those years ago.

The other possibility is that Kroenke just sees Arsenal as a 'trophy' asset. It's difficult for most people to relate to this, but is seems that if you are amongst the world's elite plutocrat billionaires you simply have to have a top football club, in the same way that you have to have a superyacht, a small tropical island, a large American ranch, beautiful mistresses and a European mansion. In such circles, the status conferred now by owning a football club seems to be second to none and of course the more prestigious the club, the better. In this respect Arsenal fans can reassure themselves. Kroenke is in Abramovich's league. Forbes magazine estimated Abramovich's net worth in 2015 as US$7.6bn. It estimated Kroenke's net worth as US$7.7bn (Alisher Usmanov: US$12.5bn). So Silent Stan is not

IT'S HAPPENED AGAIN

really like the other Americans who have owned Premier League football clubs: Malcolm Glazer gets closest with a net worth estimated in the region of US$4.5bn at his death, but the other three don't even appear on the Forbes list of billionaires.

In April 2016, Forbes estimated the value of Arsenal at £1.356bn. When Kroenke bought the majority of his shares, the company was valued at around £800m. Theoretically, if Stan sold tomorrow, he would make a profit of about £420m on the £500m or so that he has invested. In other words, he has already made more money from owning Arsenal shares than anyone else, ever. By far the most effective way for Stan to realise some of the value of his investment would be to simply sell some shares. As he owns nearly 70%s, he could easily sell a few and still retain a majority stake.

Finally, we might note that Kroenke is 69 in July 2016. He may not live forever and even if we do know his intentions, the business will be passed on at some point. Stan's only son, Josh, is the grandson (through his mother) of Walmart founder James Walton, so may end up even wealthier than his father. Josh had enough sporting talent to earn a 100% basketball scholarship from the University of Missouri (no mean feat). After college, he did a six-month internship for the National Basketball Association and - incredibly - worked as an underwriter for the Global Real Estate Group of Lehman Brothers (I'm sure it wasn't all his fault!). He is an Arsenal Director and looks most likely to be a future owner. We know even less about him....

BACK IN THE DOLDRUMS

CHAPTER TEN
THE END OF THE SECOND GOLDEN AGE

The end of the second golden age, its date and causes, are a matter of some controversy. The most common causes cited are:

1. **The end of a generation.** As the 2000s wore on, some of the great players of the invincible era began to age and lose their edge. The talismanic Patrick Vieira left in 2005 to see out the twilight of his career elsewhere. Arsenal legend Dennis Bergkamp stayed, but was into his mid-30s and retired in 2006. The mercurial Robert Pires also left in 2006, as did Sol Campbell; possibly the greatest player amongst the canon of Arsenal centre halves. Ashley Cole, the most despised member of the Invincibles team, sulked off to Chelsea. By the end of the 2005-6 season, only Gilberto, Freddie Ljungberg and Thierry Henry remained from the nucleus of the Invincibles. Henry and Ljungberg spent most of the season injured and left at the end of it for a last hurrah at Barcelona and West Ham respectively. Gilberto had one more good season for Arsenal, but lost his place in the team the year after. This was an exceptional group of players who bought glory to our club. It is hardly surprising that results suffered when they left

2. **The new stadium.** In 2006 Arsenal moved to the new Emirates Stadium. The creation of the stadium was a highly complex project involving the relocation of the waste processing facility on a new site; the conversion of the old stadium into flats and the sale of the variety of residential and commercial properties that resulted. The board, in this period, were accused of being focused on property management rather than football; and my, there was a lot of property to manage. The costs of building the new stadium were incurred before the flats in the old stadium

were sold, so large loans were required to bridge the gap. In order to reassure the lenders, Arsenal agreed to various temporary restrictions on player purchases and wages. This severely restricted the Manager's ability to acquire new players. Some of the Invincibles came to the end of their Arsenal careers a bit earlier than Wenger might have anticipated: he was suddenly left with a lot of vacancies, and no money to fill them

3. **The oil men.** When Arsenal took the self-limiting decision to move to the Emirates, their main rivals were Manchester United, both on the pitch and in terms of revenue. The new stadium was really an attempt to match the revenue that Manchester United were able to generate from Old Trafford. However, after the decision had been irrevocably taken, some new players emerged. In June 2003 Russian oil plutocrat Roman Abramovich took over Chelsea FC and started spending money in a way that nobody could compete with. Ambramovich, 36, was a self-made man who lost both his parents by the age of four and was adopted by his uncle. He made his fortune initially in the murky world of the Russian oil industry and by 2003 his wealth was estimated to be in the region of £7.5bn (£7,500m). He thought nothing of blowing £30m on a player and no-one could compete with him, especially not Arsenal. Abramovitch hired Champions League winning coach, Jose Mourinho to lead Chelsea, a moderately successful mid-table team, who went on to win the Premiership in both 2004-5 and 2005-6.

In 2008, possibly inspired by Abramovich's example, an even less successful team - Manchester City - were purchased by the oil-rich Abu Dhabi royal family. They also threw money around in an Abramovichesque style and won the Premier league in the 2010-11 season. Arsenal were used to being 'second dog' to Manchester United in financial terms. Now they had to get used to being 'fourth dog'

IT'S HAPPENED AGAIN

4. **Boardroom machinations and the demise of David Dein.**
Many of the greatest Managers of all time are based on great partnerships. There are many examples of this, including Shankly-Paisley, Paisley-Fagan, Clough-Taylor. It is unreasonable to expect any one individual to hold all the skills necessary to manage a great club and some fans believe the successful period of Arsène Wenger's time as Arsenal Manager was actually the period of his partnership with Vice-Chairman David Dein, whose story was discussed in the previous section. The two were (and are) great friends. Many fans believe that Wenger has been indecisive and reluctant to do transfer deals in subsequent years. It is certainly true that Dein was a natural deal maker and negotiator and had a natural boldness, which Wenger seems to lack.

All great leaders need someone to tell them when they are wrong. Arsène Wenger is a formidable and intimidating figure. This is not a matter of style, or aggression, but one of knowledge and experience. Anyone who challenges Arsène needs to accept that they don't know as much about football as him. The ability to challenge such people is sometimes called 'speaking to power' and it is a remarkably difficult thing to do. David Dein was able to do it for several reasons: he had been at the club longer than Arsène; he was a substantial shareholder; he was well connected in European football; he was the de facto chairman, Arsène's friend, and knew a lot about football. Nobody at Arsenal today has a comparable moral authority. Gazidis and the Kroenkes have been with the club much less time than Wenger and while of course Kroenke has the authority to instruct Wenger, I suspect he rarely - if ever -does so. Apart from it being out of character, Kroenke would undermine his own credibility by such action.

By this analysis, the second golden age ended when the partnership behind it broke up in April 2007

5. **Treacherous players.** In the late 2000s, Arsène Wenger tried to build a young team from players he had acquired as teenagers and developed to first team standard. With the club's financial resources tied up in the stadium project, and so unable to compete with the oil clubs, this was the only strategy really available to him (this attempt is sometimes referred to as 'project youth'). In some ways we will never know if his plan could have succeeded, because the team didn't stay together. A series of players left in search of more money, or better chances of winning titles: many of them are reviled to this day by Arsenal fans. Football supporters see the world through the lens of their own club and prize loyalty above all other qualities (after all, fans will never switch clubs). This naturally puts them at odds with players. Very few players spend their entire career with one club (Tony Adams, 1983-2002 is the only major Arsenal player in recent times to have done so). So professional footballers tend to see their attachment to a club as temporary. The following players left acrimoniously in the late 2000s and early 2010s:

- **Ashley Cole** (Cashley was 25 when he left) was trained by Arsenal as a boy. A supremely talented left back, he was a mainstay of the Invincibles. He left for more money at Chelsea, after narrowly avoiding a car crash
- **Emmanuel Adebayor** (25) spent three and a half seasons at Arsenal. He matured into a top striker, but left for more money at Manchester City in 2009. He subsequently taunted Arsenal fans and is perhaps the most disliked of this august crew
- **Samir Nasri** (Na$ri) spent three seasons at Arsenal, leaving at the age of 24 in the summer of 2011. Manchester City offered him (a lot) more money than Arsenal. He has won titles with City, but always seems a bit too keen to justify his decision to leave Arsenal, seeming to know that he did the wrong thing

IT'S HAPPENED AGAIN

- **Cesc Fabregas** is the most controversial of this group. Fabregas is still held in affection by many Arsenal supporters. Fabregas, a prodigiously talented midfielder, was poached from Barcelona's academy at the age of 16. They were quite annoyed. He matured into a wonderful midfielder, the centre around whom the rest of the team rotated and became captain after Gallas' collapse, but never seemed entirely comfortable in the role.

  Some fans have been harsh on Cesc in recent times, because he signed for rival teams. I don't share this point of view. I can forgive his decision to return to Barcelona. He is a Catalan, and Catalans see themselves as an oppressed minority in Spain. The closest thing we have to it is a Scottish or Welsh identity, but even those analogies are weak. FC Barcelona is an icon of Catalan identity, a source of nationalistic pride and hope. The siren call of his hometown proved too much in the summer of 2011: Barcelona had become the best team in the world and were being managed by his boyhood hero, Pep Guardiola. It is rumoured that he accepted a pay cut to move

- **Robin van Persie** (29) became Arsenal's leading player after Fabregas left in the summer of 2011 and succeeded him as club captain. He responded to the challenge by being the Premier League's top goal scorer for the following two seasons. Unfortunately, by the second of those seasons he was playing for Manchester United.

  RVP had always been a talent, but had suffered from endless injuries. Many Arsenal fans felt that he owed the club a debt of gratitude for sticking by him and paying his wages through all his time out. Some were also angered by Arsenal's decision to sell for £20m. Perhaps Arsenal felt they were getting a bargain for a player who was nearing the end of his peak years and had only one year left on a contract he was refusing to renew. Unfortunately, his goals in 2012-13 were just what Man U needed in Fergusson's final season and propelled them to the title. In fact, 2012-13 proved to be van Persie's last effective season, but by then the damage had been done

6. **Injuries.** Arsenal suffered a lot of injuries in the decade following the Invincibles season. The reasons for this are controversial, with some blaming training methods or bad luck. It was certainly commonly accepted wisdom that Arsenal were easily intimidated during this period. The previously described Game 50 was one of the most controversial league games of the Premiership era and was endlessly debated and reshown. It certainly appeared that other teams learnt from the way that Man U approached the game that day. The 'rotational fouling' tactic that was used by them against Arsenal was widely emulated, being seen by many to be the best way to beat Arsenal.

Three young players suffered compound leg fractures in incidents that still anger fans today. All resulted from the kind of late tackles the Neville brothers made particularly liberal use of in Game 50. Abou Diaby (leg broken 2006) never really recovered and a promising career was destroyed by perpetual injury. The story of Eduardo's broken leg (2008) is told below. He never recovered to the same level and left Arsenal in 2010. Aaron Ramsey (leg broken 2010) has probably recovered the best of the three, and at the time of writing is having a reasonably successful career with Arsenal, but lost the best part of two years of his career to the injury.

CHAPTER ELEVEN
FLATTERING TO DECEIVE

Back on the pitch it was far from obvious that the second golden age was over. Patrick Vieira won the FA Cup for us with his last kick in an Arsenal shirt, by scoring the decisive penalty in the 2005 Final. The following season was the last at Highbury and was full of celebrations and reminiscences. The team had a glorious run to Arsenal's first ever Champions League Final in Paris which was lost to a club on the up, Barcelona. But even then a bit of misfortune was involved; with a red card and two late Barcelona goals converting triumph to defeat. The emergence of Cesc Fabregas briefly seemed like ample compensation for the loss of Patrick Vieira

In the wake of defeat, and to widespread relief, Thierry Henry decided to stay at the club, plus we had a shiny new stadium to move into. The stadium was due to be opened by lifelong Arsenal fan Queen Elizabeth II, but on the day she injured her back and sent her husband, Prince Phillip as substitute. She subsequently held a reception at Buckingham Palace for the Arsenal players and employees by way of compensation, but it was a bad omen for the new palace of football.

The 2006-7 season was a tough one on the pitch with a number of the Invincibles ending their Arsenal journeys at Highbury, including three of the back four: Campbell, Cole and Lauren. The magic of Bergkamp and Pires left too, meaning that nearly half the Invincibles starting line-up left in one summer. The spectacle of 60,000 sell outs at every match in the new stadium steadied our nerves. Arsenal was the proud owner of the most advanced stadium in the world, generating more match day income than any other club on earth, but we finished 21 points behind champions Manchester United. A youthful team lost the final of the League Cup to Chelsea, and we entered the 2007-8 season with some trepidation. There was a suspicion that our new home was not intimidating opposition teams like the old one had. When Thierry Henry left to join Barcelona in the summer, the faithful were beginning to get concerned.

But 2007-8 went better than anyone expected. Arsenal were trying to convince us all that the golden age wasn't over, by leading the Premiership. It looked like we might win our first title at the new Emirates stadium. The team was showing promise following the departure of the talismanic duo of Vieira and Henry. Over the summer, the last vestiges of the Invincibles team - Thierry Henry, Fredrik Ljungberg and Jose Antonio Reyes - had left but there was a sense that the next chapter had begun, and the future looked bright.

Our new captain was a combative and very talented centre half called William Gallas (Arsenal fans adore centre halves perhaps more than any other players). He had come to Arsenal from Chelsea's championship team, as part of the deal that took much-reviled Ashley Cole to Chelsea. A host of new players were threatening to continue the glories of the past decade. Cesc Fabregas was the closest we had ever come to replacing Liam Brady in midfield and up front, a bright young striker of Croatian-Brazilian extraction called Eduardo was getting the pulses racing.

Eduardo had joined in the summer, and was establishing himself as a deadly striker. He was a classic Wenger 'left-field' signing. Having hardly played in the first part of the season while he acclimatised to English football, he was fresh and lively as the title run-in approached. This was a physically lightweight team compared to the great teams of a few years earlier (Vieira, Pires and Campbell). They had developed a delightful style that relied on quick passing and sharp movement and almost danced their way around the opposition.

The worst game ever

IT'S HAPPENED AGAIN

On the morning of 23rd February, 2008, Arsenal led the Premiership by five points and took their lead to an away match with the struggling Birmingham City (who ended up being relegated).

There was a common view in the game at the time, that the only way to stop Arsenal was with violence. Man U had pioneered the idea in the 50th Game (as described in the previous section), assisted by some shocking refereeing, while Allarydyce's Bolton had further popularised the idea in a rugby game which cost Arsenal the 2004-5 Premiership title.

The struggling Birmingham City players must have been fearful before the game that we would simply play around them: footballers are curiously sensitive to humiliation. Perhaps they had talked about how to combat this before kick-off. If a violent approach wasn't specifically in their team talk, it was probably in the backs of their minds.

After three minutes, Arsenal's elusive style was already in evidence. They were playing the ball with control and poise, with the Birmingham team already chasing shadows and showing signs of frustration. As Eduardo played the ball gracefully to a teammate, Birmingham defender Martin Taylor piled in with a late, dangerous tackle. Eduardo's eyes were on the ball, and he didn't seem to see Taylor coming. Football is a sport of many things: beauty, competition, sporting endeavour, controversy, dispute and joy. Occasionally, it bares its ugly teeth. Occasionally, we are confronted with the reality that these supermen, these balletic, overpaid, primadonnas, are really just flesh and blood. This was one such occasion. Eduardo's ankle and lower leg were shattered by Taylor's challenge. It looked as if his foot had been amputated and was only being held on by the sock. It was one of the most shocking injuries you will ever see on any sports pitch.

Taylor was sent off and had the privilege of leaving the scene of the crime immediately. It took seven minutes for St John's Ambulance to remove the stricken Eduardo from the pitch.

Eduardo was strapped onto a stretcher and to an oxygen machine, leaving the field barely conscious. It was seven long minutes, when the players and spectators had little choice but to reflect on what they had just witnessed. Eduardo claims to have no memory of those minutes. Arsenal's Brazilian midfielder Gilberto was the only player present (he was a substitute) who could speak Eduardo's native Portuguese; and Eduardo hadn't been in England long enough to learn fluent English. Gilberto stood by Eduardo, acting as translator between him and the first aiders. The look of horror on Cesc Fabregas' face told a thousand stories. He looked like what he was: a young man who loved his sport, but was suddenly confronted with a horrible reality that had never occurred to him - his legs, the tools of his trade, were not the indestructible objects he had imagined.

The game eventually continued in a kind of daze, as if no-one could believe what they had seen. 10-man Birmingham scored after 28 minutes. After about half an hour, the players' instincts re-established themselves and a game of football broke out. Walcott scored on 50 and 55 minutes (his first league goals for Arsenal) and we drifted towards a comfortable 2-1 victory. It had been a horrible day, but at least the title challenge would live to fight on.

Then, in injury time, Arsenal left back Gael Clichy, under no pressure, mis-hit a pass and gave away the ball just outside his own penalty area. Birmingham's Stuart Parnaby controlled the ball and made a run into the area. Clichy, perhaps over-eager to atone for his error, made a clumsy challenge on Parnaby which was unnecessary and a bit wild, but wasn't a foul. The referee, whose brain was probably as addled as everybody else's, awarded a penalty which Birmingham duly scored to deny Arsenal three points.

The Arsenal community was left with an empty feeling. Sport can be crushing when everything conspires against you. We didn't know whether to be upset about the lost points, or to consider it irrelevant in the face of Eduardo's injury. We didn't

IT'S HAPPENED AGAIN

know whether to be angry with Clichy's carelessness, or to sympathise with a traumatised young man.

Arsenal captain William Gallas seemed to descend into a state of mental breakdown. When the penalty was awarded he removed himself from the scene and stood in the opposite half of the pitch, in apparent silent protest, while it was taken. At the end of the match he vented his frustration by viciously kicking out at an advertising hoarding and sitting down on the pitch, again in apparent defiant protest. None of his teammates joined him: they all trudged off the pitch, probably just relieved it was all over. Only Wenger approached Gallas to console his desolation. I have never seen a player protest in this manner before or since. Gallas cut a lonely figure, sitting on the pitch for about five minutes as the stadium emptied. Over the next few weeks he was widely ridiculed for his behaviour.

I rather felt for Gallas. We often misuse words like tragedy, disaster and triumph in football. We dismiss the sadness of footballers on the grounds that 'how sad can you be when you are paid £5m a year to play football?' But what had happened to Eduardo was genuinely shocking, on a human level. I think that many of the players on that team were traumatized and suffered from genuine mental health problems as a result. Gallas had summoned every ounce of will in his body to put the Eduardo incident to the back of his mind and to concentrate on winning the game. As captain, a role he was new to, he tried to lead by example. And he succeeded. His team was coasting to a hard-worked victory. When his teammate and countryman Clichy made an inexplicable mistake at the end of the match, compounded by a refereeing error, Gallas had nowhere left to go. He felt he was a man wronged, and boy did he have a right to feel that way. In the finest of French traditions he protested, silently but insistently. When I look at those pictures of Gallas, I see a man who is genuinely in a dark place, and doesn't know what to do. As human beings, surely we can all relate to that.

Our hearts (and William Gallas' face) told us the title challenge was over. Our heads told us we were still top of the league with all to play for. Our hearts told us a bright future had been shattered. Our heads told us not to be so ridiculous - how could one game, and one injury, define an era? Our hearts were right.

The devastation was total. Arsenal's title challenge unravelled over the next few weeks and we finished third. As the 2015-16 season dawned, Arsenal had still failed to better this performance. Perhaps the saddest aspect of this tale is that none of its protagonists (except perhaps Eduardo) are now held in any real affection by the Arsenal community.

CHAPTER TWELVE
WHAT HAPPENED TO THEM ALL?

The mercurial 22 year old **Cesc Fabregas** was well on the way to hero status at Arsenal that day. He was probably the most imaginative footballer we had seen up to that point (Ozil came later) and had narrowly failed to bring us the European Cup 18 months earlier: now it looked like he would bring us the League. We were looking forward to ten years of Fabregas inspired success. Of all the players on the pitch, he looked the most disturbed by the Eduardo incident and never really recaptured the form that had lifted Arsenal to the top of the league. He eventually left Arsenal to join his boyhood club, Barcelona, in the summer of 2011. Some of us felt that the violence of the English game, as epitomised by Birmingham, played a major part in his decision to leave. He didn't prosper at Barcelona, who got rid of him in summer 2014 and Arsenal didn't take up their option to re-sign him. He further tarnished his reputation with Arsenal fans by joining Chelsea in the same summer; subsequently playing a part in the sending off of Gabriel in Game 4 of the 2015-16 season.

Eduardo was lucky to avoid an amputation. It took nearly 18 months for him to return to the Arsenal first team, but he was clearly not the same player. He played a handful of games for Arsenal and was sold to Shakhtar Donetsk in 2010. The day Taylor broke his leg had been two days before his 25th birthday.

William Gallas never recovered his reputation. The press were merciless and he was finally removed as Arsenal captain in November 2008, when he gave an interview in which he criticised his younger teammates for lacking courage. Fabregas replaced him as captain, but never looked comfortable in the role. In August 2010, Gallas (by then in decline) joined arch rivals Tottenham Hotspur, eventually becoming the team's captain. Any sympathy for him amongst Arsenal supporters went out of the window.

Martin Taylor didn't prosper either. His tackle was a symptom of the fact that he was out of his depth playing Arsenal that day. He simply didn't have the skill to deal with attackers like Eduardo, and made a clumsy mistake. Taylor had never been able to establish himself as a regular player in the Premiership for Birmingham. Manager Alex McLeish had already tried to sell Taylor earlier in the season. He only played against Arsenal because of an injury crisis at Birmingham, and was starting only his second game of the season. His tackle caused such controversy that it was reviewed by FIFA, who cleared him of any intent. Taylor only played two more Premiership games for Birmingham over two seasons before they sold him in 2010 to Watford and he saw out the rest of his career playing a handful of games for lower league clubs.

Mike Dean was the referee that day. He sent off Martin Taylor and awarded the controversial last minute penalty. He remains a figure of hate for the Arsenal faithful to this day and went on to referee the infamous League Cup Final between the same two teams in 2011, as well as a string of other dubious matches involving Arsenal. He finally capped his reputation in Game 4 of 2015-16, with one of the worst (and most result-altering) refereeing performances ever seen in the Premiership, gifting Chelsea a blatantly unearned victory. Arsenal fans gathered a petition with over 100,000 signatures after this game, asking that he never be allowed to referee another Arsenal game. The FA, which seems to be completely immune to accusations of corruption and malpractice, appointed him to referee his next Arsenal match on 20th February 2016.

The rest of the Arsenal players. When I researched this, I was genuinely shocked at what happened to the men who played for Arsenal that day. Including the substitutes, all but two had left the club by the summer of 2011, just over three years later. I list their ages on that day, to make the point that this was a young

IT'S HAPPENED AGAIN

team. In normal circumstances we would have expected many of them to have long careers at Arsenal. This is what happened to them:

Manuel Almunia, aged 30, played 109 games for Arsenal and was first choice for much of 2007 to 2010. He was never loved by the fans and lost his place in the team in September 2010. Arsenal allowed his contract to run out (the ultimate insult for a modern footballer) and released him in the summer of 2012

Bacary Sagna was 25. Of the players who played that day, Sagna arguably prospered best. He was a stalwart of Arsenal during the lean years which followed. We won the FA Cup in his final game in 2014. He deserved it. He joined Manchester City for a higher salary in the summer of 2014, but as he was past his best, Arsenal fans didn't begrudge his decision

Phillipe Senderos. Along with Fabregas, who he roomed with as an Arsenal youth, the 23 year old Senderos was seen as the core of the Arsenal team of the next decade. He was part of the legendary 2006 back four who still hold the record (919 minutes) for not conceding a goal in Champions League play. However, he never quite made the grade and left Arsenal at the end of the 2007-8 season on loan. He never re-established himself in the Arsenal team and left permanently in the summer of 2010

Gael Clichy, 22. Clichy's mistake that day turned out to be the first in a series of mental errors which have held back the career of this otherwise highly talented full back. He left to join Manchester City for a higher wage in July 2011. We were not really sad to see him go

Theo Walcott was 19 at the time. His career is another story of unfulfilled talent that has been massively blighted by injury

Matthieu Flamini was 23. Flamini left to join Milan on a free transfer at the end of that season. His career was plagued by injury and he made only 97 appearances for Milan over five seasons, returning to Arsenal as a free agent to become an occasional squad player in the summer of 2013

Alexander Hleb, 26. Hleb also left at the end of the season to join Barcelona. His career nosedived and he made only 36 appearances for Barcelona, then playing for a series of ever-lesser teams, including a loan spell with Birmingham City

Emmanuel Adebayor, aged 23, left Arsenal for a higher wage at Manchester City fifteen months after this match, becoming a hate figure for Arsenal fans after exuberantly celebrating a goal he scored against Arsenal. He suffered numerous personal problems as his career went inexorably downhill and he descended into a tragi-comic figure. He sealed his infamy by joining Tottenham in 2011

CHAPTER THIRTEEN
DARK DAYS & DAWNING HOPE

The period that followed the Birmingham game was emphatically trophy less and the media began to count up the years that had elapsed since Arsenal's 2005 FA Cup victory. The low point on the pitch came at Wembley in the 2011 League Cup Final with Birmingham City again providing the pain. We were the overwhelming favourites. Superstar captain Cesc Fabregas flew his whole family over to watch the game, to see him lift his first trophy as Arsenal captain. But Fabregas got injured in the run up to the game and didn't play. Arsenal missed him and put in a turgid display. With the game locked at 1-1 extra time beckoned. Arsenal goalkeeper Szchezny and centre back Koscielny then managed to conjure a horrendous mix-up. Both players looked on, expecting the other to collect the ball while Birmingham striker Martins nipped between the two of them, singing 'thank you' as he went through and scored into an empty net.

The low point off the pitch came the following summer, when both Fabregas and Nasri jumped ship, thus delivering an eloquent verdict on 'project youth' that was difficult to misinterpret. The club looked to be in disarray: Wenger appeared to panic for the first time in his Arsenal career. He signed five players just before the transfer deadline day in August 2011 including the infamous singing of South Korean striker, Park Chu-Young. At first it appeared that Park would have to return to South Korea to perform military service. When that problem was resolved, it emerged that he wasn't very good at football. In two years at Arsenal, he made one substitute appearance in the League and scored one goal in the League Cup.

The high points of this dire period were a series of increasingly unlikely and ever-more amusing incidents by which local rivals Tottenham conspired to finish below Arsenal in the league. These incidents are lovingly described later in this book. Arsenal fans adopted the tradition of celebrating St Totteringham's Day. This was a saints day celebrated, not on the same day every year, but on the day that it became mathematically impossible for Tottenham to overtake Arsenal in the League table. The two teams had been considered to have a roughly equal status before the arrival of Arsène Wenger, but Tottenham hadn't finished above Arsenal since 1995. By the start of the 2015-16 season Arsenal fans had, with increasing glee, celebrated holy St Totteringham's Day for 20 years in succession.

Arsenal's finances also seemed to improve during this period. The Emirates continued to sell out, even for minor games. The money accumulated on Arsenal's balance sheet, and the team continued to qualify for the Champions League, often at the expense of Tottenham.

In many ways it was a fabulous achievement to keep Arsenal playing in the Champions League in this period. But the fans begun to smell a rat. They suspected the club's new owners were milking them for cash and thought the club's ambition was only to finish in the top four rather than making any genuine attempt to win silverware. The atmosphere around the club deteriorated, and for the first time, some fans begun to question Wenger's suitability for the job. Arsenal seemed to be getting left behind.

All hail the Messiah

By August 2013 some fans had descended to chanting 'spend some fucking money'. Arsenal did, blowing £42m (more than double the previous record signing) on German wonder kid Mesut Ozil, from Real Madrid. Everyone was boosted. The oil men seemed to have wearied of spending silly money and oil prices had fallen, meaning they had less to throw around. It felt like we were back in with a chance. Ozil's performances were often

IT'S HAPPENED AGAIN

underwhelming but undeniably elegant. The team led the league for much of the season before falling away in spring, but the 9 year trophy drought came to an end with an FA Cup final win over unfashionable Hull City. It was a dramatic day. With the team 2-0 down inside ten minutes, memories of the humiliation of the 2011 League Cup flooded into our hearts. Santi Cazorla and Laurent Koscielny got us back in the match before Aaron Ramsey, our player of the season, scored an extra-time winner. We were back!

I watched the game with my five year old son, bringing back memories of watching the 1979 Cup final with my dad on the day I became a six-year-old Arsenal fan. Passing on your 'fandom' to your son is a magical thing. I'm a first generation fan. I didn't inherit Arsenal from my own dad, and this confers a slightly reduced status from some fans. You are always viewed with a little suspicion in some circles, a bit like a first generation immigrant, or the outsider who moved into a tight knit Cornish village 20 years ago and is still seen as an alien. The look on my son's face when we went 2-0 down also reminded me that football supporting is not all fun. Several members of my family had questioned whether Arsenal was a good thing to share with my son, and I had genuine concerns over it. A five year old can't really make an informed choice on these things, and football supporting is something that you can be stuck with for an awfully long-time. In the end though, there wasn't any real decision to make. I didn't even need to encourage him. He just wanted to join in with his dad; and what could be more natural than that?

The 2014-15 season

The story of the season was Chelsea, with Jose Mourinho in the second year of his second spell in charge at Stamford Bridge. His team looked good and he strengthened it by signing former Arsenal player Cesc Fabregas from Barcelona and Diego Costa, the striker from Champions League runners up Atletico Madrid. Fabregas and Costa were unstoppable for three months at the start of the season. By Christmas, Chelsea had won 13 of 17 games and were 15 points ahead of Arsenal.

Arsenal, with new signing from Barcelona Alexis Sanchez, started slowly and never looked like threatening Chelsea. Ozil and Mertesacker had won the World Cup with Germany in the summer and they seemed tired even before Ozil picked up an injury and missed half the season.

In the Champions League, Arsenal qualified for the knockout stages for the fourteenth consecutive year. We then catastrophically lost 3-1 to unfancied Monaco at home in the first leg of the last 16. A brave away performance was not enough to make up the deficit and Arsenal lost the only tie Arsène Wenger had ever played against his former club.

In the second half of the season, Arsenal had looked like the strongest team in England. In particular, Francis Coquelin emerged as the legendary defensive midfielder that Arsenal fans had been yearning for, for the past decade.

Arsenal briefly threatened to catch Chelsea, but a 0-0 home draw at the Emirates with five games to go was effectively enough for Chelsea to hold them off. Arsenal finished third as Man City made a late run to second.

We did, however, convincingly retain the FA Cup. The highlights of the run were a 2-1 victory at Old Trafford in the quarter final, with Danny Welbeck scoring the winner against the club he had grown up with but who had sold him to Arsenal at the start of the season on the grounds that he wasn't good enough. The 4-0 victory over Aston Villa in the final was a lovely contrast to the previous year's nail-biting finish.

Overall it was a season of improvement. The FA Cup represented another trophy, and all seemed rosy in the Arsenal tent. Fans were optimistic that we would be real challengers for the League title in 2015-16.

CHAPTER FOURTEEN
SUMMER 2015

And so we arrive at the summer of 2015, the prelude to our season. Like many football fans, I am a bit ambivalent about summer. I can see the attractions of the heady long evenings, the briefly Mediterranean climate and the glorious sunlight. I take the opportunity to be interested in other sports. Wimbledon is good, the Tour de France, the British Open golf, sometimes a World Cup or European Championship, or an Olympics. It occurs to me also that other things happen in the world, and I might turn a bit of attention to politics or world affairs. The truth is though, that I miss Arsenal. A sense of relief washes over me as August wears on and the new season approaches. So here's a few things that happened in the summer of 2015, the backdrop to the 2015-16 season:

- Wars and conflicts rumble on in Syria, Iraq, Afghanistan
- The newly elected Conservative government settles in (no longer in coalition with Lib-Dems)
- After a hissy-fit that was impressive, even by the standards of the modern footballer, Liverpool finally sell Raheem Stirling to Man City for around £49m
- Europe plunges ever deeper into a refugee crisis. People are desperately escaping the world's conflict zones, particularly Syria
- European governments decide that their naval patrolling of the Mediterranean is encouraging refugees, by making the crossing from North Africa safer, so they withdraw the patrols
- This leads to mass drownings in a series of heart-wrenching sea accidents with no rescue available
- The Germans (who I find it increasingly impossible to dislike, no matter how hard I try) show the world moral leadership by actively welcoming desperate refugees. Can it

really be true that German people are just nicer than everybody else?
- The British economy continues to show signs of coming out the long recession that has lasted since 2008 (with bizarrely little effect on football)
- England defeat Australia to regain the Ashes. Joe Root is England's hero. In the decisive fourth test, Australia are bowled out for 60 before lunch on the first morning (Stuart Broad is the hero)
- World football governing body FIFA descends into farce. President Sepp Blatter is increasingly desperate to prove that his hands are clean of the widespread corruption (they are clearly not)
- USA celeb-entrepreneur Donald Trump emerges as the frontrunner for the Republican ticket in the 2016 Presidential election
- A horrific roller-coaster accident at Britain's most popular amusement park, Alton Towers, leaves 4 people trapped at 60ft for four hours.
- USA win the women's World Cup (played on artificial turf - the sign of things to come?). England lose 2-1 in the semi-final to Japan. Japan's winning goal was a spectacular, and heart-breaking, freak own goal in the 92nd minute.
- Chile (including Alexis Sanchez) win the Copa America for the first time. Sanchez scores the winning penalty in a shootout to decide the final. He is even more revered in Chile than in Islington
- The never ending Greek debt saga lurches from crisis to crisis
- The 800th anniversary of the signing of the Magna Carta is celebrated. The document represents the origin of freedom in the English speaking world
- The scandal of paedophilia in the Roman Catholic church rumbles on

IT'S HAPPENED AGAIN

- Periodic mass shootings in the USA continue (to the visible frustration of President Obama, who finds his countrymen's endless opposition to gun control unforgiveable)
- Israelis and Palestinians continue to tragically kill each other
- Vladimir Putin's Russia continues to provoke the West with various acts of brigandage in an attempt to distract attention from the Russian economic crisis that has resulted from the fall in oil prices
- Usain Bolt wins the 100m and 200m at the World Athletics Championships, to establish himself beyond doubt as the greatest sprinter of all time. To widespread delight and relief, he defeats the favourite, convicted drug cheat Justin Gatlin (USA) into second.
- Much loved British athlete, Mo Farah (a Gooner!) comes under pressure following unproven accusations of doping against his coach. He wins the 5k and 10k at the World Championships, to become one of Britain's most successful athletes of all time
- Debris is found washed up on an island from Malaysian flight MH370, which mysteriously disappeared in March 2014. All hope is lost for relatives, but hopes of solving the mystery are revived
- NASA's New Horizons spacecraft completes a flyby of Pluto and its moons. Spectacular pictures were taken amid much scientific hyperventilation

The summer transfer window

One of the great frustrations for intelligent football fans is the silliness of transfer speculation over the summer. This has become more and more detached from reality as time goes on. And yet it is difficult to ignore, because somewhere amongst the dross will be important news of genuine signings. If you care, it is hard to block it all out. And it is very tricky to distinguish the small amount of real news from the vast quantities of rubbish.

TIM CHARLESWORTH

Nobody wants to pay for journalistic content any more, whether on the internet or in newspapers, but writers of all sorts need to earn money and cover publishing costs. Most writing nowadays is funded by advertising. Advertisers are interested in how often their adverts are seen, and this is usually measured by views or 'clicks' on the internet. This results in 'click baiting'.

'Click baiting' involves writing sensationalist, but vague headlines. The idea is that the reader is suckered into clicking on the headline to find out what it means. The 'baiter' doesn't care that the reader is disappointed to discover that the headline was misleading. The baiter is only interested in the click, which allows advertising sales. Disappointing the reader is of no concern.

For example a click baiter might scream: 'Wenger set to leave Arsenal!' Wow! Big news, thinks the reader, but when he clicks on the headline, he discovers that the article is about an interview which Wenger gave six months ago in which he mentions that 'one day' he will retire. This is not news, but the baiter has his (dishonestly obtained) click.

'Click baiting' is responsible for the rather strange headlines that we tend to see nowadays, such as: 'Arsenal midfielder to miss Liverpool' game. We click on this, thinking it is an important development, only to discover that it is simply saying that a player who broke his leg (say Wilshere for the sake of an example) two months ago, will not play against Liverpool. We already knew this, but if the headline had said 'Wilshere to miss Liverpool game' nobody would have clicked on it.

So the football writers, devoid of any real news, find it hard to resist the click baiting temptation, and the poor reader ends up wading through all the excrement that results. The main speculations of summer 2014-15 were:

1. Petr Cech to leave champions Chelsea for Arsenal
2. Arsenal to sign Karim Benzema from Real Madrid
3. Arsenal desperate to sign any striker (not true in my opinion)

IT'S HAPPENED AGAIN

4. Raheem Sterling desperate to leave Liverpool
5. Chelsea repeatedly bidding to sign Everton Centre Half John Stones
6. Chelsea reject Kevin de Bruyne to come to England from Germany
7. Cavani to join Arsenal from Monaco (never happening)

In the end Arsenal did sign Petr Cech, but nobody else. Apparently they were the only team in any of the major European Leagues not to sign an outfield player. Raheem Sterling signed for Manchester City, as did Kevin De Bruyne. Chelsea Manager, Mourinho failed to sign John Stones and seemed quite upset about it, but Chelsea entered the new season as favourites to retain their title anyway. Man City were considered second favourites with their shiny new players and most bookies had Arsenal third favourites.

But by far the most momentous (although curiously under-reported) event of the summer was that I decided to take my wife's advice. I started writing for Untold Arsenal, my favourite Arsenal website. The rest of this book is the story of the season and what I wrote about it. The next chapter is my very first article.

CHAPTER FIFTEEN
WHO SHOULD ARSENAL BUY?
THE COMPLETE GUIDE

June 15th 2015

Following the successful FA Cup campaign there was a general consensus in the 'commentatorsphere' that Arsenal would challenge for the Premiership next season, but only if they bought 'two or three high quality improvements'.

This started me thinking about who, or what, these reinforcements might be. So here is a view of Arsenal's players and options for next season.

But we must remember that us Gooners are a little bit misled by the Alexis Sanchez experience, which has encouraged us to forget that most big money transfers are a failure (after all there is usually an unspoken reason why the selling club was prepared to let him go). In fact, Sanchez is an exceptional player - there are not lots more like him sitting on a shelf ready to be plucked.

IT'S HAPPENED AGAIN

First Choice

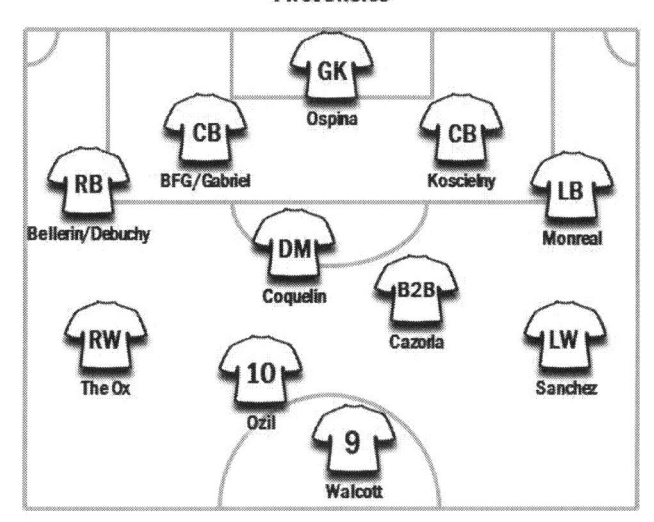

GK	Ospina
CB	BFG/Gabriel
CB	Koscielny
RB	Bellerin/Debuchy
LB	Monreal
DM	Coquelin
B2B	Cazorla
RW	The Ox
LW	Sanchez
10	Ozil
9	Walcott

Second Choice

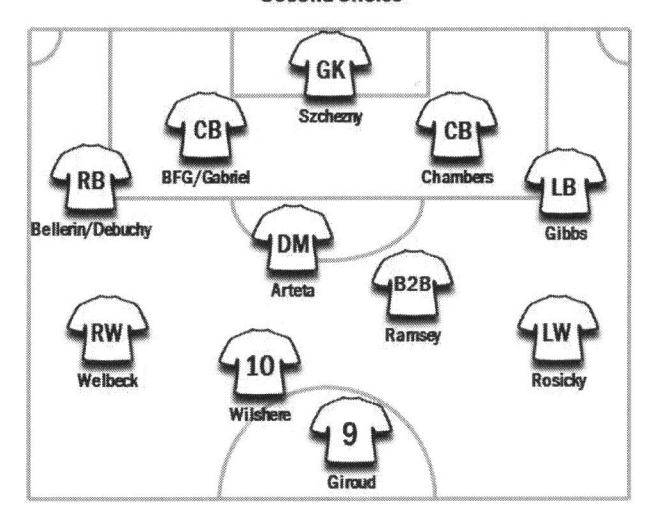

GK	Szczesny
CB	BFG/Gabriel
CB	Chambers
RB	Bellerin/Debuchy
LB	Gibbs
DM	Arteta
B2B	Ramsey
RW	Welbeck
LW	Rosicky
10	Wilshere
9	Giroud

Not included in either: Diaby, Gnabry, Bielik, Akpom, Sanogo, Hayden, Martinez, Toral, Podolski, Flamini, Daniel Crowley, Joel Campbell, Wellington Silva

There aren't that many positions where the first choice players are clearly much better than the second choice ones. (Ozil is probably the best no. 10, Koscielny is better than Chambers, Sanchez is clearly the best winger/AM option and Le Coq is head and shoulders above Arteta).

We can clearly see why pundits think Arsenal have enough 'depth' and 'cover'. This leads to the conclusion that the only real way to improve is to sign some exceptional players. However it is not really obvious which positions these signings could be in. Let's look at the positions most commonly talked about:

GK: This position looks like a weakness for Arsenal, albeit not a terrible one and Petr Cech looks like he might be better than either of our top two.

However, I am always suspicious about players who lose their place in a team. Their supporters work hard to argue that the place is lost due to some 'view' held by the Manager. In reality, terminal decline is often found to be the true explanation (Arshavin, Podolski).

You certainly can't trust anything that comes out of the mouth of Mourinho, the man who knows best what is going on with Cech.

Cech is 33, and may well have his best years behind him. Alternatively, he might not (see Pat Jennings). I don't see any other realistic options. Only Lloris, De Gea and Courtois look better (possibly Casillas), but are unobtainable.

CB: Mertesacker looks under pressure here, but he is still a good player. Remember he had a hard 13-14 season, followed by a long World Cup and then played 48 games for us in 14-15. He is entitled to be tired and looked it when celebrating his goal at Wembley - and in the post-match interview.

We may find he is an improved player next season with a bit of rest and international retirement.

IT'S HAPPENED AGAIN

Gabriel looks excellent, apart from a tendency to make over-eager mistakes. I presume these errors are a function of newness, and not a permanent feature of his game. I don't think any incoming centre back is going to do better than him. Koscielny is obviously excellent.

Chambers is the best no. 4 choice CB I can remember at Arsenal (Squillaci, Stepanovs, Ceasar). Monreal and Debuchy also appear to be good options. Liverpool and City managed to piss away large sums of money by trying to improve this position last summer, and I don't think it likely that Wenger will make a similar mistake.

DM: I think the brilliance of Coquelin is killing this debate. I think we all still feel his performances are a bit too good to be true (how can he suddenly be this good? Why didn't we - including Wenger - ever notice the potential?).

However strange it is, we must probably accept that he is a world class player who is likely to prove this point over the next couple of seasons. I am in awe. At the very least, Wenger is going to give him the chance to prove he is as good as he looks over the next season.

Arteta is not a world-beater, but has done very well for us, and is surely good enough to be no. 2 in this position. I feel certain that he will be given that chance. Surely Flamini is redundant with Bielik, Wilshere and Chambers available in emergencies?

CF: Neither Giroud nor Walcott are proven world class options here. However, it is perfectly conceivable that one or both will be very good next season. Giroud is massively improved on the player that arrived at Arsenal, and the limit of Walcott's potential is still unclear (but exciting).

I would probably swap either of them for Suarez, Aguero or Costa, but this is not an option. I'm not sure that any of the available players (Cavani, Falcao, Higuain, Benzema, Ibrahimovic, Martinez, Van Persie, Benteke, Lukaku) are obviously better (even before we consider a settling in period). As a general rule, it is easy to spend a lot of money on a No 9, and the majority of such transfers fail. There is also an argument that the traditional No 9 position is on the way out. Barcelona don't really play with one at all, and all No 9s are much more involved in general team play than they used to be (Giroud, Van Persie and Walcott are all more integral that Ian Wright ever was). Even Thierry Henry recorded far more assists than was decent for an out-and-out no 9. So could the answer to the no9 question, simply, be that you don't need one?

All in all, it is hard to see where these three world class signings could possibly fit in.

THE CURATE'S EGG

Pre-season to the second Interlull
July to October 2015

CHAPTER SIXTEEN
PRESEASON

| Wed 15th July | Singapore Select XI | N | Barclays Asia Trophy | W | 4-0 |
| Sat 18th July | Everton | N | Barclays Asia Trophy | W | 3-1 |

WENGER'S SELECTION DILEMMAS FOR 2015-16
July 22nd 2015

As the new season approaches I cannot remember ever being so uncertain about our 'first choice starting eleven'. So I thought it might be useful to consider some of Wenger's upcoming selection dilemmas.

For simplicity I have assumed a traditional back four; a defensive midfielder, a box to box midfielder and an attacking midfielder/no. 10. I have then added two wingers/wide midfielders and a central striker/no. 9. This is a bit of an over-simplification, but it is essentially the way Arsenal have lined up for the last five years.

The lack of clear 'first choice' players is both a strength and a weakness. It indicates that we have good strength in depth, but also that we are short of real 'stand-out' performers who have proved themselves so consistently excellent in recent years they are nailed-on starters. I think the Community Shield line up will give us the first real indication of what Wenger thinks our first 11 is (albeit Sanchez will not play following the Copa America).

Uncertain positions

GK: Szchezny or Ospina or Cech

We have to assume that Cech will get an opportunity to establish himself as first choice in goal. He left Chelsea due to a lack of first team games and surely Wenger gave him some assurances when he signed.

TIM CHARLESWORTH

I remain to be convinced that Cech is as good as he used to be (and he was very good). I have a nagging doubt that Mourinho has tricked us into buying a dud: Maureen's protests against selling Cech seemed a little surreal to me. At the end of the day Mourinho is a good judge of players and will know if Cech is in decline or not, whereas Wenger is in a less good position to conduct an objective judgement (of course the Tots thought Pat Jennings was in decline...).

That leaves Ospina and Szchezny. I don't think many of us are convinced that Ospina is the long-term solution here, but he did finish the season as first choice in a successful team. Szchezny seems like a young keeper who may still be the long-term option in this position, but has not quite lived up to expectations yet*. The general assumption is that Ospina will leave and Szchezny will settle in to play the long-game. This is probably correct. Wenger will probably allow one of them to play in cup games, but third choice keepers generally get very little opportunity and I cannot see either of them settling for third choice.

CB: Mertesacker or Gabriel

I fear for Mertesacker. He is a lovely chap, and I really enjoyed his headed/shoulder goal in the Cup Final. His 'Big Friendly Giant' moniker is well earned (I reject alternative interpretations of BFG). But he lost his place in the German team on merit and now looks under threat for Arsenal.

His ability to turn like an oil tanker - and his general lack of pace - can expose our team on occasions. He seems to rely on Koscielny (and the full backs sometimes) to cover for him, which can work very well (teamwork being the essence of football after all), but is a potential point of failure when the team is really under the cosh. Wenger likes his defences to push high up the pitch and the BFG's lack of pace is a barrier to this.

---

* Szchezny eventually spent the whole season on loan at Roma

IT'S HAPPENED AGAIN

On the other hand, Mertesacker is going to have a proper summer off for the first time in a while. Last season he played 49 games for us on the back of a long World Cup campaign. He looked tired at the end of the season and a rest might make all the difference. He has also retired from the German team and this will make 2015-16 easier for him. So let's hope we see an improved BFG next season.

Gabriel looks like the real deal; a bit skittish and prone to errors when he played last season, but I think this might go away as he settles down and plays regularly. Athletically he looks superb, so I expect that Wenger will use pre-season to compare the two. My bet is that Gabriel will get more playing time than Mertesacker and that Chambers will get some minutes too. I have a sneaky suspicion that Gabriel will establish himself as a starter for Brazil as well (possible rotation/horses for courses).

LB: Monreal or Gibbs

Monreal has talked recently about feeling that he has finally settled in here, which struck me as a slightly strange thing to say. Was there something odd about his transfer? Did he not really want to come?

Cazorla and Monreal were both signed from Malaga in the period when we seemed to be looking for bargains. Malaga had financial problems and appeared to be forced to sell these players at knock down prices. Moving from Malaga to London is not a trivial change in life and I wonder if Monreal was really ready for, or expecting it. Did he just take a really long time to settle in?

Whatever the reason, he appears to have displaced Gibbs for now and to have done so on merit. However Wenger seems to think that Gibbs is an important player in the long-term (English core etc.). Gibbs doesn't seem to be far behind and I suspect he will rise to the challenge and win his place back at some point next season (possible rotation/horses for courses).

TIM CHARLESWORTH

RB: Debuchy or Bellerin

This one is genuinely hard to call. Bellerin had a breakthrough season and was the man in possession at the end of 2014-15. Many of our fans are very excited by his prospects, but he is still young and relatively inexperienced. Debuchy is a high class international player who looked very good in his few appearances last season: many of us were delighted to get an 'upgrade' on the excellent Sagna last summer. He will be fully recovered at the start of the season. I suspect Debuchy will start the season (possible rotation/horses for courses).

DM: Coquelin or a new player

I thought the emergence of Coquelin was the most exciting thing to happen last season. How long have we fans cried out for a genuinely brilliant defensive midfielder? Was the answer really under our noses all these years? The team looked completely different with him in it.

BC (Before Coquelin) I beat myself silly with frustration as we got caught on the counter attack over and over again. With him, the counter attack problem has virtually disappeared (I think others, particularly Cazorla, must take some credit as well).

I am just so grateful to this enigmatic man. His positioning is freakishly good - next time you watch the mighty Arsenal, ignore the ball and just watch him - it's nearly as good as watching Sanchez trying to get the ball back after he has lost it! His tackling is wonderful and he seems to have magically eliminated the tendency to get carded for it.

He also seems to have strength, balance and pace in abundance. His aerial ability is fantastic. During the FA Cup Quarter Final Man U pumped aerial balls up the middle and he dominated Fellaini in the air (apparently not even flinching when Fellaini used his elbow to break his nose). For a man listed as 5'10", this is inexplicable.

During the FA Cup Final, just like that, he decided to add Messi-like close control to his list of attributes. Is there no end

IT'S HAPPENED AGAIN

to this man's talents? Anyway, I must stop going on about this wonderful player or my wife will get suspicious.

The fact remains that he hasn't played a full season for us, and thus hasn't proved his ability to do so. I still have a nagging fear that he is 'too good to be true'. Could he just be an illusory 'flash in the pan'? Perhaps I don't really understand what I am seeing (I am an experienced observer, but I am just an amateur and not always a good judge of players).

It is also very rare for players to suddenly become brilliant at the age of 24, after showing relatively limited promise before that. I get the firm impression that Wenger was genuinely surprised at how well Le Coq played (if not, then why did he let his contract get so close to expiring?). Will opposition teams work out how to play against him, how to find his weaknesses? Will his body hold up to a full season? Will Wenger sign another DM - the rumours are incessant. Will our club captain even get his place in the team back?

Of all the 'uncertain' positions, this is probably the one where I feel most strongly that I do know what will happen next season. As the summer wears on, it increasingly looks like Wenger is not looking for another player in this position. I see no evidence that Arsenal ever expressed any serious interest in Khedira, Schneiderlin, Schweinsteiger, Vidal, Bender, Carvalho, Pogba, or anyone else who can play this position. All the rumours seem to be based on interest that was expressed BC and could be described as 'vapour rumours'.

Wenger is probably happy with Arteta as back up; and the experience of the Asia Cup suggests that he is considering alternatives such as Ramsey/Cazorla in deeper roles. Wenger has an odd tendency to deny that he plays a Defensive Midfielder at all, and I sometimes think he is looking for midfield arrangements that avoid the need for one. However all things considered, I think Coquelin will be first choice and that he will have an excellent season.

TIM CHARLESWORTH

B2B: Cazorla or Ramsey (or Wilshere)

Cazorla has firmly established himself as the no. 1 in this position and I suspect this will carry over into the new season. I don't see how we can drop a player that is playing that well.

However Ramsey is a wonderful player who may well be on course to become one of the best in the world. In 2013-14 he was clearly our best player. It must be a terrible wrench to leave him out of the team. Some of his appearances on the right wing at the end of last season suggested how reluctant Wenger was to bench him. Cazorla is in his 30s: can he really hold Ramsey at bay? Either way, we look pretty strong here, especially with Wilshere as an alternative.

RM: The Ox or Ramsey or Walcott or Wilshere

My feeling is that The Ox is the no. 1 choice here in Wenger's mind. Only injury seemed to lose him his place last season, but he can hardly be considered an established starter here. The array of talent competing with him is stunning. Walcott (if not playing centre forward), Welbeck (ditto), Sanchez (ditto), Cazorla (if not playing B2B) and Gnabry are all great options here. In addition, Wilshere and Ramsey had some very good games in this position last season. My suspicion is that The Ox will get the most minutes here in the coming season (possible rotation).

CF: Giroud or Walcott

Arguably Walcott is the man in possession here. There can surely be no suggestion that Wenger did not pick his strongest 11 for the Cup Final (Goalkeeper excepted). However the last two weeks of the 2014-15 season were probably the only time in this 26 year old's career when he really looked convincing in this position. Four goals in two games against WBA and Villa is hardly sufficient to convince anyone that he is a long-term option as a no. 9 for one of Europe's top teams.

Yet somehow, my gut tells me that after all these years, his moment has finally arrived. Wenger has been talking about him as a Centre Forward for years. And when Wenger talks persistently about something, it usually turns out to be right, no matter how outrageous (I remember the derision he got for talking about an unbeaten season c. 2001). Somehow Walcott now looks more robust and confident in this position.

I wouldn't be surprised if he ends up as the man who plays most minutes in the no. 9 role next season. Remember the precedent of RVP turning into a no. 9 quite late in his career?

At the same time, Giroud has improved every year he has been with us. He is still in his prime and is a very difficult player for defenders to handle; making an instant difference to the team when returning from a broken leg last season. He also makes an underestimated defensive contribution in the air at set pieces, which Walcott is unable to offer.

I don't think much of Danny Welbeck's chances in this position next season and I think we won't sign a new player (mainly because no good ones are available). My bet is that Walcott will prevail in 2015-16, but I'm really not sure.

Safe positions

No. 10: Ozil

Ozil has to be the man in possession, and Wenger seems to play him here when he is fit: the brief experiment at left midfield in the early games of last season appears to have been abandoned. However he is still to prove that he can consistently produce world class performances and there are an absurd number of alternatives to play here. Sanchez was the best alternate last season, but Cazorla, The Ox, Wilshere, Ramsey and Rosicky have all put in good performances in this position in the past.

CB: Koscielny

Surely only injury can keep this man out the team. He has been our top performing CB for a number of seasons now.

LM: Sanchez

This is a bit of a simplification, because Sanchez might play in a number of positions next season (notable games at no. 9 and no. 10 last season). My assumption is that he was so good - and such a good 'team player' - that he cannot be left out when fit. This could change next season, but let's hope he goes from strength to strength rather than suffering the 'sophomore effect'/burnout from a very long season that has only just finished.

Conclusions

In a few instances I have recognized that players might be rotated or that Wenger might use 'horses for courses'.

This is a bit of a cop-out, as Wenger is a reluctant rotator. He is more likely to rotate higher up the pitch, but even then it is usually clear who is first choice. I can't think of any examples in the past where Wenger has used a 'horses for courses' approach by selecting different players depending on the opposition and I think this is an unlikely solution to our selection dilemmas. In the unlikely event that Wenger does want to adapt the team depending on our opposition, the following would seem to be the main options:

1. Play Mertesacker when we want to defend deep (Europe away?) or want extra aerial protection; play Gabriel when we want to push higher up the pitch
2. Play Debuchy when we want to defend deep (Europe away?); play Bellerin when we want to push higher up the pitch. We may also be interested in defensive and aerial balance depending on whether Monreal or Gibbs are playing on the opposite side, or if Giroud is playing.
3. Play Walcott against immobile/slow CBs (he will run them ragged) and Giroud against smaller/quicker ones (he will dominate them in the air). Also play Giroud if we are concerned about having enough defensive strength in the air

Finally, we also have to remember that Wenger can be a bit unpredictable. If I had been penning this article twelve months

IT'S HAPPENED AGAIN

ago, I would have discussed the merits of Cazorla as no. 10 or Wide Midfielder/Winger, not as a box-to-box Midfielder, which is where he seems to have ended up. In the past Touré, Eboue, Lauren, Song and RVP all seem to have changed position without prior notice. Of course, injuries will also negate some of these selection dilemmas.

At the moment we only seem to have three certain starters. I may have exaggerated slightly here because I think Cech and Coquelin are reasonably safe bets. Nonetheless, I cannot think of a time when there was so much uncertainty about our best 11. If some of our players can solve this problem by out-performing expectations and establishing themselves as a clear first choice, we will have a great season.

| Sat 25th July | Lyon | H Emirates Cup | W 6-0 |
| Sun 26th July | Wolfsburg | H Emirates Cup | W 1-0 |

It doesn't pay to read too much into the preseason, but Gooners were generally excited by this one. Four games and four wins, three of them by more than one goal. Opposition was reasonable but not too strong. The standout performer was 17 year-old Jeff Reine Adelaide who was particularly impressive during the worst of the pre-season performances - against Wolfsburg - as the best player on the pitch; setting up Walcott for the only goal of the match. We have been deceived by great preseason performances from young players before, only for them to fail to live up to expectations. This guy looks like the real deal though, and a genuine 'Wenger gem'.

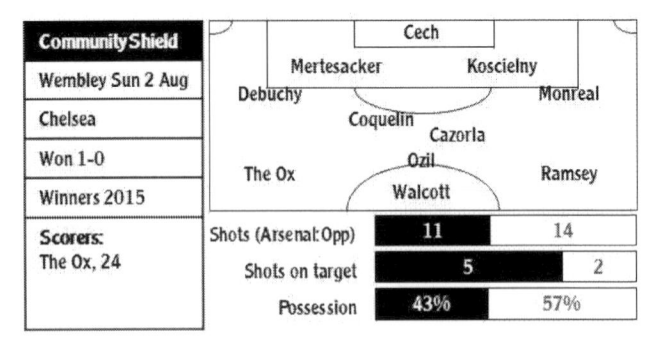

Community Shield		
Wembley Sun 2 Aug		
Chelsea		
Won 1-0		
Winners 2015		
Scorers: The Ox, 24	Shots (Arsenal:Opp)	11 — 14
	Shots on target	5 — 2
	Possession	43% — 57%

Lineup: Cech; Debuchy, Mertesacker, Koscielny, Monreal; Coquelin, Cazorla; The Ox, Ozil, Ramsey; Walcott

What a lovely match. 'Wenger's first win over Mourinho' was the most popular headline. Our first chance to see the Arsenal line-up for the season. All players were fit and well except:
- Alexis Sanchez (unfit due to late return from Copa America)
- David Ospina (unfit due to late return from Copa America)
- Danny Welbeck (suffering from a long-term knee injury)
- And of these, Sanchez was the only likely starter anyway. Everybody else was fit and available. Significant selections were:
- Mertesacker kept his place in defence over Gabriel
- Bellerin retained his place over Debuchy at RB
- Walcott started up front with Giroud on the bench
- Wilshere on the bench

Janet and Ryan Rocastle were Arsenal's guests of honour (widow and son of Rocky - see 'A Potted History of Arsenal FC'), bringing back happy and sad memories to those of us who loved him all those years ago.

And so we entered the 'real season' with hope and optimism. Our team had finished strongly in the second half of last season; we had won another FA Cup; new players were bedding in; we had solved the old goalkeeper problem; we appeared to have solved the old DM problem; some fans still held out hope of a Centre Forward signing; we had a great pre-season; we didn't have the dreaded CL qualifier to play; and we were second

IT'S HAPPENED AGAIN

favourites for the Premier League after Chelsea, who we had just beaten. The long and lazy summer was over and I hadn't been so excited about a new season for years. Happy days are here again.

CHAPTER SEVENTEEN
THE LONG WAIT IS OVER

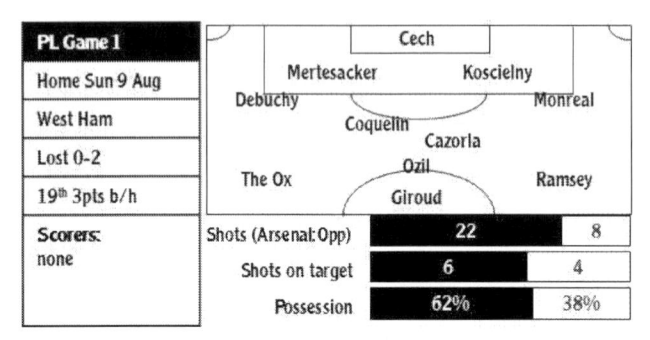

PL Game 1	
Home Sun 9 Aug	
West Ham	
Lost 0-2	
19th 3pts b/h	
Scorers: none	

Formation:
- Cech
- Mertesacker, Koscielny
- Debuchy, Coquelin, Cazorla, Monreal
- The Ox, Ozil, Ramsey
- Giroud

	Arsenal	Opp
Shots	22	8
Shots on target	6	4
Possession	62%	38%

What a horrible start after a wonderful preseason. Cech looked culpable for one - possibly two - of the goals on his home league debut. Gooner balloons were well and truly popped. To make it worse, it was announced a few days before the game that eternal injury victim but fan favourite, Jack Wilshere, had a 'hairline fracture' of his fibula. He had played a good preseason and there was much talk of how he needed an injury-free run.

West Ham played with 16-year old Reece Oxford in midfield, who was excellent. For Arsenal, Debuchy came in for the injured Bellerin, and Giroud came in for Walcott. A sluggish first half ended in a West Ham goal. In the second half Arsenal chased the game unconvincingly, conceded again and never looked like coming back after that. The general reaction was surprisingly restrained (compared to the vitriol that followed some of last season's defeats). Perhaps fans were remembering 2 years ago when we lost the first game at home to Villa, but were top of the league within a month.

With the benefit of hindsight, the Chelsea and West Ham games were misleading. This is often the case in the early weeks, as we presume that Arsenal's opponents will continue their form of the previous season. We were impressed by the defeat of

IT'S HAPPENED AGAIN

Premier League Champions Chelsea. As it turned out, Chelsea got eight points from their first eight games (including 3 underserved ones against Arsenal, as we shall see). So hindsight tells us that beating Chelsea 1-0 was not that impressive. West Ham on the other hand had 14 points after eight games and had beaten both Man City and Liverpool away, as well as Arsenal.

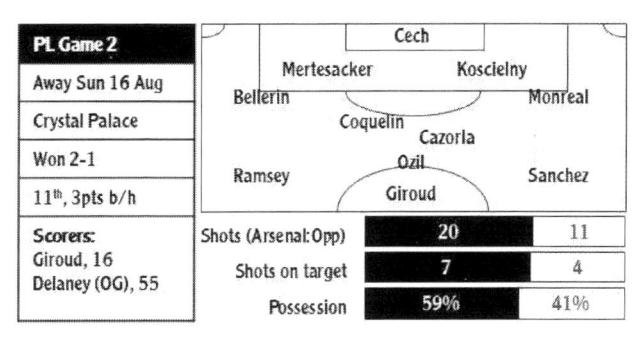

PL Game 2		
Away Sun 16 Aug		
Crystal Palace		
Won 2-1		
11th, 3pts b/h		
Scorers: Giroud, 16 Delaney (OG), 55	Shots (Arsenal:Opp)	20 / 11
	Shots on target	7 / 4
	Possession	59% / 41%

Lineup: Cech; Bellerin, Mertesacker, Koscielny, Monreal; Coquelin, Cazorla; Ramsey, Özil, Sanchez; Giroud.

This was by no means a comfortable game. Giroud kept his place over Walcott up front (to add defensive and aerial presence?) and Bellerin came back for Debuchy. Sanchez started his first game as the expense of The Ox. We took the lead, but were pegged back on 28 minutes. It was a tight game and Palace hit the post.

It was tense, with the game in the balance and Arsenal needing the win. Eventually, we got an own goal thanks to the persistence and aggression of Sanchez, after which we looked relatively comfortable and solid in defence. Palace Manager, Alan Pardew was outraged that Coquelin had not received a second yellow card following a series of semi-cardable fouls in the second half. He had a point, and the PGMO (Professional Game Match Officials, the organisation that manages refereeing for English football matches) thought so too. Referee Lee Mason was rewarded with a month on the side-lines for his performance. Any less than three points after two games is really a bad start so this was a must win on which the team delivered.

TIM CHARLESWORTH

ON VISITING REAL MADRID: THOUGHTS ON EXPANDING THE EMIRATES STADIUM

21st August 2015

I was recently on holiday in Madrid and took the opportunity to tour the Bernebau stadium (home of Real Madrid) with my son. It was a great chance to look at a famous stadium and compare it to our own.

My first impression was how small the stadium seemed (narrower, but also higher than the Emirates/Grove). This was an interesting observation as it is an 85,000 capacity stadium (compared to our own 60,000).

My second impression was how steep the stands were (the steepness of the stands probably explaining how you can get more people into an apparently smaller stadium).

I haven't attended a match there, but it was instantly obvious to me that this was a much more intimidating stadium than the Emirates. The words 'cauldron', 'bear-pit' and 'arena' sprung to mind.

This led me to think about a subject which seems very important to me, but I see remarkably little discussion of: our future plans for stadium expansion. We are clearly able to sell more tickets than we currently do (stadium is always sold out, season ticket waiting lists, ever growing popularity of the Premier League etc.).

If we were able to add 20,000 seats, I am confident we would sell them for an average of £20 per match (they wouldn't be the best seats). This would produce a revenue of c £500,000 per match for roughly 25 matches per season, so about £10m per annum. If such an expansion could be done for £100m it would seem to be profitable, but not massively so. I can see a number of other possible barriers:

Planning permission. This was a major issue when the stadium was first built. The main problem is disruption to the

IT'S HAPPENED AGAIN

local population on match days, plus safety and transport issues. I feel the resident objections can be overcome. The safety considerations seem more problematic. Certainly the crush on/just after North Bank (Ken Friar) Bridge on the way out doesn't feel like you could comfortably add another 20,000 to it.

But this is hardly a unique problem. There are a lot of 80,000 plus stadiums around the world. Surely, better use of Drayton Park and Holloway Road stations is possible. The cost of such solutions could, of course, be a barrier to expansion plans. Wikipedia suggests a £60m cost for upgrading Holloway Road.

Is the stadium designed for it? This matters. For example, did they over-engineer the foundations so that they could bear more weight from future expansion? If not, then expensive and difficult reinforcement might be necessary. Was the roof designed in such a way that it could easily be jacked up to accommodate another tier? What are the problems with filling in the 'airflow' gaps at the back of the stadium?

I remember when the plans for the Grove were first announced. It seemed obvious to me that the stadium would be designed with future expansion in mind, but in the following fifteen years I have seen no evidence that this was the case.

Would it be possible to do the work in the summer? If the team needs to leave the stadium for a period, that adds significant costs.

Could it be done in stages (this would ameliorate many forms of risk) - North Stand, West Stand etc.? The stadium is a bowl rather than the traditional four stands design of Highbury. Is this distinction cosmetic or integral to the design (the roof certainly looks like one structure not four)? Can its design stand a staged expansion?

The stadium was designed to allow sunlight and air to get to the pitch. Surely this can be overcome with the use of mirrors/UV lamps/air fans?

Would the raising of the necessary funds restrict the club financially again? No-one wants to return to the days of financial parsimony.

So I guess the financial case for expanding the stadium is not clear cut. It seems like, subject to better information, it would probably be marginally profitable but may come with risks and possible financing restrictions (Usmanov level anyone?). However it seems to me there are a number of non-financial reasons for expanding the stadium that our board should be considering:

Home advantage is an important factor in football and especially in Champions League. Football people often talk about the 'fortress' mentality. Some stadia appear to be very intimidating in the right circumstances: Real, Barca, Dortmund, Old Trafford, Anfield, even Stamford Bridge.

This intimidation works on both players - and perhaps more importantly - referees. Just imagine how it feels to be a lone referee resisting the howling demands for a free kick from 80,000 screaming Barca fans - all within 100m of you - you have a fraction of a second to make your decision! As a general rule, modern bowl stadia seem to be less intimidating. It seems that 'size' and 'steepness' are both factors which contribute to the intimidation advantage. An extra tier at the Emirates would increase the 'steepness' as well as its capacity (obviously this would not be true of the 'fill in the gaps' option).

People in football talk about 'big clubs'. In some ways this is a puerile debate, but 'perceived bigness' does influence decisions in the world of football. This is most obviously observable in the series of poor decisions that Arsenal players have made to wreck their careers by leaving Arsenal to join Barcelona (list too long to show). A number of factors influence perceived bigness (history, money etc.), but the size and intimidation factor of the stadium seems to be one of them.

When at the Bernebau, I couldn't help considering what impression it must have made on Mesut Ozil when he first looked at the lower, more gently sloping Emirates Stadium. I think it must have felt like a 'step down' to him.

Acoustics are also relevant to intimidation and 'atmosphere', two factors in which the Emirates seems deficient to me. Some stadia seem to 'channel' sound. The addition of a new tier - and possibly roof - would allow the acoustic properties of the stadium to be reconsidered. We might even consider a retractable roof, which seems to add to the atmosphere at Cardiff's Millennium stadium and Wimbledon's Centre Court. I particularly dislike the way in which the current roof blocks the view of the opposite stand for fans at the top of the upper tier - I think this really reduces atmosphere.

Getting more fans into the stadium will increase the size and loyalty of the fan base (another factor in 'perceived bigness'). Fans feel closer to the team if they can actually attend a match.

Overall my feeling is that, if we are to fulfil our potential to compete on a level playing field with the likes of Real Madrid, our stadium needs to fit the bill. I think another tier of seating is the best way to do this as it will not only add capacity, but also add to the 'intimidation factor' and 'perceived bigness'. I would like to see more debate about this among fans; and for questions to be asked of the Board on the subject.

I was disappointed in the reaction to this article. Nobody seemed to know any answers to the questions that I posed, and not many others seemed to agree that we needed to expand the stadium. I feel that this is a major strategic priority for Arsenal. If I were a director, this would be the thing I spent most time working on.

TIM CHARLESWORTH

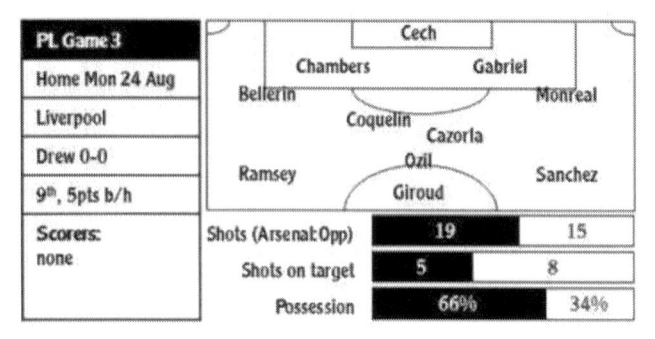

PL Game 3	
Home Mon 24 Aug	
Liverpool	
Drew 0-0	
9th, 5pts b/h	

Formation:
- Cech
- Chambers, Gabriel
- Bellerin, Coquelin, Cazorla, Monreal
- Ramsey, Ozil
- Giroud, Sanchez

	Arsenal	Opp
Scorers: none		
Shots	19	15
Shots on target	5	8
Possession	66%	34%

The pre-match news was a bit shocking. Merts (flu) and Koscielny (injury) were both out (Chambers and Gabriel in). No indication of either problem had been given before. This was really ripping out the heart of our defence and I was nervous about what would happen. No other changes; and Giroud continued to keep Walcott out of the team at no. 9.

The performance was nervous, particularly in the first half, with Calum Chambers looking very shaky. But Cech made a few saves and Chambers seemed to get stronger as the match went on. Liverpool hit the post twice, Alexis once and Ramsey had a goal incorrectly ruled out for offside. All in all, we did OK to draw in the circumstances. We failed to score at home again (although this is a silly statistic).

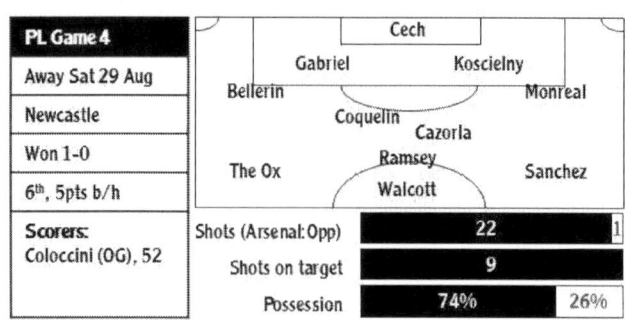

PL Game 4	
Away Sat 29 Aug	
Newcastle	
Won 1-0	
6th, 5pts b/h	

Formation:
- Cech
- Gabriel, Koscielny
- Bellerin, Coquelin, Cazorla, Monreal
- The Ox, Ramsey, Sanchez
- Walcott

	Arsenal	Opp
Scorers: Coloccini (OG), 52		
Shots	22	1
Shots on target	9	
Possession	74%	26%

Koscielny returned for Chambers. Ozil had a minor injury and was replaced by The Ox with Ramsey moving to the middle

IT'S HAPPENED AGAIN

and The Ox playing on the right. Walcott came in for Giroud. Mitrovic was sent off after 20 minutes for a foul on Le Coq. A harsh decision, but probably correct. This gave Arsenal a big opportunity and, truth be told, they struggled to get the win against ten men.

Walcott and The Ox failed to grab their opportunities. This game produced the rather startling statistic that Arsenal had only scored one goal in four Premier League games (if you discounted two own goals). But seven points from four games is acceptable and we went into the first Interlull* in reasonable spirits.

---

* The Interlull is the rather derogatory name given by most modern fans to a break in the season to accommodate international matches. These matches are mostly meaningless friendlies, usually of little interest. Even qualifying matches for international tournaments are getting a bit dull nowadays. Europe used to consist of nations like France and Germany who would give you a good game of football. Now it is full of fixtures with Monaco, the Faroe Islands, Bosnia Herzegovina, the Czech Republic and others. These matches are primarily designed to allow national football associations to make a bit of money. From a fan's point of view, they break up the rhythm and continuity of the season. This is particularly so in the early months of the season, when there are always 2 fortnight-long Interlulls. We have just survived a whole summer with no football and now we are subjected to this!

CHAPTER EIGHTEEN
THE FIRST INTERLULL

WHAT'S GOING ON WITH ENGLISH REFEREEING?
September 3rd 2015

I love all things 'Untold' with one exception. I find myself constantly disagreeing with the analysis of refereeing. Unlike many readers of this site, I don't see any evidence of a systematic refereeing bias against Arsenal.

I certainly see a lot of mistakes, and have some sympathy with the view that PGMO standards are poor (the self-assessments are risible). I also feel frustration at the mistakes (Ramsey Liverpool, Bellerin Newcastle). However there are a number of reasons why refereeing may appear to be biased against you:

1. If you are a team like Arsenal which generally dominates possession, you will be the victim of more fouls than you mete out. This is because most fouls are committed by the team without the ball. If the referee makes mistakes with a fixed percentage of fouls, he will fail to award you a foul more often than your opponents
2. Similarly, if you do most of the attacking, you are going to be unlucky with penalty shouts and offsides more often than your opponents
3. A lot of fans watch home matches live, and away matches on TV. Referees are generally biased against away teams, due to sub-conscious crowd influence. They make most mistakes in favour of the home team. If you are watching on TV with the benefit of replays, analysis etc. you will easily see the mistakes made against you. It may not be so obvious that the same thing is happening to your opponents when they play at the Emirates and you are watching live with 55,000 like-minded friends.

IT'S HAPPENED AGAIN

4. Arsenal's style is a difficult one for referees. A lot of our players deliberately try to draw players in to a tackle and then play the ball after the opponent is committed to the tackle (I call this the 'offload pass' after the similar tactic in rugby). This is an effective tactic, as it creates space for the player receiving the pass. It also, inevitably, leads to late tackles which may be made worse by the fact that the passing player is concentrating on making the pass and not preparing for the impact. This is what happened with Coquelin and Mitrovic: Coquelin didn't evade the descending boot because he was focussed on the pass.
5. Perception bias (see below)

In my life, I have been involved in a number of institutions, including political parties, public limited companies and football teams. All of them, without exception, see the world as biased against them. This is not always a bad thing as it promotes cohesion. Maureen goes to great lengths to create the 'us against the world' spirit at Chelsea. The fortress mentality also did us a lot of good during the '2 point deduction for fighting at Man U and Tony Adams imprisonment' season (1990-91). We won the league comfortably.

I think the root cause of this perception bias or 'bias paranoia' is mostly to do with perspective. When we are emotionally invested in something, we tend to see the world differently.

For example, over the last ten years Wenger has tried to play a fast paced passing game. We fans therefore see this type of game as 'real football'. We see those who play a physically aggressive form of football (Stoke) as playing 'the wrong way'.

As a result, when we see referees allowing Stoke to rough us up in an attempt to disrupt our passing game, we think the referee is biased against us. Without spending time on Stoke blog sites, I am pretty sure that they think referees are biased against them because they:

TIM CHARLESWORTH

- 'Over-protect' namby-pamby southerners
- Protect the 'big teams' (who are more likely to play the passing style game)
- Are influenced by Stoke's reputation even before a ball is kicked

In reality, the referees are picking a 'middle way' between allowing Stoke to play their way and protecting Arsenal from physical abuse when we try to play the beautiful game. Both sets of fans perceive bias because neither team is being allowed to play the game exactly as they want it to be, and believe it should be, played.

It is interesting to note that things look a bit different so far this season. The most extraordinary aspect of the season so far is that away teams are doing well and home teams are doing badly (Arsenal are a good example, not the exception). This is interesting in particular, because most home advantage arises from subconscious intimidation of referees by home fans. Is it possible that PGMO have become aware of this and are making a deliberate effort to counteract it by being hard on home teams?

This certainly looked like the case against Newcastle. I wasn't there, but I understand that the referee came under incredible pressure from the disgruntled home fans, but resisted it. Marriner was consistently carding the home team for violent conduct right from the start of the game.

Usually referees allow this kind of fouling to go unpunished, seeming to think that players are still 'adjusting to the pace of the game', when in fact they are deliberately assaulting their opponents. They are usually particularly generous with home players in this regard. This kind of refereeing laxity is particularly dangerous at the start of the game as it sets the tone for the match and leads away players to expect to be fouled every time they touch the ball, thus restricting their play.

Newcastle appeared to be trying to carry out something that has become a pretty standard tactical approach for non-top-four

IT'S HAPPENED AGAIN

teams at home against Arsenal over the last ten years. That tactical approach is what I call 'hometown roughing', a variant of the old 'kick 'em off the park'.

Basically, you persistently rotationally foul Arsenal, particularly in the first ten minutes. You are trying to make us uncomfortable on the ball. You hope that this makes players pass too quickly, miscontrol, or take their eye off the ball to look at the incoming tackler. This should then lead to mistakes or misplaced passes.

This is particularly effective if you are the home team, because the home crowd will prevent the referee from giving too many cards and fouls against you. Fergie invented this tactic, in desperation, at the end of the 49 game run. It was much admired and widely copied (Bolton were its earliest imitators). It is interesting that Wenger never seems to comment on this tactic (perhaps he doesn't want to encourage it). Diaby, Eduardo and Ramsey all suffered their injuries during away matches.

The tactic didn't work on Saturday because the referee was on top of violent conduct right from the start. Is this just a coincidence or is there some concerted effort by referees to address the home advantage problem? Is this why away teams are doing so well in the Premiership? Is this a sign of things to come?

I doubt it. Even if there is a new PGMO initiative, most such initiatives peter out, maybe with a little lasting effect. The home advantage bias is embedded in most sports around the world. If it is to be eradicated, I find it hard to believe that PGMO is the institution to finally root it out.

It would certainly be to Arsenal's advantage if there was a crackdown on violent conduct and 'hometown roughing'. This would probably also advantage the other top teams, as high quality teams tend to pass the ball more, but Arsenal might benefit the most, as the most extreme example of a 'passing team'.

TIM CHARLESWORTH

'Hometown roughing' is a tactic that gives the smaller teams a chance against the more skilful teams. If it were to be eradicated, the League might become slightly less competitive, and a bit more like the Spanish league. I get the firm impression that the lesser teams are not allowed to rough up Real Madrid and Barca.

And this brings me to my final point. The performance of English teams in Europe is inexplicably poor compared to their financial muscle. Money is not everything in football, but other things being equal, it is a big advantage. I suspect that the relatively lax attitude of English referees towards violence is one of the major factors explaining the poor performance of English teams (lax compared to Spain, strict compared to 20 years ago).

I think English teams are playing more 'tough' games than their Champions League opponents. A close game, say a 1-0, is more tiring than a 3-0 because the close game will be played at 100% right to the end. In a 3-0, both teams will ease off in the latter stages.

Also, physical contact is tiring. Players use a lot of strength in preparing for and receiving 'a hit' and the blunt force leads to muscle fibre damage (that's why boxing is so incredibly physically tiring). This effect is also cumulative over a season; and so the form of English teams seems to deteriorate as the competition progresses (note also how poorly Premier League players perform in World and European cups - it's not just the English ones - Per and Mesut were probably the most disappointing performers in Germany's World Cup winning team.)

As a result of the close matches and the physical contact, English Champions League players are less physically fresh than their Spanish opponents (Real and Barca win most of their games by several goals, as do Bayern Munich).

There is also a consequence that the physical conditioning of English players is not quite right. English teams are built to

IT'S HAPPENED AGAIN

withstand Stoke, not Barcelona. There is too much emphasis on strength and not enough on agility. As a crude generalisation, heavy muscling, particularly in the upper body, will make you stronger but less agile. This means that in Champions League matches which are not overseen by English referees, the English teams give away too many fouls and struggle to match Barcelona's speed of movement. Note how much Mesut Ozil and Theo Walcott seem to have 'bulked up' in recent times.

So, if the PGMO really are coming down hard on 'hometown roughing', we can expect a few things to happen:

1. Arsenal should benefit at home and in Europe
2. The Premier League may become less competitive
3. English teams will do better in Europe (Premier League players may also do better in World Cups)

TIM CHARLESWORTH

STATE OF THE ARSENAL NATION: PHASE ONE OF THE SEASON IS OVER

September 7th 2015

And breathe...

So phase 1 of the season is over, and the reviled Interlull is upon us. The first four League games are played and the transfer window is closed.

This was perhaps the least important 'phase 1' for years. There were several reasons for this. Firstly, we had no major squad gaps to fill (I appreciate that not everyone agrees on this point). Secondly, the results are not that important at this stage of the season. Thirdly, and most importantly, we didn't have to play the dreaded Champions League qualifier, a terrible tie, with very little to gain and an awful lot to lose.

Overall, the start is mildly disappointing. We have scored 7 points from 4 relatively benign games. This is not good enough to win the title (1.75 points per game - Chelsea won with 2.26 pts per game last season and we scored 1.97 in 2014-15). We are level with most possible competitors, significantly behind City and slightly ahead of Chelsea (way ahead of the tiny tots, if you are interested in such things). This is OK but we have a tough run of away fixtures coming up, so don't be too perturbed if we slip back a little.

I think a few things have combined to make the start seem a bit worse than it really is:

1. Losing at home on the opening day against a minor team is always going to be a horrible shock which is difficult to recover from psychologically (for the fans particularly)
2. There was a lot of talk about how important it was to make a good start, after failing to recover from a bad start last year
3. Our poor start last season was repeatedly blamed on the 2014 World Cup - I think we all hoped to start better in the absence of a World Cup

IT'S HAPPENED AGAIN

4. Both indicators of 'form' - the finish to last season and the pre-season games - suggested that Arsenal would start well. The team failed to live up to these form guides

It is tempting to say that if only Ramsey's goal against Liverpool had stood we would have 9 points at 2.25 per game and all would be well. I don't really like this analysis and think the 7 points is generally reflective of how the games have gone.

In fact there were a few turning points. Some went our way - Palace hitting the post, Liverpool failing to convert their chances - whilst some went against us; Ramsey's offside goal, missing chances against Liverpool and West Ham and, most of all, the terrible defensive positioning mix up that led to WHU's first goal.

So to the transfer window. The standard of journalism surrounding 'transfer rumours' is increasingly ludicrous. The rise of the blogs and the importance of 'click-baiting' suggest that even in mainstream newspapers, all sense of integrity has died. Everyone makes stuff up and it's just a game. This year's prime silliness was the (never ending) stories that Benzema/Madrid had agreed to various things. Clearly no such agreement had happened, yet it was widely reported.

One consequence of all this silliness is that it's very difficult to ascertain what really happened. This is particularly difficult for us Gooners, because Wenger repeatedly makes statements that are simultaneously meaningless and true. His basic line was that: 'We will sign someone, if a quality player becomes available at a sensible price' (I will overlook the fact that he said something similar just before the Kallstrom signing). This is a bit like saying 'if a beautiful girl wants to have sex with me I will do it' (in my bachelor days obviously).

This statement actually imparts no new information and I think that's quite deliberate. Unusually, our club likes to conduct its transfer business in private. So what really happened?

TIM CHARLESWORTH

My guess (and it's only a guess) is that very little actually took place. It looks as if we may have made a genuine enquiry about Benzema and possibly some others, but were easily put off by lack of availability or high prices. From this, I conclude that Wenger is largely happy with his squad, but thinks there is a small amount of room for improvement with an 'exceptional player'.

Wenger's opinion is important here. He sees a lot more of the players than we do (particularly in training) and is in a much better position to judge form, fitness, skill, development etc. than we are. This is especially true of those not regularly playing 90 minutes; we hardly see these players at all and have no idea how they are progressing. If Wenger is largely happy with the squad, this is a good sign that it is strong (although his record is not unimpeachable on this point).

I have read and heard some pretty daft analysis of our transfer window (only team in Europe not to buy an outfield player etc.). There is a kind of conspiracy of cynical Arsenal fans and excitable journalists/ex-pros who argue roughly along the following lines:

1. Chelsea beat Arsenal by 12 points last season
2. Arsenal have only signed Cech
3. Do they really think that this one signing is enough to close a gap of 12 points

In fact Arsenal's team has changed out of all recognition from the one that started last season. I struggle to recall a period when the team has changed so much. So let's compare the current team to the one that started in 2014-15:

Gabriel is an excellent player, who hardly played at all last season and was signed in January

Petr Cech appears to be an improvement at Goalkeeper

Francis Coquelin is a gem. Possibly the most important player to emerge since Fabregas, he only played half of last season

IT'S HAPPENED AGAIN

Theo Walcott will be an important player and hardly played at all last season

Internationally retired **Per Mertesacker** is fresh (he looked exhausted last season)

A number of players look to have improved since last season, most notably **The Ox**, who may well have a great season.

Ozil should be available for the majority after only half a season last time out. He is Arsenal's most creative player. His return to the side coincided with the successful second half of last season.

Bellerin is doing very well. He only played half of last season (again, like Ozil, it was the successful half)

Cazorla only played in Central Midfield for half a season (he was pretty peripheral in the first half of last season). Like Bellerin and Ozil, the half a season he played was the one in which Arsenal scored more points than any other Premier League team.

Monreal seemed to get a new lease of life and is a 'new player' compared to the one we had at the start of last season. Gibbs was first choice left back at the start of 2014-15. I think Monreal has improved rather than Gibbs losing form (note his England selection this week).

Overall, you might observe that comparing this team to the one that started last season, there are in fact eight high quality new players (brackets show what they were doing in the first half of last season):

- Cech (a Chelsea player)
- Coquelin (on loan)
- Ozil (injured)
- Monreal (second choice, not the same player)
- Cazorla (poor form, appeared to be ageing)
- Gabriel (playing for Villarreal)
- Walcott (injured)
- Giroud (broken leg)

TIM CHARLESWORTH

Now I know that not all these players are likely to play simultaneously. However, most are starters, not squad players. The only real exceptions to this are that Walcott and Giroud tend not to start together and Gabriel is still in the process of establishing himself as a starter (again, note the international selection this week).

We should not be misled by the fact that most have come via internal routes rather than big signings. Eight players is a substantial portion of an 11 man football team. It seems to me that more than half the team is different to the one that started last season. The idea that Arsenal has only improved in one position is absurd!

On the downside, there are probably other players who will not do as well as last season:

1. At least one player will probably miss half a season with injury. Last season Walcott, Ozil, Debuchy and Giroud fell into this category. I suspect, based on recent experience, that 2 (+/-2) first team players will fall into this category this season
2. There is a risk that Sanchez will suffer 'second season syndrome' and will not be as good as last year.
3. Some of our players are older, but actually it is quite a young squad. Ageing seems to mostly apply to Mertesacker (nearly 31) who looks fresher than last season. Cech is also ageing (33 not that old for a keeper) but can hardly be compared to the younger Cech of last season. Koscielny is pushing 30 but seems to be in as good a form as ever. Cazorla (30) seems to be maturing rather than ageing. Rosicky is ageing, but a fringe player.

My thoughts are that any comparison of the two lists above (ten improvements against three 'downsides' will conclude we are considerably stronger than in the first half of last season and remember that in the second half we scored more points than anyone else.

IT'S HAPPENED AGAIN

Finally, I feel obliged to comment on the Welbeck hysteria (following the announcement of a significant setback in his recovery).

It is true that the no. 9 Striker position looks like a possible weakness. I am also genuinely sorry for Welbeck, who seems a nice lad. But, the truth is that he is our third choice behind Giroud and Walcott (possibly fourth choice behind Sanchez), and an auxiliary reserve Winger/Wide Midfielder. He is not a great loss. The loss will look worse if Walcott or Giroud pick up a serious injury, but actually, even at Arsenal, most players go through the season without a major injury, so we would be a bit unlucky if this happened.

He will also be back and fresh in the New Year. It would have been a gross waste of money if Wenger had bought someone to replace him, when Joel Campbell (not a bad player actually) was available for free.

Conclusions

Overall, I am mildly disappointed with the results, mildly disappointed with the form, but happy with the transfer window outcome.

We are much stronger than at this point last year. Some of our improvements are still to prove themselves (Coquelin for a whole season, Walcott as a striker, Gabriel, The Ox).

I don't guarantee that we will win the league, but I think we have a good team with strength in depth.

Accidents (like Monaco and West Ham) will still happen, but hopefully are becoming less frequent and stability should further that reduction: there were a lot of accidents in 2013-14, but less in 2014-15. Most bookies have us as second favourites for the title at around 5-1, although bookies do tend to overvalue transfer window success at this time in the season and I think they are overestimating how good the ageing Man City are.

TIM CHARLESWORTH

Last season was quite unusual in the respect that the team who had the best transfer window won the league. Chelsea's new players (mostly Courtois, Fabregas and Costa) did well, but most big signings take a while to bed in. To be fair, I think that the team that negotiated a deal to sell David Luiz for £40m deserved to win the league. 5-1 is good value for Arsenal and I have invested appropriately. Chins up fellow Gooners; quiet confidence is the order of the day.

CHAPTER NINETEEN
HOSTILITIES RESUME

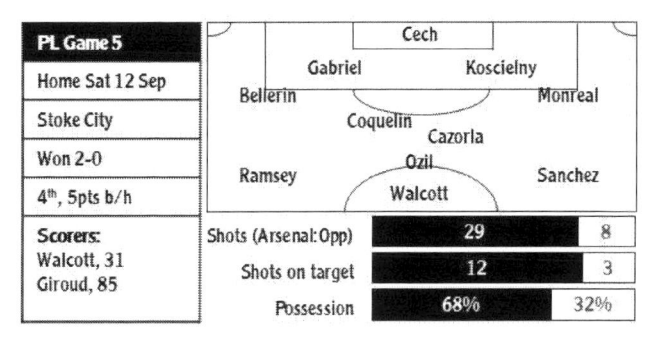

PL Game 5	
Home Sat 12 Sep	
Stoke City	
Won 2-0	
4th, 5pts b/h	
Scorers: Walcott, 31; Giroud, 85	

Formation:
- Cech
- Gabriel, Koscielny
- Bellerin, Monreal
- Coquelin, Cazorla
- Ramsey, Ozil
- Walcott, Sanchez

	Arsenal	Opp
Shots	29	8
Shots on target	12	3
Possession	68%	32%

With Mertesacker still unfit Gabriel continued and did well again. The Ox made way for Ozil's return, with Ramsey reverting to the right. Walcott - surprisingly - started (is this rotation with a hard week ahead?). Sanchez hit the post twice before Walcott scored: the goal that broke the deadlock was a wonderful pass from his own half by Ozil to Walcott, who finished very efficiently.

I felt like I had waited a long time to see this goal. The best passer in the world hitting a ball over the top to Walcott, surely the best player in the world to have running in behind the opposition defence. He just controlled the ball and scored. Why can't we just do this all the time?

After that, it was always comfortable, although supporters are inevitably nervous until the second goal goes in. The press are making a big thing about Sanchez not scoring, but he looks dangerous and in my book he did score against Palace. A nice routine home win, bringing an end to the Interlull purgatory.

15th September injury news

Having been told repeatedly that Jack Wilshere was 'in the post', we had to digest the news that he was undergoing surgery on his broken leg and would be out until the New Year. It felt inevitable and sad at the same time that this young man's career has been destroyed by injury. Having followed the wonderful Abou Diaby for years, we are all concerned that Jack might go the same way, although hopefully he is still young enough to make it. It turned out Wilshere wouldn't start a game until the final match of the season. What a sad waste.

TROUBLED WATERS AHEAD

September 16th 2015

What can we learn in the next three weeks?

As we head into a tricky looking run of fixtures, us Gooners are torn between optimism and fatalism. On the one had Walcott is coming good, the team looks solid, we have three clean sheets and the form of the second half of last season looks to be returning. On the other hand, we lost at home to West Ham, we are still short of a striker, our finishing is abysmal and we are vulnerable to injuries in key positions.

On the whole, I am in the optimistic camp (as most 'Arsène Knows Best' fans will be). But a string of bad results up to the next Interlull will make even me anxious. The fixtures are:

- Zagreb, Away, Champions League, 16th Sept
- Chelsea, Away, Premier League, 19th Sept
- Tottenham, Away, Carling Cup, 23rd Sept
- Leicester, Away, Premier League, 26th Sept
- Olympiacos, Home, Champions League, 29th Sept
- Man U, Home, Premier League, 4th Oct

These games come at the rate of two a week for three weeks: successive away fixtures like this can be draining and the sequence will certainly test the depth and endurance of our squad. I suspect we will see the wonderful looking Reine-Adelaide at least once. Tottenham is a Carling Cup game, so we may see a reserve/youngsters team, although defeat in this fixture would be bad for morale. In order not to fall back too far in the Premier League, we would really want a minimum of four points from the three League fixtures and this looks far from certain (we got no points from Man U home and Chelsea away last season - we drew away to Leicester).

So the shape of our season may well become clearer during these three weeks. Football games are wonderful things (hence their popularity). There is so much to see and discover on so many different levels. When I watch Arsenal play, I struggle to see beyond the questions of 'Are Arsenal going to score?' and 'Are the opposition going to score?' So I have had a little think about the things we should look out for, which will really shape this crucial part of the season:

1. **Can Coquelin keep it up?**

In some ways, this is the most important question of all. If Coquelin continues to be as good as he was last season (and avoids major injury), we have a genuine big time player. Early signs are good this season: if he plays 90% of games, I feel we will be defensively solid. I am still somewhat mystified by his failure to earn a France call up. Is this because non-flair players are easier to overlook in the short-term? Is his game more suited to the Premier League than international football?

2. **Will Walcott go prolific?**

This is another big one. The most obvious potential weakness in our side is at centre forward. If Theo scores a lot of goals this season, this concern will go away. The signs are very good here:

- Walcott is getting a lot of chances. Actually getting into scoring positions is the real test of a striker's skill and class - finishing rates can be deceptive or 'cyclical' as Arsène has observed

- He has all the attributes of a top class striker: speed, skill, balance, imagination and accurate finishing. He has been a consistent goal scorer for the last three seasons now (despite being massively injury disrupted and generally playing wide).
- He has missed a few sitters this season. If he had scored two or three of these, we would be raving about his exploits, but all top class strikers miss sitters, and we shouldn't read too much into a small number of games. He clearly does not lack the skill or 'calmness' to finish sitters and he doesn't have a record of doing it, so there is no reason to think that this is a long-term problem.
- Wenger's record in moving players to new positions has a lot more successes (Henry, RVP, Lauren, Kolo Touré) than failures (Eboue, Song, Wiltord)

3. **Is Gabriel as good as he looks?**

This guy also looks like a big time player. He is beginning to establish himself in the team and has all the attributes of a top class defender (although yet to prove consistency). If I was an attacker, I wouldn't fancy my chances of getting past a line-up of Koscielny and Gabriel protected by Le Coq and any combination of our full backs

4. **Ozil**

I love this player. He has wonderful skills and great stats. However, I still feel there is more to come from him: he doesn't seem to 'dominate' games, but looks capable of doing so. Perhaps he never will and will always just be a great team player. Instinct however, tells me that he might start overpowering the opposition in the way that Pires, Fabregas, Bergkamp, Vieira and Henry have all done at various times. If he does, then our rivals are in big trouble.

5. **Is Wenger going to rotate?**

IT'S HAPPENED AGAIN

Historically our Manager is not an enthusiastic rotator. But this squad is deep and there are a number of positions where the first choice is not much better than the reserve.

Strikers are the most common position to rotate. Walcott in the Champions League, Giroud in the Premier League sounds good, but can anyone resist the temptation to play Walcott against Terry? Expect Joel Campbell to get minutes. Full Back looks like a good candidate for rotation, with four strong players.

Can Wenger bear to rest Ozil? Can we afford to play Arteta instead of Coquelin? Can we chance working Coquelin into the ground? Will we try Ramsey in the middle again and give the ageing Cazorla a rest? Will we rotate the top three centre backs - is it conceivable to rest Koscielny? Will Wilshere and The Ox be important? Is it possible to rest Sanchez and does he know the meaning of the word?

Or will too much rotation disturb the team? If we don't see rotation in this series of matches, we can probably look forward to the 'rotation by injury' policy that we have suffered in the last few years. If we do see rotation, it could be a sign of things to come: the success or failure of that rotation could determine our season.

Of course there are many other important players at Arsenal and their performances will also make a big difference to the team. Questions of secondary importance seem to me to be:

- Can Sanchez maintain last season's form?
- Is this the year that The Ox finally establishes himself?
- Can our Full Backs keep up the good work?
- Will Cech make a real difference?
- Will Koscielny be as good as ever?
- Can Cazorla keep it up in the new position?
- Will we get the 2013-14 Ramsey back?
- Will Giroud do well?
- Will our BFG have an Indian summer?

TIM CHARLESWORTH

All in all, I expect the next few weeks to start answering some of these questions. We are now into the season proper. There is no more 'early season form' and this is our first big test.

CHAPTER TWENTY
MORE SETBACKS

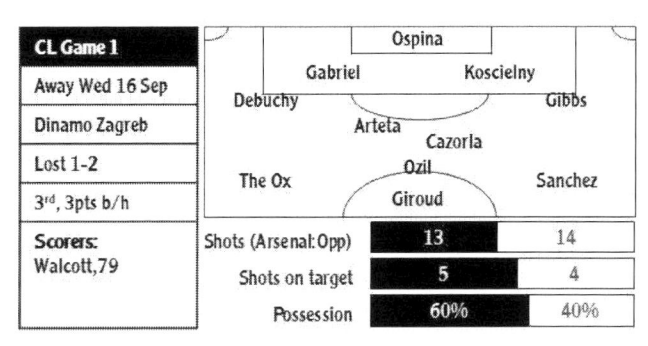

CL Game 1		
Away Wed 16 Sep		
Dinamo Zagreb		
Lost 1-2		
3rd, 3pts b/h		
Scorers: Walcott,79		
	Shots (Arsenal:Opp)	13 / 14
	Shots on target	5 / 4
	Possession	60% / 40%

Formation:
- Ospina
- Debuchy, Gabriel, Koscielny, Gibbs
- Arteta, Cazorla
- The Ox, Ozil, Sanchez
- Giroud

This was not a good night. Wenger went boldly for rotation with Ospina, Gibbs, Debuchy, Arteta, The Ox and Giroud all coming in. Cech, Monreal, Bellerin, Coquelin, Ramsey and Walcott were all rested.

We dominated early, but Dinamo looked dangerous on the break, and scored. Then Giroud got a second booking and a red. Both bookings were questionable, but also understandable. Dinamo scored again from a good header from a corner. Walcott came on, looked dangerous and got one back. A disappointing start to our Champions League campaign and a reminder that no European away game is easy.

A DISAPPOINTING NIGHT, BUT PLENTY MORE TO PLAY FOR

September 17th 2015

Two days ago, I eyed a tricky looking set of upcoming features and wrote an article about it.

My article tried to focus on the really important things to look out for, other than the obvious ones of whether we scored goals and whether the opposition did. After the match in Dinamo, I'm sure we would all welcome the chance to focus on something other than the result, so here is a review of the questions I asked and what we have learnt so far.

Firstly, I can't avoid observing that this tricky set of fixtures hasn't started well, but actually, of the six, this is possibly the best one to lose (depending on how you feel about Carling vs. Totts).

Of the questions I asked, the most obvious one we now have answers to is the one about rotation - Wenger was prepared to gamble; and more than I expected him to. My question over whether the rotation would work was also answered. Full marks for courage, less marks for achievement. With the benefit of hindsight, Wenger gambled too much.

I must say I was initially pleased when I heard the line-up for the Dinamo game. I thought it was a bold gamble and indicated Wenger's confidence in his squad. I was expecting to see 2-3 changes tonight, but we got 6. The Goalkeeper change really surprised me - are we going to see Ospina in all cups including the Champions League? I expected only one change at Full Back and the use of Arteta really surprised me (in my original article, I considered this rotation unlikely).

Looking at the longer term implications of the game I expect we will still qualify, but will probably have to play full strength teams right to the end of the group and this will have knock on effects for domestic fixtures. We are also likely to come second in the group, although you could argue we were favourites to do that anyway. Second and third is likely to be a battle between us and Dinamo, and in the Champions League group stage, head to head results matter.

So Theo's goal could be surprisingly valuable in the case that we tie with Dinamo and beat them at home (not that unlikely). If this happens the away goal - and the reduction of the deficit to one goal - could be important. We play Dinamo on match day five and this could also be a tactical advantage.

IT'S HAPPENED AGAIN

Unfortunately, I also have to observe that confidence will suffer going into a big game on Saturday (Chelsea's resounding victory may also be unhelpful in this regard). In terms of the other 'real questions' identified in my original article:

Coquelin: Unfortunately reinforced how good he is by how much we missed him. Looked good when he came on as well, setting up Walcott's goal with a typical piece of athletic and aggressive play. Arteta's form is a worry. Many fans have expressed doubts about Arteta as a DM backup and unfortunately those concerns looked real tonight. Let's hope Arteta improves as the season goes on and he gets more minutes.

Walcott: Could hardly have done better in terms of conversion rate (100% I think). He also constantly looked dangerous. He looks, just a little bit, more like a 'real no. 9' after this game and his impact from the bench. Showed the kind of great finish we know he is capable of.

Gabriel: Looked fantastic. Massive presence, great defending and tackling. He made one mistake at the end, but this was a calculated risk by a man chasing the game, I think. I'm really interested to see whether the BFG can get his place back (other than by rotation).

Ozil: Looked good in patches. He threatened to turn in a dominant performance at the start of second half, but then fell short and seemed to drift out of the game a bit.

Others:

- The Ox looked poor
- Sanchez did OK, without setting the world alight. Sanchez's form is slightly worrying and the 'sophomore effect' still seems like a possibility, but really it's too early to tell. He did some good things such as the goal assist and a lovely pass to Ozil that looked onside to me
- Giroud was obviously disappointing and he will feel hideous, but he was harshly dealt with by the referee and did OK whilst he was on the field

- Koscielny looked good, albeit not his best performance. I don't think he really could have done anything about the second goal, which was a good leap by a player with momentum on his side

So let's set aside the result, on the grounds that you can't read too much into a single score line, especially when a red card is involved in an away game. Overall, the answers to the big questions were quite encouraging. Most of the answers were good. Wenger may have slightly overdone it on the rotation, but I would rather see over-rotation than under-rotation (as a gymnastics coach would say). Overall, on balance, this match actually produced evidence that we will have a good season. Chins up Gooners. Mood will soon change if we get a good result on Saturday.

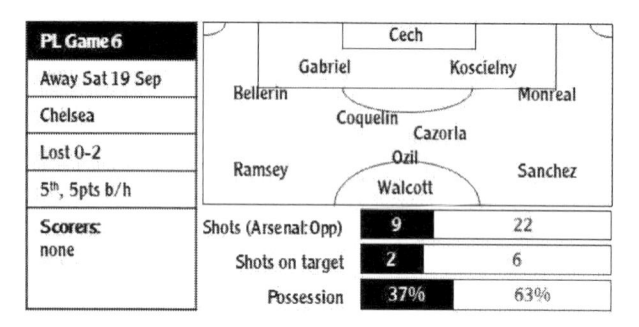

PL Game 6		
Away Sat 19 Sep		
Chelsea		
Lost 0-2		
5th, 5pts b/h		
Scorers: none		
	Arsenal	Opp
Shots (Arsenal:Opp)	9	22
Shots on target	2	6
Possession	37%	63%

Formation: Cech; Bellerin, Gabriel, Koscielny, Monreal; Coquelin, Cazorla; Ramsey, Ozil, Sanchez; Walcott

Horrible, horrible day. The team that played Stoke played again, with Mertesacker still out. The match was cagey for the most of the first half. Then the series of events that decided it require a little recollection here:

- Chelsea striker Costa hit Koscielny in the face several times and then knocked him to the floor
- The referee and all his assistants apparently didn't see it
- Gabriel came to his teammate's defence and engaged with Costa. Costa and Gabriel quarrelled and were both booked

IT'S HAPPENED AGAIN

- They continued to quarrel as they went back to the half way line and Gabriel flicked out a boot at Costa
- The Chelsea players (including Fabregas) surrounded the referee and joined the baying crowd in demanding a red card. They got it

With a man advantage, Chelsea got a goal early in the second half when Arsenal defended a free kick poorly. Coquelin went off injured and to add further insult, Cazorla was dismissed (probably correctly) for a second yellow. Chelsea managed to score another one against our nine men.

Chelsea had had a terrible start to the season and were under a lot of pressure. They were jubilant and Mourinho gloated by describing Costa (who played poorly apart from getting Gabriel sent off) as 'Man of the Match'. Arsenal fans were outraged by the injustice.

In a highly unusual development, the FA confirmed the game was a farce by rescinding Gabriel's ban (on the grounds that he hadn't touched Costa), effectively saying he should not have been sent off. They also gave Costa a ban (effectively admitting that he should have been sent off). So instead of Arsenal having a man advantage if the match had been properly refereed, Chelsea had a man advantage. Arsenal fans protested by gathering a petition of over 100,000 signatures to the effect that Mike Dean should never be allowed to referee another Arsenal game. Petitions with over 100,000 signatures must be considered for debate by Parliament. This was funny, but actually Parliament didn't consider the petition very seriously. Mike Dean was kept away from Arsenal for a while but did referee us again before the season was out.

LET'S SEE THE FUNNY SIDE OF MOURINHO
September 23rd 2015

I'm really going to stick my neck out here and post a defence of public enemy number one, Jose Mourinho.

TIM CHARLESWORTH

Everything I have ever read about this highly successful Manager suggests that he is a perfectly reasonable chap, who spends time with his family and has a sense of perspective about football, which he sees as a job, not a calling. Some of the comments that he makes are really quite funny if you step away from the emotion of it all. He is quick-witted, intelligent and has a real eye for the one liner ('the Special One' resonates almost as strongly as Shankly's joke that football was much more important than life or death).

It's a curious thing that in the world of football we don't seem capable of giggling. So when Mourinho describes Costa as 'Man of the Match', instead of laughing at what is actually quite a good joke, we are outraged by it. Anyone who watched the match - Mourinho is obviously an intelligent observer - knows that Costa played poorly and should have been sent off. Actually, by a huge stroke of luck and refereeing incompetence, Costa won the match for Chelsea.

This is ironic on a number of levels. Lest we be in any doubt that Mourinho is joking about Costa being Man of the Match, he says he is looking forward to going to the rugby tomorrow, directly after talking about Costa's performance. This comment is unnecessary and redundant, unless we understand the implication that Costa's behaviour was more appropriate to the rugby field. Mourinho is not only making a joke, but goes to the trouble to add on a comment of such stupidity that one can be left in no doubt he is being ironic. Yet of all the things I have read about the match, no-one comments on what a good joke this is. Now certainly, it is not so funny if you are an Arsenal fan. The joke is very much at our expense, but it's still only a joke. As football fans, we can surely live with a bit of banter (or even admire it)?

It's not really Mourinho's fault that no-one appears able to see the joke. To make it worse, we read all sorts of nonsense into Mourinho's comment. We think that Mourinho's game plan was to cheat and wind Arsenal up. We conclude that he knew what

IT'S HAPPENED AGAIN

he was doing all along and his cheating master plan came up trumps. This is ridiculous. Maybe this is why Mourinho likes England so much. I don't think his jokes are taken so seriously elsewhere.

Let me assure you, Mourinho is not clever enough to orchestrate what happened on Saturday. (We will assume for the sake of this article that the referee wasn't bribed - I know it looked like he was, but this is actually quite unlikely). Mourinho is not omnipotent. He is just a normal human being who is quite good at managing football teams. Mourinho may well have suggested to Costa that he try to irritate the Arsenal defenders, he certainly wouldn't be the first sports coach to suggest such a thing. Costa doesn't need much encouragement from his Manager on this front; he is naturally annoying.

Mourinho wouldn't have based his whole game plan on this idea (he is far too good for that) and he certainly wouldn't have suggested the kind of assault on Koscielny which in normal circumstances would lead to a red card and a ban (as of course happened, although it took a while).

So why don't we laugh at Mourinho? He is quite clearly funny. His witticisms are in the same class as Shankly and Clough and we had no trouble laughing at them (actually we laughed with them, not at them). Is it something to do with him being foreign? Does his Portuguese accent somehow make us less inclined to think he is joking? Do we incorrectly ascribe his humourful tones of delivery to a lack of familiarity with English pronunciation? Are we fooled by his deadpan mode of delivery - surely not, this style of comedy is as old as the hills, or at least as old as Jack Dee.

I suspect that the standard of journalism is partly to blame. Most football commentators nowadays are ex-pros rather than professional journalists. Can we be surprised that ex-pros in a sport that encourages people to leave school at sixteen don't make very insightful journalists? The shocking standard of journalism in English football is often commented on by Arsenal blogs. In fact, people are increasingly turning away from mainstream media towards sites such as Untold Arsenal in search of reasoned analysis.

Mourinho's jokes are also perhaps a bit more edgy than those of Shankly or Clough. For example, his descriptions of Wenger as a 'voyeur' and a 'specialist in failure' are quite funny, but also lack grace. They are memorable because they have a ring of truth to them. Wenger is a voyeur (dedicated student of the game is a kinder description), compared to Mourinho, who does not live and breathe football in the way that Wenger does.

Mourinho also feels a little upset that he was sacked by Chelsea in 2007 despite being considerably more successful than Wenger during the preceding three years. I think Mourinho bears a genuine grudge about this incident which forced him to move his family away from a home they loved. Wenger was kept on for a number of reasons; he was working with less money than Mourinho and also generates value for the club by developing young players in a way that Mourinho does not (Mourinho sold De Bruyne, Wenger kept Coquelin).

Wenger is also a good corporate man who looks after the long term interests of the club by building new facilities, investing in coaching and seeking value in the transfer market. Mourinho, by contrast, is only interested in winning football matches. And we must sympathise with Mourinho's point. After all, winning is the most important function of a Manager. He feels aggrieved that he was rewarded with the sack, despite doing better in his primary function than a rival, Wenger. The 'specialist in failure' comment is a pithy and witty way of expressing this frustration.

So let's look at what has really happened. A Manager is under terrible pressure because his (champion) team has had a terrible start to the season. He has then had an immense slice of luck. He should have had a player sent off and lost another game at home. Such a result would have threatened his job, his livelihood and a reputation he had spent nearly twenty years

IT'S HAPPENED AGAIN

building. Instead of sending Costa off, the referee made a horrific error, and actually sent off one of the opposition players for retaliating to the original, unseen, offence. This is even better (from Mourinho's perspective) because the opposition is a genuine rival. As a result, you have been gifted your first, desperately needed, home league victory of the season, lazy pundits will talk of a 'turnaround' and confidence around the club will be generally boosted.

At the end of this game, you are naturally on a high. Being an intelligent and witty man, you then make a joke about it. You say that Costa was the Man of the Match. Of course he was, in a way. He really did win the match. He did it by cheating in a manner which is an affront to the sport of football. But actually this makes it even better, because it's the unearned victories that really make a difference to your final league position.

Mourinho is a competitor who sees football as a competition, not a pure art (he is very different to Wenger in this). Annoying a 'poncy', 'snooty' purist like Wenger (who thinks he is better than you, despite the relative lack of silverware!) actually makes the whole thing better from Mourinho's perspective. He doesn't really care how Chelsea won, he just wanted to win.

What I think cannot be denied, is that my favourite Manager of all time does not like Mourinho. He doesn't like him one little bit. The handshake nonsense is not all a media invention. If you look at Wenger's body language, he genuinely doesn't want to touch Mourinho. By contrast, Mourinho sees the funny side and never wants to miss a chance to make Wenger uncomfortable by shaking his hand (Wenger had a similar issue with Ferguson).

Wenger doesn't like what Mourinho stands for, the way he does it, and the sort of football be promotes. I love Wenger, but he singularly lacks a sense of humour when it comes to football matters (his sincerity is one of the reasons that he is so good). Wenger most definitely does not find Mourinho amusing. This is a genuine clash of personalities.

TIM CHARLESWORTH

Wenger's teams have been consistently more fluid passers, less inhibited and less defensive. Mourinho's teams are consistently more defensive, more physical and more disciplined. Wenger sees magic in football, Mourinho sees a battle. They are both great Managers and actually their rivalry is good for the game, just as Borg/McEnroe was good for tennis, Prost/Senna was good for F1 and Ashour/Matthew was good for squash (sorry, I'm a squash fan and couldn't resist this one).

My suspicion is that history will be kinder to Wenger than Mourinho, because Wenger has contributed positively to the overall way that the game is played. I also suspect that history will treasure Mourinho's witticisms for what they are.

I love Wenger and will always support him. But let's not deify him. His lack of a sense of humour about football allows Mourinho to wind him up. By taking Mourinho's comments seriously we add to some kind of nonsense mythology about the man. He is not that clever; and dignifying his jokes with serious analysis implies some kind of mystic power, which he most certainly does not have. So can I politely suggest to my fellow fans that we draw the following conclusions from Saturday:

1. Mourinho was incredibly lucky
2. He is an enemy of pure football, as Wenger sees it, but 'vive la différence' as they say in Alsace
3. He is a witty man and his comments about Costa are actually quite funny. Don't let him wind you up. Have a giggle, see him for what he is, and move on. Actually the injury to Coquelin worries me far more than the result on Saturday

In my final attempt to cheer the Goonersphere up, I simply have to include a Shankly joke that I came across in researching this article. I desperately tried to work it in, but failed. Nonetheless, I think it stands on its own:

[Dismissively responding to a journalist who asked if he had taken his wife to see Rochdale as an anniversary present] *"Of course I didn't take her to see Rochdale as an anniversary*

IT'S HAPPENED AGAIN

present... It was her birthday. Would I have got married in the football season? Anyway, it was Rochdale reserves."

This was my most unpopular article yet. Copious quantities of metaphorical tomatoes were thrown. My idea that 'surely we can live with a bit of banter' was clearly wrong. The theme of 'Mourinho as amusing man' had been running about in my head for a while, but this may not have been the best moment to air my ideas! Perhaps the article will look better in this book than it did at the time on the website.

CHAPTER TWENTY ONE
GETTING BACK ON TRACK

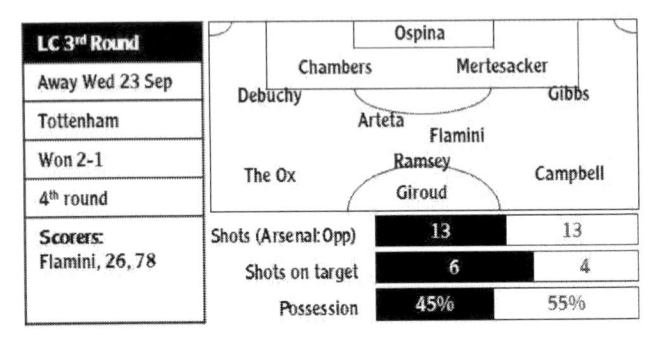

LC 3rd Round			
Away Wed 23 Sep			
Tottenham			
Won 2-1			
4th round			
Scorers: Flamini, 26, 78	Shots (Arsenal:Opp)	13	13
	Shots on target	6	4
	Possession	45%	55%

Lineup: Ospina; Chambers, Mertesacker; Debuchy, Arteta, Flamini, Gibbs; The Ox, Ramsey, Campbell; Giroud

Well this was really good fun. A run out for the under used members of the squad and a nice antidote to our post-Chelsea despair. It may have been a minor game, but we always enjoy a win at the Lane. Flamini even won it with an uncharacteristic screamer. The Totts actually played quite a lot of first team players too.

No real youngsters this year. I was hoping to see the wonderful Reine-Adelaide, from pre-season, but he was injured. It was quite a strong team in the sense that all the players are experienced Premier League professionals, but also a much changed team, none of them being current first choice players. It reflects well on our strength in depth that we can produce such a strong reserve team as this.

IT'S HAPPENED AGAIN

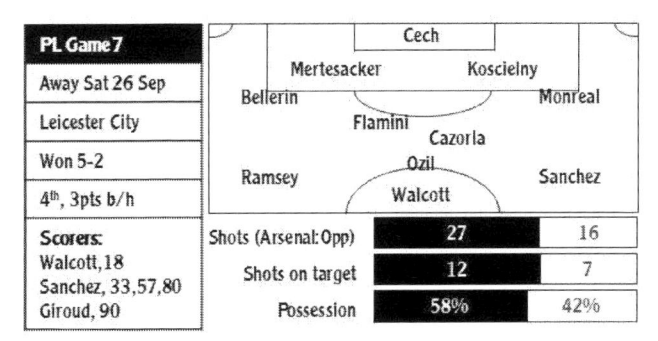

PL Game 7	
Away Sat 26 Sep	
Leicester City	
Won 5-2	
4th, 3pts b/h	
Scorers: Walcott, 18; Sanchez, 33, 57, 80; Giroud, 90	

Formation:
- Cech
- Bellerin, Mertesacker, Koscielny, Monreal
- Flamini, Cazorla
- Ramsey, Ozil, Sanchez
- Walcott

	Arsenal	Opp
Shots	27	16
Shots on target	12	7
Possession	58%	42%

This was an overdue spanking against an unbeaten Leicester team, away from home. There was a lot of talk that Arsenal had had more shots than any other team in the League, but the goals were not coming. Up to this point in the season Arsenal had only scored 3 Premier League goals and Alexis had had more shots than anyone (with no goals). Finally, the dam burst.

Gabriel had been banned*, so the BFG came back into defence. Walcott started rather than Giroud. After his midweek heroics, Flamini came in for Coquelin, but picked up an injury and was replaced by Arteta after 20 minutes. The defence looked a bit shaky without Gabriel and Coquelin, but when you score five it doesn't matter!

In hindsight, this match was not much remarked upon at the time. Actually it was incredible. Leicester only lost two more games all season (one to us) and never again lost by more than a single goal. This was also their only home defeat of the season. This was a thrashing of the champions by a weakened Arsenal team, away from home! Bravo!

---

* Gabriel's red card from the Chelsea game was rescinded on appeal, and therefore his three game ban was overturned, but the review panel took the view that he didn't leave the pitch quickly enough after being given the red card that he didn't deserve. For this second offence, he received a one game ban. Hmmmmnnn

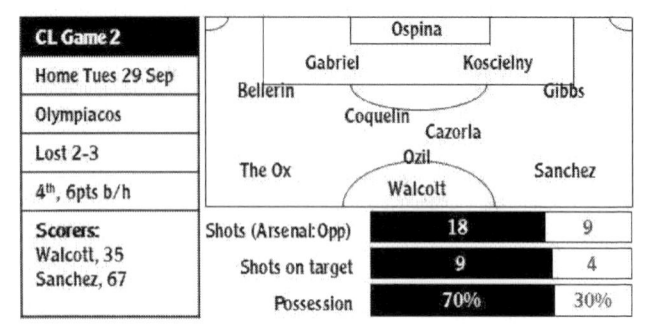

CL Game 2	
Home Tues 29 Sep	
Olympiacos	
Lost 2-3	
4th, 6pts b/h	
Scorers: Walcott, 35; Sanchez, 67	

Formation:
```
              Ospina
      Gabriel        Koscielny
Bellerin                      Gibbs
         Coquelin
                Cazorla
         Ozil
   The Ox                 Sanchez
              Walcott
```

	Arsenal	Opp
Shots (Arsenal:Opp)	18	9
Shots on target	9	4
Possession	70%	30%

Oh dear. This one really came from left field. We had all assumed that this was an easy three points and he team looked like it was going well. Less rotation than Champions League game 1 with Gibbs and The Ox coming in and Ospina in goal again. Gabriel returned after suspension, relegating the BFG to the bench (sign of things to come?). The BFG came on after 57 minutes due to a Koscielny injury. Walcott played as Giroud was suspended from match day 1. Coquelin returned from injury, but was substituted as we chased the game.

After a horrible start we got back to 1-1, when Ospina inexplicably dropped the ball over the line when fielding a corner. A true howler! Sanchez equalized irresistibly, but we gave the lead back within a minute. Our defence looked panicky without Le Coq and Koscielny on the field. They all chased the ball like schoolboys until Olympiacos slotted home.

Our spirit looked broken and we couldn't equalise a third time. Much gnashing of teeth ensued, amid silly comments that Wenger shouldn't have played Ospina (obviously true in hindsight, but a Manager cannot be held responsible for random errors). We had qualified from the group stage for the last 15 years in a row. Suddenly qualification this season looks almost impossible.

The next two games are against Bayern Munich, one of the top three teams in the world right now. We need at least three,

IT'S HAPPENED AGAIN

probably four, points from the two games to have a real chance of qualification.

HYSTERIA AND DISAPPOINTMENT

September 1st 2015

So the Goonersphere is full of hysteria and disappointment again. Olympiacos was a horrible game and a horrible performance, however you look at it. We're all full of blame and recriminations.

The hysterical attacks on Wenger for picking Ospina are plain silly, as if to imply that it was predictable that Ospina would make a mistake, or that Cech is immune from mistakes (West Ham anyone?). We have discussed the pros and cons of rotation on a number of occasions and I have yet to see a sensible argument that Wenger should never rotate. So, if we accept the principle of rotation, it is then a judgement about how much and how often. This is a difficult judgement that Wenger has to make without the benefit of hindsight.

It is important for any top club to have two high quality Goalkeepers, but Goalkeepers don't get that many injuries and it is difficult to retain a good keeper who never plays. Lots of clubs manage this situation by playing one in the League and one in the Cups: it is quite common practice. We have won the last two FA Cups with this policy (Fabianski and Szchezny playing in the Finals). Real Madrid won the 2014 Champions League doing this (using Casillas in the Champions League, but not in La Liga). So it's hardly an unusual rotation policy and - arguably - is one that has proved very successful in the past.

My last article defended Mourinho after the Chelsea game, for which I received quite a lot of negative feedback (actually I just tried to look at him from a different point of view, but passions were running high, and senses of humour running low). So perhaps it is a little risky to write about another well-established enemy of Untold, Piers Morgan, but here goes anyway.

In some ways, I quite like Piers Morgan. He quite often says what I am thinking. Watching Arsenal lose is a desperate situation for me and I hate it. It provokes all sorts of negative thoughts in my head about Wenger, our players, and life in general. As a rule I keep these to myself and try to subject my thoughts to a filter of 'common sense' and 'rationality'.

However, I must admit, thoughts such as 'Walcott is useless', 'Klopp would never let this happen' and 'Wenger's past his best' do fly uncontrollably into my brain. Actually I disagree with all these opinions and soon remind myself of my disagreement, thereby banishing the silly thoughts.

Piers appears not to apply a 'common sense filter' and, as a result, some of his comments are not very well thought out. During the Olympiacos game he engaged in a torrent of Twitter abuse. He didn't think about saving it up for the end of the game, after having a chance to reflect on the matter. He just regurgitated his gut reactions in real time.

The result was some very daft comments (of which a claim that he could run faster than the BFG was the highlight), drifting into his old 'Wenger out' mantra. Piers is a man who likes to run with his gut reaction (he is, after all, a tabloid journalist by background). There are only so many times that you can complain publicly about Arsenal's performance and remain faithful to Wenger.

If you have complained too many times in public (and he has), then eventually you can only maintain credibility by demanding significant change. Eventually, you have to publicly call for the Manager's head; this is a difficult position to back out of once entered into (if we win the League this season, I am really looking forward to seeing how Piers reacts).

I sometimes wonder what would happen if you could talk to Piers privately. I have a sneaking suspicion he would confirm

IT'S HAPPENED AGAIN

that, in Stan Kroenke's position, he would stick by Arsène as well. I suspect that even he, deep down, really knows that Arsène is the right Manager for Arsenal. Unfortunately, he has backed himself into such a position that he can never admit to this opinion.

I am extremely impressed by Walcott this season and even wrote a pre-season piece that we didn't need another striker, because he would be the solution. So I can certainly claim to be a Walcott loyalist. However, when I see him miss a chance toward the end of the game, the thought 'Walcott is useless' comes straight into my head (actually my subconscious brain uses less polite words than that). No matter that I actually think he is brilliant, no matter than every striker misses chances, the angry thought still comes to me.

Now, to my mind, part of being an adult is learning not to say the first thing that comes into your head. But I also recognise that, in the name of sanity, we all need to escape from the 'real world' on occasions. Some people escape the real world by going to a football stadium. Perhaps the chap who was yelling about 'useless Walcott' the other day knows that Walcott is not useless. Perhaps he goes to football to escape the real world and was just expressing a gut reaction. Perhaps he is normally a rational and sensible human being, but suspends common sense when he crosses the Ems threshold (or bridge).

So let's not be too harsh on Piers Morgan, or the chap who shouts 'useless Walcott'. It's not the way I like to behave. Like most Gooners, I believe in positively supporting our team, but the inner, angry me, can see their point of view and feel their pain. Maybe by expressing their ill-considered gut reactions, they avoid the need for me to do so, thereby freeing me to have a sensible dialogue about the world's greatest team. Football is all things to all men. I can forgive someone for venting a gut reaction, even if it is Piers.

TIM CHARLESWORTH

PS Please can someone arrange a BFG vs. Piers Morgan 100m race? I would pay good money to see this.

This was another very unpopular article. It may have been unwise to publish this one so soon after the Mourinho article. Sometimes football fans can be a little narrow minded. Some commenters even made the connection with the Mourinho article, and were pretty aggressive towards me (there may have been more abusive comments, but filters block the most unpleasant ones). I wasn't quite accused of trolling, but some people came pretty close. Like the Mourinho article, I still stand by it, and hope it looks better to you, reader, with a bit of hindsight.

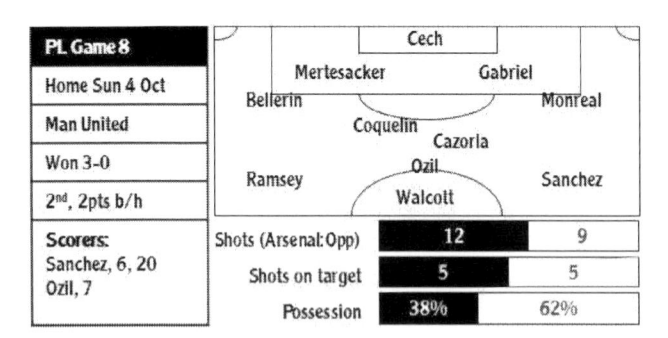

PL Game 8		
Home Sun 4 Oct		
Man United		
Won 3-0		
2nd, 2pts b/h		
Scorers: Sanchez, 6, 20 Ozil, 7	Shots (Arsenal:Opp)	12 / 9
	Shots on target	5 / 5
	Possession	38% / 62%

Formation: Cech; Bellerin, Mertesacker, Gabriel, Monreal; Coquelin, Cazorla; Ramsey, Ozil, Sanchez; Walcott.

Wow, what a treat. As good as match day 1 (and Champions League match day 2) was bad. Man U humbled, humiliated in a way that Arsenal haven't dispatched a top team in years. Almost makes us believe we might beat Bayern and survive in Europe. Walcott started up front again. The BFG retained his place due to Koscielny's injury. It was a low stress match for us fans. 3-0 up after 20 minutes and we can sit back and enjoy the magic. Nice memories to take into the two week Interlull.

IT'S HAPPENED AGAIN

The team

A clear first choice 11 has emerged at this point in the season, with only one of the Centre Back positions looking uncertain. Gabriel and Mertesacker have hardly ever been simultaneously fit this season, so it is difficult to see which one Wenger prefers:

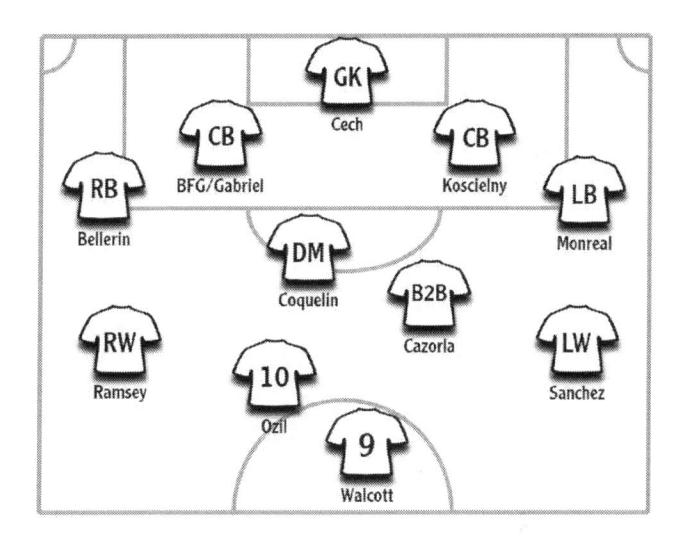

```
                    GK
                    Cech
           CB                CB
  RB    BFG/Gabriel       Koscielny    LB
Bellerin                              Monreal
                    DM
                  Coquelin
                             B2B
                            Cazorla
  RW         10                       LW
Ramsey      Ozil                    Sanchez
                     9
                   Walcott
```

TIM CHARLESWORTH

The table

	Team	P	W	D	L	GF	GA	GD	PTS
1	Manchester City	8	6	0	2	19	7	12	18
2	Arsenal	8	5	1	2	13	7	6	16
3	Man United	8	5	1	2	12	8	4	16
4	Crystal Palace	8	5	0	3	11	7	4	15
5	Leicester City	8	4	3	1	17	15	2	15
6	West Ham	8	4	2	2	17	11	6	14
7	Everton	8	3	4	1	12	8	4	13
8	Tottenham	8	3	4	1	11	7	4	13
9	Southampton	8	3	3	2	13	10	3	12
10	Liverpool	8	3	3	2	8	10	-2	12
11	Swansea City	8	2	4	2	10	10	0	10
12	Watford	8	2	4	2	6	7	-1	10
13	Norwich City	8	2	3	3	12	14	-2	9
14	Stoke City	8	2	3	3	8	10	-2	9
15	Bournemouth	8	2	2	4	10	12	-2	8
16	Chelsea	8	2	2	4	12	17	-5	8
17	WBA	8	2	2	4	6	11	-5	8
18	Aston Villa	8	1	1	6	8	13	-5	4
19	Sunderland	8	0	3	5	8	18	-10	3
20	Newcastle United	8	0	3	5	6	17	-11	3

HOPE SPRINGS ETERNAL

The second Interlull to Christmas
October to December 2015

CHAPTER TWENTY TWO
WHAT IS HAPPENING TO OUR PLAYERS?

13th & 14th October 2015

We have seen some very significant improvements from a number of our players over the last twelve months. Coquelin and Monreal are the most conspicuous - but not the only - examples and this got me thinking about what is really going on.

Nacho's case is really a great mystery. How did he suddenly change, from a failing player who was struggling to hold on to his place in the squad, to a top performer? Did he just have a bad run of form after he joined us? After all, he was an established squad member of that exceptional World and European Cup winning Spanish team when he arrived. Is this a case of a player just taking a very long time to adapt to the Premier League? He joined us in January 2013, so an improvement towards the end of 2014 is nearly two years later. Was there some connection between his improvement and his period playing at Centre Back? This seems unlikely, because I cannot see a mechanism by which such a thing might occur, but the coincidence of timing is difficult to ignore.

Whatever the cause, his improvement last season was unexpected. It is difficult to think of a similar case of a mature player having been with us for so long and suddenly showing a big improvement. Obviously this happens with young players, but that is easy to explain, as they develop physically and gain experience. This cannot be the explanation for the improvement of a 29 year old, established international player. It happens sometimes with players taking time to adapt to the Premier League, but surely two years is too long for an adaptation period?

The case of Coquelin has been discussed on many occasions, and I don't want to get repetitive. However, this player really is the most mysterious case I have ever seen in all my time observing Arsenal. At the start of last season, I had totally lost interest in him. He was one of many promising youngsters at Arsenal who had simply failed to make the grade. The list of these is long and distinguished. If a player hasn't made, at least, a partial breakthrough by the age of 21, they are not going to. This is true throughout the football world, not just at Arsenal. I was even beginning to fear for his career. Some of the youngsters who fail to make it at Arsenal go on to have good careers elsewhere, but the long list of (not particularly successful) loans for Coquelin made it look to me like Arsenal were struggling to find a home for him. Usually the players who are going to make it have conspicuously successful loans (Wilshere, Cole, Szczesny); and usually at the first attempt.

Maybe Arsène knew better and always expected Coquelin to come good? If so, he went about it in a strange way. By January 2015, one of the best players in the Premiership had less than six months on his contract. I don't know how much he was being paid, but all the indications are that in February 2015, Arsenal signed him up to a contract paying circa £40k per week; and that this was a considerable pay rise. The lack of a good contract wasn't because he was a contract rebel, it was simply because Arsenal had not offered him a new deal. If Wenger had a secret plan to turn Coquelin into an exceptional Defensive Midfielder, he seems not to have shared it with Coquelin, who appeared to have been genuinely annoyed at having his loan cut short at Charlton due to Arsenal's injury crisis.

And the story doesn't end there either. Cazorla is also a player transformed. His case it perhaps a little less outrageous than Monreal and Coquelin, but nonetheless worthy of comment. He was already a first team regular last season, so he hardly came from nowhere, but he did change from being a peripheral to an essential player. He is also not the first player to find a home in Central Midfield late in his career: John Barnes did something similar at Liverpool. However, the success of Cazorla's

IT'S HAPPENED AGAIN

move is unusual. Usually when a player ages and adapts to a new role, they become competent at the new position and do a job for their team. John Barnes was never as successful as a Central Midfielder, as he was as a youthful, pacy winger. Cazorla looks better than that; in fact he is making more contribution to the team than he ever has and some of his performances have been truly exceptional.

And then there's Bellerin, whose case is only a little less strange. On the face of it, this is just a young player growing up and establishing himself. But the pace of his improvement is exceptional. The most similar cases in recent times were Cole and Clichy, who were also young Full Backs who established themselves as they matured. Both Cole and Clichy were part of the squad as teenagers, Clichy at 18 and Cole at 19. Bellerin was nearly 20 before even making a meaningful debut. And he has gone very quickly from an unknown to a top performer. Keeping Debuchy out of the team is no mean achievement. His rise is actually not that different to Ashley Cole; they share a similar physique, but even so, it is quite remarkable. Cole (despite the loyalty bypass) is probably the finest product of the Arsenal youth system in the last 20 years. He is the only major player who has left Arsenal during the Wenger years and looked as good at his next club as he did at Arsenal. If we have another Ashley Cole on our hands in Bellerin then wow, what an amazing development that is (and how ironic it would be if this Barcelona boy proved more loyal than Cashley!).

So there are quite a few of our players showing considerable improvement over the past twelve months. These cases are important because they explain why it was not necessary to make a lot of additions to the squad which finished third last season. The shallow commentators didn't notice, but actually Arsenal effectively have a lot of new players. Some of these cases are more unusual than others and this requires a bit of explanation. I can't think of another period when we have seen so many dramatic improvements in existing players (arguably, something similar happened in 1996-97 just after Wenger joined, and in the mid to late eighties when the young George Graham team of Rocky, Adams, Thomas and Groves emerged).

So what is going on?

Why is all this happening? There are a lot of things that, as supporters, we don't see at a football club. Most of the real action goes on at training grounds behind closed doors. What we see on match day, is really just the results of that preparation work. It is difficult to know what is happening to explain these unusual player developments. One possible explanation is strength and conditioning. Certainly the improvements in Monreal and Coquelin are at least partly attributable to apparent increases in speed, agility and strength.

In the summer of 2014, Arsenal hired Shad Forsythe, who had been working with the World Cup winning Germany team as 'Head of Performance'. There didn't seem to be any immediate impact. The start of the 2014-15 season seemed to be as bad as ever for injuries. But slowly, our injuries seem to have reduced to at least a 'normal' level compared to other Premier League teams and this has been true for about ten months now.

And this is the kind of impact we might expect an improved strength and conditioning regime to deliver. No strength and conditioning can eliminate injury entirely. What we can do is build up the strength and flexibility of players, enabling them to better withstand the inevitable impacts that they sustain in a football match. As a result, a given impact or stretch is less likely to result in injury, or will result in a more trivial injury. We might expect it to take six months to see a genuine improvement in player conditioning: strength is not improved overnight, especially with professional sportsmen who are playing and recovering twice a week; and most of whom have played a summer World Cup. And this is exactly what we have seen. From the start of 2015, six months after Forsythe joined, our injury record has subtly improved. And we have also seen these extraordinary improvements in some of our players. So why only some?

Well, I'm speculating here, too. But it seems unlikely to me that Arsenal had never thought of having strength and conditioning training before Shad Forsythe arrived. Wenger has always been interested in player conditioning: this was much commented on in the early Wenger years. I think we are seeing the effect of an improvement in quality, not quantity. I suspect that the pre-Forsythe regime was a bit generic and Forsythe has made it more specific to individual players. Arsenal have talked publicly about our increased use of individualised data (and the acquisition of the StatDNA company in December 2012). So the old regime was probably great for Koscielny and Gibbs, but not ideal for Monreal or Coquelin. Perhaps the new regime is better tailored to individual players?

And there's another possible explanation. The players who have improved are mostly the ones who had time off the pitch. Again, this is what we would expect to see if strength and conditioning were the explanation. We cannot build up a player who is playing twice a week, as they spend virtually all their time playing or recovering. Muscles need to recover from strength work. Generally speaking, strength is improved via micro-tears in muscle fibres caused by slightly overworking the muscles (by, for example, lifting heavy weights). The body rebuilds the small tears stronger than they were before. But this process takes more than three days. So if you do serious strength work with a player who is playing three days later, you will impair his performance.

If we pursue this line of thinking a little further, we might note changes in a few players I didn't even mention above. Walcott shows signs of being a changed player. He always had pace to burn, but it was too easy for defenders to knock him off the ball. Now he seems much more able to hold onto the ball under physical pressure. Is he just stronger? He looks less lean and more heavily muscled than he used to (as does Ozil).

And we cannot ignore the case of Sanchez, who joined at the same time as Forsythe. This guy is a freak. He plays virtually every match, usually for 90 minutes; and has played major tournaments with Chile for the past two summers. This might be understandable if he were a quiet, genteel player, but he is the opposite. He is a kind of Duracell-bunny-Tigger-love-child. He is all action and never seems to stop running. By all common sense, he should be breaking down with a major injury (rest assured, I am touching wood as I write this). Sanchez obviously has natural athletic talent, but is the new regime playing a part in his story too?

We might also note that Arsène Wenger has form on this front. A decade ago there was a lot of talk about how Wenger had achieved his spectacular success at Arsenal. In recent years, this interest has waned, for obvious reasons. A commonly cited explanation ten years ago was the radical changes that Wenger made to the fitness regime at Arsenal in the late 1990s (Tony Adams talked a lot about his new stretching regime, diet and stopwatch training). It was also notable that Wenger didn't bring an assistant with him like most new Managers do. Instead, he retained Pat Rice. What he did do was bring in Boro Primorac, who Wenger had worked with before, as 'first team coach'. Primorac is a shadowy figure, whose contribution on match day is not obvious, yet as Arsène has retained him for 19 years he must be playing an important role. I suspect he is the implementer of the fitness regime on a day-to-day basis. The Arsenal teams of the late 90s and early 00s certainly seem to have had physical advantages. Their pace and strength often seemed to overwhelm the opposition.

But football is not a closed world. Players and staff move from club to club and there is constant press scrutiny. So if you are doing something that gives you an advantage, you can expect to be copied in due course, even if you are as private as Primorac. Over the years, other teams emulated Arsenal's regimes and

IT'S HAPPENED AGAIN

maybe even moved ahead. Alex Ferguson has commented several times on how he studied Wenger's methods.

Certainly, the game of football seems to have become faster and more physical over the last fifteen years; many commentators have made this observation. Wenger is also widely credited with changing the English game after his arrival.

By the late 00s, our teams looked comparatively frail in a physical sense, and the injuries started to mount up. Many fans have complained that referees failed to protect the Arsenal teams of this period; and there is truth in this complaint, but it also strikes me that Martin Keown, Patrick Vieira and Emmanuel Petit didn't need anyone to protect them. Perhaps, over time, Arsenal lost the edge the Wenger/Primorac training regime bought to North London in the late 90s. Maybe Forsythe has come in and helped reinforce the physical conditioning regime, thereby helping Arsenal to catch back up with the other teams. Maybe Arsenal are even a little bit ahead again?

Really, this article is quite speculative and could be totally wrong. However, it does seem to me that we have seen significant improvements in strength and conditioning at Arsenal since Forsythe arrived. Those improvements appear to date from about six months after his arrival - much as one might expect - and seem to have affected some players more than others. I have no insider insight into Arsenal's strength and conditioning regimes, but I suspect we will find out more about Shad Forsythe in the years to come. After all, as observed above, football is an open world. But certainly, something unusual is going on at Arsenal. Long may it continue.

TIM CHARLESWORTH

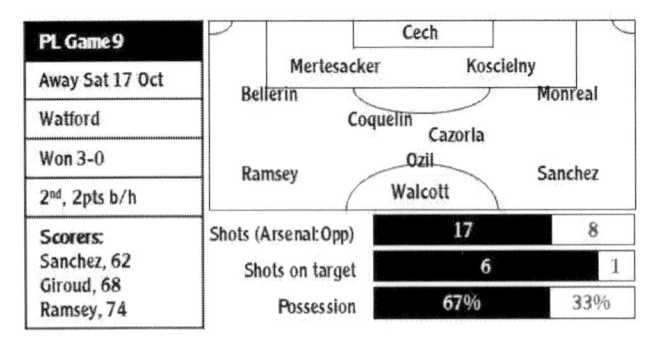

PL Game 9	
Away Sat 17 Oct	
Watford	
Won 3-0	
2nd, 2pts b/h	
Scorers:	
Sanchez, 62	
Giroud, 68	
Ramsey, 74	

Formation:
- Cech
- Mertesacker, Koscielny
- Bellerin, Monreal
- Coquelin, Cazorla
- Ramsey, Ozil, Sanchez
- Walcott

	Arsenal	Opp
Shots (Arsenal:Opp)	17	8
Shots on target	6	1
Possession	67%	33%

Not as comfortable as Man U, but the team did well. Koscielny returned to the team. Gabriel dropped out with a minor injury. Walcott started again with Giroud on the bench. Nice game. We were patient until we scored and then Watford crumbled a little. Good routine away win with no major dramas. This sort of win is championship form! Nice to see Giroud scoring from the bench and Ramsey is looking more dangerous. Bellerin excellent again. This guy seems to be still developing!

CHAPTER TWENTY THREE
BAYERN & BRILLIANCE

WILL WENGER GO FOR PACE AGAINST BAYERN?
October 20th 2015

During the summer I speculated on the Walcott vs. Giroud choice at no. 9. Walcott seems to have got the upper hand in this selection battle, but Giroud is now scoring lots of goals, so it will be interesting to see who is selected against Bayern. In my summer article I tried to look beyond the 'who will score most goals' question, as there didn't seem to be a clear answer to this; and to see what other contributions the players made.

I suggested that Giroud brought a defensive advantage to the team. This is most obvious in his work defending corners and free kicks, where his aerial presence in the penalty box brings a clear advantage. Walcott does not bring this to the team. As the season goes on however, it is increasingly clear that Walcott does bring a threat 'on the break'. With him in the team, we are more able to rapidly turn a defensive situation into an attacking one.

In days gone by, when watching Arsenal, I used to hope the opposition would win a corner. This slightly bizarre hope was all to do with Arsenal's ability to counter-attack from deep. As soon as an Arsenal player picked up the ball, Vieira, Bergkamp, Henry and Pires would surge forward, often assisted by torrents of Wiltord or Ljungberg. The opposition would have too many players committed forward for the corner, facing the wrong direction. By the time they turned, the wave of red shirts was gone. It was almost unfair on the other team. One minute they are in with a sniff of a goal, next minute they are picking it out of their own net, with a somewhat bemused expression.

In modern parlance this is called 'being good in transition' and wow, were we good at it! Our current team is beginning to remind me of these days. Sanchez, Ozil and Walcott, in particular, can be very dangerous in transition. We saw it against Manchester United and we saw it again against Watford. Although Walcott didn't score in either game, he seemed to be making dangerous runs in transition that defenders were obliged to cover and were thus getting out of position, creating space for other Arsenal players to exploit.

One of the reasons we are seeing this danger in transition is the increased amount of pace in the team. Sanchez and Walcott are conspicuously quick. Ozil is pretty fast too (albeit specializing in Bergkampesque 'speed of brain' rather than Henryesque 'afterburner pace').

The current team don't quite do it the same way as the Vieira-era teams. They are physically less overpowering than the Henry/Pires generation, but I think also a little faster and more skilful. So they seem to rely more on pace and trickery than the intimidating tidal wave of yesteryear. We're not quite back to the old days and our weakness at defending corners still means that I prefer Arsenal not to give corners away, but this is starting to look like a significant change in the way Arsenal play.

It seems that Coquelin is playing a part in this too. Flying forward creates gaps for the opposition to exploit if they can get the ball back. Because the Arsenal players feel confident in Coquelin's ability to cover them, if they lose the ball they feel they can run at the opposition with impunity. I think Gilberto and Petit played similar roles in the past. Cazorla is often the deep playmaker who unleashes the modern-day torrent.

So, to return to my original theme, the replacement of Giroud with Walcott obviously adds significantly to the aggregate pace of the team. Replacing Arteta with Coquelin has a similar effect. The use of Bellerin and Gabriel also contributes to the overall pace of the team (faster than Debuchy and Mertesacker). Overall, we can see a very significant increase in pace compared to the team of 12 months ago.

IT'S HAPPENED AGAIN

This increased pace seems to be resulting in counter-attacking goals at the moment. We might expect opposition teams to adapt: the obvious response is to defend with a 'deep line', especially when in possession. This means we might see opposition Defenders and Midfielders reluctant to commit forward, fearful of Arsenal's transition speed. Obviously, this blunts the effectiveness of opposition attacks and we can see a defensive advantage which Walcott brings to the team and Giroud does not.

It is difficult to measure, but I sense teams are already 'standing off' Arsenal because they are worried about Walcott's pace. Those teams that fail to do so (e.g. Man U) are paying the price. I will be interested to see if Walcott and Gabriel start against Bayern. If they do (and I suspect they will), we will have a very pacy team. Look out for the effects of this:

1. Will Arsenal have the confidence to launch all-out counter attacks? If we do, we are relying on the pace of Le Coq, the Boss and Gabriel (and, to a lesser extent, the Full Backs) to cover counter-counters. Bayern have extremely quick and talented counter attackers (a different proposition to Man U or Watford)
2. Will Bayern recognise this danger and sit deeper when in possession? If so, you may see Bayern attacks which peter out due to lack of support, or a lot of sideways and backwards passing (Guardiola teams like possession). Alternatively you might see Bayern players working to create their own opportunities. Players like Lewandowski are quite capable of doing so

The Bayern game will be fascinating on a number of levels. It is a real chance for Arsenal to test out their newly (re)discovered speed based tactics against top class opposition. Arsenal will need to go for the win, especially if the game is level going into the last third. In this scenario, spectacular open play is likely. Hold your breath...

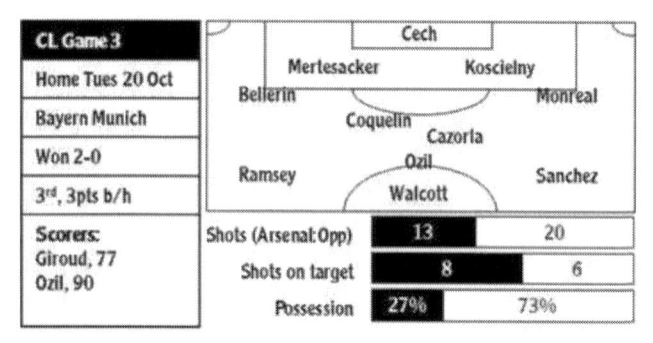

CL Game 3	
Home Tues 20 Oct	
Bayern Munich	
Won 2-0	
3rd, 3pts b/h	
Scorers: Giroud, 77 Ozil, 90	

Lineup:
- Cech
- Bellerin, Mertesacker, Koscielny, Monreal
- Coquelin, Cazorla
- Ramsey, Ozil, Sanchez
- Walcott

	Arsenal	Opp
Shots	13	20
Shots on target	8	6
Possession	27%	73%

What a night, what a result to put us back in with a chance of qualifying. Bayern had won their last 12 and never fail to score!

The same team played as against Watford. Gabriel still injured, but a good performance by the BFG will give him hope of keeping his place. Giroud made a big difference when he came on, but Walcott also played well. It must be close between those two for the starting berth. Bayern dominated possession (nearly 75%), but we looked very dangerous on the break.

In truth it was a 50:50 match and we edged it, with the 2-0 flattering us. But perhaps we were due a bit of luck after the Chelsea, Dinamo, Liverpool and Olympiacos games. Olympiacos winning away makes it still appear very difficult for us to qualify. We looked solid in defence and Cech made some very good saves. Ospina was injured (diplomatic or real?). Ramsey got yet another hamstring injury. Apparently the club staff cannot work out what is causing them.

	Team	P	W	D	L	GF	GA	GD	PTS
1	Bayern Munich	3	2	0	1	8	2	6	6
2	Olympiacos	3	2	0	1	4	5	-1	6
3	Dinamo Zagreb	3	1	0	2	2	7	-5	3
4	Arsenal	3	1	0	2	5	5	0	3

Arsenal are below Dinamo because we have a losing record against them.

IT'S HAPPENED AGAIN

HOLD THE FRONT PAGE, WENGER IS TALKING TACTICS
October 26th 2015

Amidst all the joy and celebration following the Bayern result, we may be forgiven for missing something unusual: Wenger made a comment about tactics. This is remarkable because of its rarity. For some reason, Arsène doesn't like to talk tactics. Perhaps he feels it gives an advantage to opponents to provide an insight into his tactical thinking. He has a pretty similar attitude to transfer plans.

An interesting article in The Telegraph reported Wenger as saying (after Bayern) 'I decided to drop Ozil a bit deeper to make it tighter around the box and to catch them on the break, because we have the pace to do it'.

This sort of statement is very common in football, but not from Wenger. There are two particularly atypical things about it:

1. Normally he is keen to keep any tactical considerations close to his chest - did he just get carried away in the moment of victory and forget himself?
2. It is very 'un-Wenger' to instruct a player in this manner. He usually likes his players to work things out for themselves within a structure. This quote however, suggests that he gave Ozil a very clear almost 'Mourinhesque' instruction, which he expected Ozil to follow

Wenger's failure to discuss tactics has led to quite a lot of speculation over the years that 'Wenger doesn't do tactics'. This is a bit of a silly observation, as tactics are clearly part of a football Manager's armoury and even the most pessimistic assessment of Wegner must conclude that he is, at least, quite good. It would be strange if he achieved his success without using one of the tools available to him, i.e. tactics.

TIM CHARLESWORTH

So what do we mean by tactics?

Tactics can be confused with analysis.

For example, in the Bayern game, Arsenal went for fairly aggressive passing, looking to move the ball forward rather than sideways and often going for long passes. I don't think that this was really a 'tactic' in the sense of a pre-planned strategy, more the case that Bayern forced us to play like this.

Bayern showed brilliant execution of one of Guardiola's trademarks, the 'high press'. In a high press, Midfielders and Attackers aggressively pursue the ball, rapidly closing down the man in possession and trying to cut off the available outlets for him to make a simple pass to.

This tactic hopes to elicit a mistake from the man in possession, thereby setting up a dangerous attacking situation. And Bayern succeeded with this on a number of occasions, notably when pressurizing Sanchez, of all people, to lose control of the ball and give away a very good shooting chance.

When you are faced with a high press, the only real option you have is to try to 'spring it', by getting the ball past the onrushing 'pressers' and up towards your attackers and midfielders. This means passing forwards, not sideways. If you can do so, you are likely to have a good attacking position because the pressing team has committed players forward to the press and will now have a lot of players in front of the ball. This will expose the opposition defenders to the space between the defensive line and the pressers.

So, if Wenger had talked about the 'tactic' of Arsenal's aggressive forward passing style, this wouldn't really be a tactic at all, but a natural response to Bayern's play. The Arsenal team may well have discussed these scenarios before the game, but the choice of passing style is not really a tactic, it is simply an inevitable response to the high press.

The decision to drop Ozil deeper, however, is a genuine tactic in the sense that it is a pre-planned action intended to shape the game. The intended effect was presumably to allow Bayern to pass it around their back four more easily, but to make it harder for them to penetrate Arsenal's reinforced defensive lines.

Indeed this is pretty much what happened. It looked to me as if Sanchez was playing deeper as well, but this may simply have been a response to Ozil's positioning rather than a pre-planned tactic.

How does Wenger approach tactics?

The rumours that 'Wenger doesn't do tactics' may also have been fuelled by Wenger's slightly unusual approach. Like many great leaders, I suspect Wenger is normally the kind of person who likes to 'ask questions' rather than 'furnish answers'.

An incident that has always stuck in my head is an often repeated story about a meeting during the second double season (1997-8). I have heard and read this story a number of times and it has sort of drifted into Arsenal folklore. Nonetheless, I believe it to be true. A fairly prosaic description of it can be found on pp 116-117 in Tony Adams' 1998 autobiography 'Addicted'.

The meeting occurred in December 1997 after a particularly dire 1-0 home defeat by Liverpool on 30th November. Arsenal were well off the pace in the Premier League and looking defensively disorganised. Arsène gave the players a couple of days off and then organized a meeting at Sopwell House, a hotel near the Arsenal training ground.

During the meeting, the Arsenal defenders, led by Adams, got a bit irate with the midfielders (particularly Vieira and Petit) for failing to provide them with enough protection. Vieira and Petit certainly seemed to amend their playing style in the second half of the season. It is also true that Arsenal went on a fantastic run after this meeting, which delivered both the Premier League and FA Cup titles.

The interesting point about this story is that Wenger appears to play a limited part in it. If it was Ferguson, one might expect to hear that the Manager launched some kind of verbal or physical assault on Vieira and Petit in order to get his message across. But Wenger seems to have made no direct intervention. All he did was tell the players that he was unhappy.

He gave them a couple of days off, to let them know that they needed to do something and to give them time to think about it. He then facilitated the meeting, but didn't try to tell the players what the answer was. He basically let them work it out for themselves. This approach seems to carry two advantages:

1. The collective wisdom of the players is likely to come up with a better answer than the Manager working alone. After all, the players are on the pitch and have the closest possible experience of what is happening. Unlike many other Managers, Wenger does not assume his players are fools
2. The players are much more likely to properly implement tactics they have worked out themselves. If a tactic is simply instructed, players may doubt whether it is right. This often appears to be the case with Mourinho, who seems to get frustrated that his players don't do what he has told them to

Conclusions

So what do we conclude from all this? Wenger did something unusual in talking about his tactics and perhaps also something unusual in the way he instructed Ozil. I can think of three possible explanations:

1. Actually Wenger quite often gives instructions like this, it's just that we don't hear about it. Perhaps he was just over excited, or maybe he was a bit too pleased with himself for getting 'one over' Guardiola
2. He slightly changes his approach in big games like Bayern and becomes more likely to 'instruct' players. If this is the

IT'S HAPPENED AGAIN

case, we might imagine such instructions would carry more weight with the players due to their rarity. Ozil certainly did look like he was sitting deeper, as requested

3. Wenger is changing his approach. This doesn't necessarily mean a permanent change. Wenger is a thoughtful man. Perhaps he has just decided that this team needs to be managed in a slightly different way than some of the other teams he has had. Over the last few years we have seen a lot of games where Arsenal dominate possession and still lose. Maybe Wenger has lost faith in this group of players to work out their own problems and decided to give them a firmer steer than usual

Whatever is behind the tactical choice that Wenger made, I am pretty sure that we won't be hearing a lot of similar comments in the future. Even if he has changed the way that he instructs his players, I am pretty sure that he will not be talking about it so openly again. We were all on a bit of an adrenalin high at the end the Bayern game. It was nice to get this unusual insight into Wenger's tactics, but we can probably expect normal service to be resumed in the coming weeks.

CHAPTER TWENTY FOUR
BACK TO EARTH WITH A BUMP

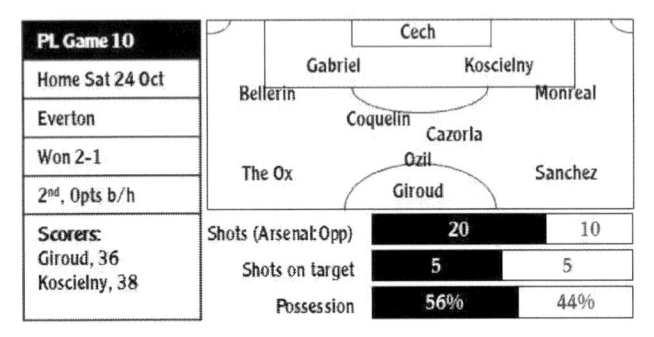

PL Game 10
Home Sat 24 Oct
Everton
Won 2-1
2nd, Opts b/h
Scorers: Giroud, 36 Koscielny, 38

Formation:
- Cech
- Gabriel, Koscielny
- Bellerin, Monreal
- Coquelin, Cazorla
- The Ox, Ozil, Sanchez
- Giroud

	Arsenal	Opp
Shots	20	10
Shots on target	5	5
Possession	56%	44%

This win took us top, but Man City got the lead back on goal difference the next day. Nonetheless, there is a feeling of quality and momentum about the team. Let's hope it's no false dawn. The Ox continued for the injured Ramsey. BFG was ill again so Gabriel came in after missing two games with an unexplained minor operation. Giroud started upfront ahead of Walcott - got his place back or rotation?

Not a classic performance. Two quick goals came from headers. Everton got one back via a lucky deflection. The performance was good but lacked brilliance. Considering the effort expended against Bayern four days earlier, they had a right to be tired and they looked it. This was especially true in the last 20, when Everton nearly equalised. But this is the sort of result you need to hold on to if you want to be champions.

IT'S HAPPENED AGAIN

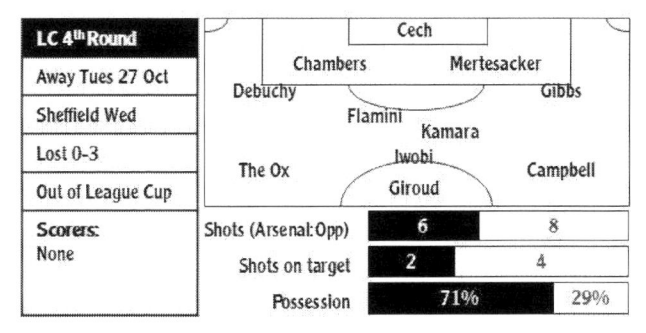

LC 4th Round
Away Tues 27 Oct
Sheffield Wed
Lost 0-3
Out of League Cup

Scorers: None

Formation:
- Cech
- Chambers, Mertesacker
- Debuchy, Gibbs
- Flamini, Kamara
- The Ox, Iwobi, Campbell
- Giroud

	Arsenal	Opp
Shots	6	8
Shots on target	2	4
Possession	71%	29%

This was a bit of a depressing night. Injuries and loans meant that Arsène had to play a weaker team than he might have liked; and it was one overwhelmed and outfought by a rampant Wednesday team on a balmy Yorkshire evening. Cech, BFG and The Ox were the only first team players involved, with Giroud starting up front. Kamara and Iwobi made debuts, with 17-year-old Bielik debuting from the bench.

To make matters worse, The Ox pulled up after only a few minutes with a hamstring injury. He was replaced by Walcott, who pulled up with his own hamstring injury minutes later. Both will now miss a few games and the squad is looking a bit stretched with tough games coming up.

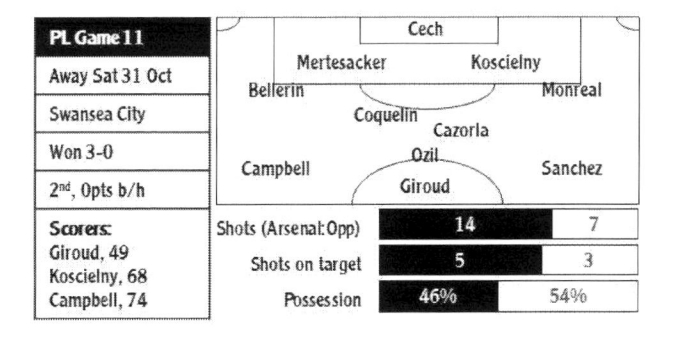

PL Game 11
Away Sat 31 Oct
Swansea City
Won 3-0
2nd, 0pts b/h

Scorers:
Giroud, 49
Koscielny, 68
Campbell, 74

Formation:
- Cech
- Mertesacker, Koscielny
- Bellerin, Monreal
- Coquelin, Cazorla
- Campbell, Özil, Sanchez
- Giroud

	Arsenal	Opp
Shots	14	7
Shots on target	5	3
Possession	46%	54%

A reassuring victory. In truth the score line flattered Arsenal, but it was a good result. A tale of two halves. Swansea were stronger in the first half, but we dominated the second.

Giroud started in the absence of the injured Walcott and the BFG retained his place, with Gabriel benched. It's beginning to look like the BFG is preferred to Gabriel. The near-forgotten Joel Campbell started on the right in the absence of the injured Ox. Ozil was exceptional again. Campbell did surprisingly well and his goal was welcome for a player who has worked hard for few chances in his Arsenal career. With Chelsea and Man U dropping points again, the league is starting to look like a straight fight between Arsenal and Man City. Bayern and Tottenham next!

IS THIS REALLY AN INJURY CRISIS?
November 2nd 2015

Based on the choices Wenger has made over the last twelve months or so, his five top players for the Right Wing/Right Midfield position appear to be (in no particular order):

- Aaron Ramsey
- The Ox
- Jack Wilshere
- Danny Welbeck
- Theo Walcott

All of these players are now injured. This is certainly an injury crisis in this position by any standards; and we could argue that Rosicky could play this position as well. But one position does not make an injury crisis.

Football is a squad game nowadays and the idea of a first eleven almost seems a bit outmoded in the days of 60 game seasons, rotation and much more frequent injuries. However, Wenger still seems to use the concept and I don't think the idea is quite dead yet. It seems to me that a clear first choice eleven has emerged, this season. It is roughly:

IT'S HAPPENED AGAIN

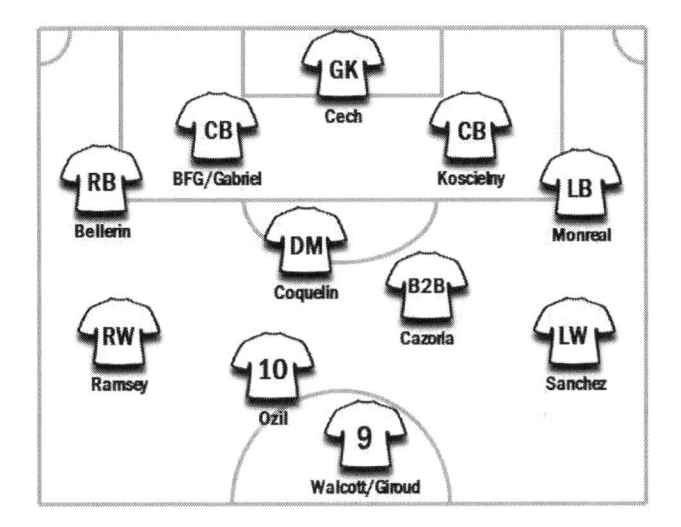

```
          GK
          Cech
    CB          CB
   BFG/Gabriel  Koscielny
RB                        LB
Bellerin                  Monreal
          DM
          Coquelin
                 B2B
                 Cazorla
RW                        LW
Ramsey    10              Sanchez
          Ozil
               9
          Walcott/Giroud
```

There are two major areas of uncertainty:

No. 9/CF: Walcott has recently edged Giroud for the starting position, but Giroud is fighting back impressively with good performances and goals after starting from the bench. Giroud seemed to be first choice at the start of the season, then it looked like there was a bit of rotation, but Walcott seems to be preferred in recent games, starting against Man U, Watford and Bayern. I think Giroud may have been a bit unlucky. He seemed to lose his place after the (definitely unlucky) Dinamo red card. It almost looks as if Wenger was a bit angry with him for losing us that match. It didn't help his cause when Walcott came on, looked good and scored. Maybe Giroud got his place back on merit, after starting and scoring against Everton. Maybe it was just rotation. Either way, he will now get a run in the team following Walcott's injury and it doesn't look like Walcott will easily recover his status as preferred starter.

Giroud is a big, physically strong player. I think he is particularly awkward for defenders to deal with when they are tired. Perhaps we could argue he is the ideal substitute, but we could make just as good an argument for Walcott - that his pace is hard to handle when defenders are tired. Perhaps tactical considerations have helped Walcott. His pace intimidates teams and makes them stand off, which makes our opponents less effective in attack. This is useful at the start of a game, as it prevents the kind of bad starts that hurt us so badly in the 2013-14 season. Everton and Swansea looked a bit more comfortable with Walcott not playing, but Sanchez still provides some pace-based threat. Giroud presents a counter attacking outlet as well because he can hold the ball up and act as a pivot to the flying midfielders. They are such different players that it is very difficult to make a clear choice between them.

Centre Back: The BFG and Gabriel are looking close. I am in the minority of fans who prefer Gabriel. They have hardly ever been simultaneously fit this season, so it is difficult to see which one Wenger favours. Earlier in the season it looked like the BFG was getting the nod over Gabriel, but Gabriel has played so well that this is no longer clear. Both were available for the Olympiacos game and Gabriel got the start, but this was a game where Wenger rotated, so it was not clear that Gabriel started on merit. Prior to that, we have to go back to Premier League game 2 on 16th August vs. Palace to find a match where both were available. Mertesacker started then, with Gabriel on the bench.

Much like Giroud and Walcott, they bring very different things to the team. The BFG brings calmness, leadership, ball control and height. Gabriel brings pace, athleticism and a fierce competitive passion. Perhaps Wenger will use tactical considerations to decide between the two, rather than have a clear first choice?

With both finally available again, I was really surprised that the BFG started against Swansea. The BFG played in midweek against Sheffield Wednesday, so I had assumed that Gabriel would play the Swansea match and the BFG would play at Bayern. I presume the BFG will still play against Bayern, but if so, why didn't Wenger start Gabriel against Wednesday?

IT'S HAPPENED AGAIN

If the BFG plays in Munich that will be three matches in 8 days. Surely this was unnecessary, when Gabriel was available? The Bayern game will suit Mertesacker. We are likely to play deep and therefore won't need too much Centre Half pace, but probably will need experience, presence and calmness under pressure.

So what is Wenger doing? I wonder if there is some rotation pattern involving the Tottenham match that I haven't considered? Is there something we don't know about Gabriel's fitness following his mysterious absence for two matches following a 'minor operation'? Is Wenger upset with Gabriel's Chelsea dismissal, just as he seems to have been upset by Giroud's Dinamo red card? Is it simply that Wenger values his BFG skipper so highly that he can't bear to bench him even against Sheffield Wednesday?

So, it may be that we really have thirteen players in our first choice eleven. The interesting thing about this starting eleven is that it has been mostly available this season. Our major injuries, so far, have been to Welbeck, Rosicky and Wilshere, but it is not clear that any of those would be in the first choice eleven (Wilshere probably closest). They are mostly backup players who haven't really been needed because the players that they back up have mostly not been injured. So injuries have hardly disrupted our team at all. Perhaps the worst instance was the Liverpool game, when we lost both Centre Backs but, even then, Gabriel was very strong and the game seemed to do Chambers good.

If I could choose which of our players would get injured, I would tend to choose the Centre Forwards or Centre Backs, where the first choice is not that obvious anyway. And these are the positions in which we have seen the most injuries and suspensions, with Walcott, Giroud, the Boss, BFG and Gabriel all missing games - Cazorla was suspended for a Carling Cup match that he wouldn't have played in anyway.

And then Ospina gets injured. He is also a backup player, but a politically difficult one. Wenger was under pressure to pick

Cech for the Bayern game (it seems he may have promised Ospina that he would start Champions League games). And then the problem goes away - if Wenger could have picked one player to come back injured from the Interlull, I am pretty sure it would have been Ospina.

If I wasn't allowed to choose Centre Backs/Centre Forwards for an injury to our first eleven, I would choose Ramsey, as he is playing out of position, so is perhaps the weakest member of that team. And hey presto, Ramsey is injured. The situation has now deteriorated slightly with the injury to The Ox, but Campbell did well against Swansea, and we are still only denied our first choice player in one of eleven positions.

The players that are really difficult to replace (Ozil, Sanchez, Cazorla, and Coquelin) have remained largely injury free. We lost Coquelin against Chelsea, but that match was already foregone anyway with a referee determined to achieve a Chelsea win. Le Coq's injury was brief. He also missed the Leicester game, but as we scored five, it didn't really do us any harm. Ozil missed the Newcastle game, but this was a good one to miss as we played most of it against ten men and managed a win without him.

So, by my reckoning, our good fortune with injuries continues. Of course, as the old saying goes, you make your own luck. Our squad is deeper with more good quality cover: our injury record seems to be finally improving following some developments at the club, not least of which is the acquisition of Shad Forsythe. Overall, our injuries are much better, in terms of numbers and severity, than in recent seasons. We have had a little blip now; certainly the number of hamstring injuries is something that requires investigation. Even so, hamstring injuries are an occupational hazard for sprinters like Theo and The Ox for obvious physiological reasons and we probably shouldn't get too worried about them.

Perhaps we are due some good fortune after several years of injury misery. I will also whisper it, but teams that win leagues tend to have reasonably good fortune with injuries. Its early days,

IT'S HAPPENED AGAIN

but it looks good so far (I am clutching lucky rabbits' feet encased in wood, with crossed fingers, as I type this). Certainly, by the standards of recent years, this is not an injury crisis.

CHAPTER TWENTY FIVE
NAUGHTY NOVEMBER

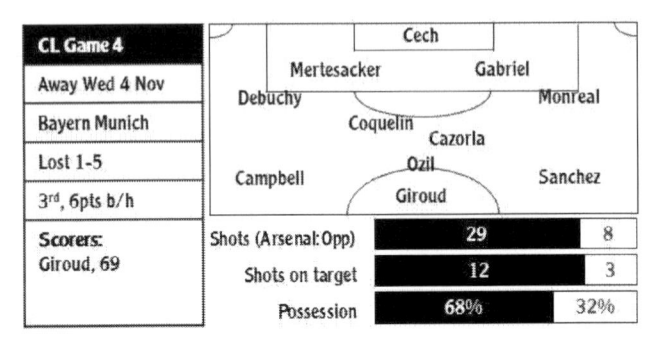

CL Game 4	
Away Wed 4 Nov	
Bayern Munich	
Lost 1-5	
3rd, 6pts b/h	
Scorers: Giroud, 69	

Formation:
- Cech
- Mertesacker, Gabriel
- Debuchy, Monreal
- Coquelin, Cazorla
- Campbell, Ozil, Sanchez
- Giroud

	Arsenal	Opp
Shots	29	8
Shots on target	12	3
Possession	68%	32%

Our first game of the dreaded November! Gabriel came in for Koscielny (minor injury - was on the subs bench) and Debuchy came in for the injured Bellerin and looked awful. Campbell kept his place.

One of my favourite players, Gabriel, had a stinker and confirmed that he won't be moving ahead of the BFG any time soon. Generally this was humiliating. Bayern opened us up repeatedly and finished ruthlessly. 5-1 was a little flattering to Bayern, but not massively so. So overall, we lost 5-3 if we take the two ties together. That is probably a fair reflection of where we are compared to Bayern, who look a very good team. Crucially we come out with three points from the two ties and still look like we have a chance to qualify.

IT'S HAPPENED AGAIN

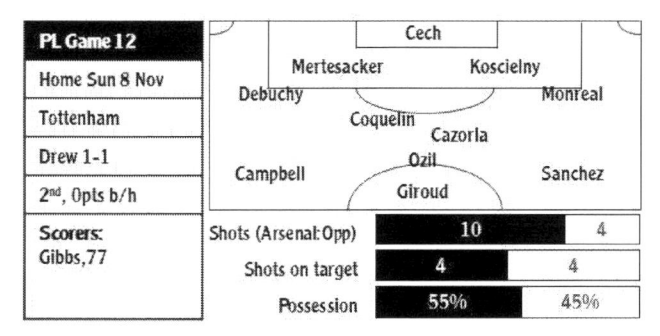

PL Game 12	
Home Sun 8 Nov	
Tottenham	
Drew 1-1	
2nd, 0pts b/h	
Scorers: Gibbs, 77	

Formation:
- Cech
- Mertesacker, Koscielny
- Debuchy, Coquelin, Cazorla, Monreal
- Campbell, Özil, Sanchez
- Giroud

	Arsenal	Opp
Shots	10	4
Shots on target	4	4
Possession	55%	45%

Overall, a bittersweet game. After Man City drew, a win would put us clear at the top of the table. The players looked like this was a game too far, with the injuries, lack of rotation and lack of quality on the bench catching up with us. Spurs looked like a good side and probably had slightly the better of the game. We did well to come back and get a point and even looked like getting a winner in the last 15 minutes.

Koscielny came back for Gabriel, but Debuchy stayed at Right Back. Santi was subbed at half time with a case that Wenger described as 'dizziness'. Giroud had a bad day at the office, missing several good chances. Gibbs came on as a sub for Campbell, played on the left wing and scored. Mesut broke a Premier League record by assisting for the sixth match in succession. What a guy!

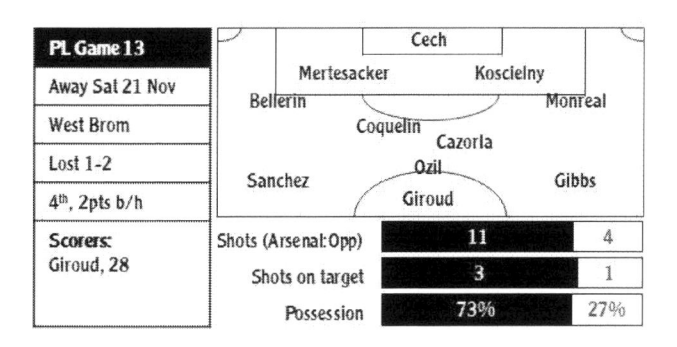

PL Game 13	
Away Sat 21 Nov	
West Brom	
Lost 1-2	
4th, 2pts b/h	
Scorers: Giroud, 28	

Formation:
- Cech
- Mertesacker, Koscielny
- Bellerin, Coquelin, Cazorla, Monreal
- Sanchez, Özil, Gibbs
- Giroud

	Arsenal	Opp
Shots	11	4
Shots on target	3	1
Possession	73%	27%

TIM CHARLESWORTH

Is the November curse (surely nonsense) striking again? This was our 13th Premier League game, so Arsenal soothsayers and astrologers were full of doom and despondency. They were absolutely right to be. I wonder if this is the game we will look back on as the one that cost us the chance to win the title. The three points are a minor blow, but Coquelin injured for (at least) three months is a major blow. Interesting that it came straight after one of Le Coq's worst performances in Bayern - fatigue?

Bellerin came back in for Debuchy (none too soon) and Gibbs came in on the left wing for Campbell after his goal scoring cameo against Tottenham. This is not a good sign for Campbell, suggesting his Arsenal career may finally be drawing to a close.

It was the kind of day that makes me want to give up watching football and find a new hobby (of course I can't). We went one up and were in complete control, but lost; a win would have taken us to the top of the table. West Brom. scored two goals from one shot on target; the free kick from which the equaliser was scored was not a foul; Campbell missed a sitter; and to top it all off, Cazorla slipped as he took a penalty to level the game at 2-2 and skied it over the bar.

Arteta had the most horrible day of all. Our captain replaced Coquelin, gave away the free kick that led to the equaliser, scored an own goal and went off injured. Wenger clearly trusts this guy and there is lots of talk that he will join the coaching team. Sadly, it looks like his playing days might be over. He has been a good player and a loyal servant, but he is ageing, looks too slow on the pitch and is repeatedly getting injured. Has he got much playing contribution left I wonder?

IT'S HAPPENED AGAIN

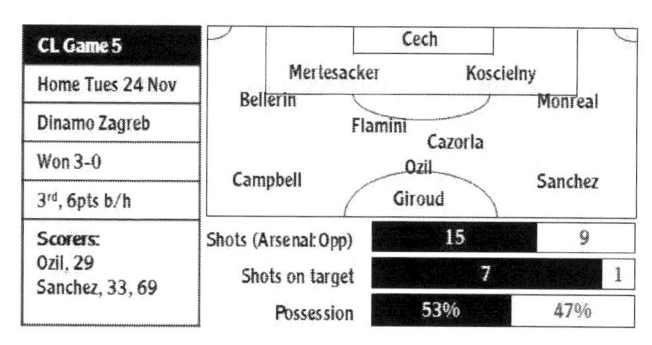

CL Game 5	
Home Tues 24 Nov	
Dinamo Zagreb	
Won 3-0	
3rd, 6pts b/h	
Scorers: Ozil, 29; Sanchez, 33, 69	

Formation: Cech; Bellerin, Mertesacker, Koscielny, Monreal; Flamini, Cazorla; Campbell, Ozil, Sanchez; Giroud

	Arsenal	Opp
Shots	15	9
Shots on target	7	1
Possession	53%	47%

Is it too little, too late?

Flamini came in for Coquelin (and Arteta), Campbell got his starting place back (a lifeline?) at the expense of Gibbs, who returned to the subs bench. Flamini did a reasonable job, but was not really defensively tested. Mesut Ozil was impressive again, having set a new Premier League record at the weekend for providing an assist in seven consecutive games. In this one he scored himself. In truth, this was a comfortable game and one which makes me wonder how we ever lost to this team.

Bayern did the business for us by beating Olympiacos, so at least it is now in our hands. If we beat Olympiacos in the final match, we will tie with them on points. Then we need to have a better head to head record. As we lost the home game to them, it will go down to goal difference and then away goals. That means we need to win by two clear goals, because they scored three away goals in Champions League game 2, or if we can score three or more away goals we only need to beat them by a single goal. If we match the Champions League 2 result by winning 3-2, the tie breaker will be goal difference in the other matches, in which case we go through (got that?!).

Olympiacos may not be brilliant, but they aren't that bad either and winning by two clear goals away is a rare result in the Champions League. Still where there's hope...

TIM CHARLESWORTH

I'M AFRAID IT IS AN INJURY CRISIS NOW

November 25th 2015

In the last few weeks, I have been desperately trying to persuade myself that we are not in an injury crisis. A genuine injury crisis is the sort of thing that destroys title challenges, while a few minor muscular injuries are not a disaster. Over a season, we are bound to get a little collection of these happening simultaneously and we are currently going through just such a period.

In the days of multi-millionaire footballers, few (if any) clubs can afford to carry a large stock of 'just in case' players. Even if we do, Mathieu Debuchy has suggested to us, such players will 'rust' on the sidelines. When we dust them off and throw them into the fray, we may just find they aren't as good as they were when we put the dust covers on.

Every team is vulnerable to the loss of key players. Man City are vulnerable to the loss of Kompany and Aguero. Chelsea are vulnerable to the loss of Courtois, Terry, and Hazard (in some cases a loss of form seems to be sufficient). We have suffered crippling injury crises in both of the last two seasons (and indeed a number before that). Chelsea were lucky with injuries last season. A club challenging for the title simply cannot afford long absences from major players.

Not all injuries are the same

We cannot expect to go through a season without injuries, so we should always be cautious about drawing conclusions from a single incident. When injuries happen, we hope they are short-term or affect less important players. The importance of the player is not just a function of how good they are, but also of how good their replacements are. So injuries to Mertesacker or Monreal are not a disaster, because their backups (Gabriel and Gibbs) are of high quality. But injuries to Coquelin and Ozil are a problem because their replacements will lead to a significant drop in the overall quality of the team.

IT'S HAPPENED AGAIN

I am still clinging to the hope that our current run of injuries is just a bit of a blip and there has been a genuine improvement in our strength and conditioning work. Unfortunately, the evidence is beginning to pile up that I am wrong about this. We suffered in the last few games before the last Interlull. Although the injuries were minor and to replaceable players, the sheer number of injuries was taking its toll. We lost the ability to rotate and started to look tired. Against Spurs in particular, we suffered by having no credible options on the bench.

Up until Saturday, we have mostly had short-term injuries to major players (Ozil, Coquelin, Walcott), and longer-term injuries to less critical players (Welbeck, Wilshere, Rosicky). But there is no hiding from the fact that the serious knee injury that Coquelin has picked up is a major blow. Wenger says he will be out for at least two months, although this may mean three in Wengerspeak. So it looks like we will have to get half way through February before we get our destroyer back.

It has been clear right from the start that we were heavily reliant on Coquelin staying fit. This situation has been exacerbated as Arteta's poor form and injury woes continue. It was always debateable whether Arteta was really a good backup for Coquelin; the gap in quality between them has looked wider and wider as the season has gone on.

We played (90% of) a game without Le Coq on Saturday and we really suffered for it. In fact, we suffer whenever we try to play without Coquelin and it looks like we are going to have to do quite a lot of it. If we are to maintain any sort of title challenge, Wenger is going to have to try to find a solution to a big problem in the Defensive Midfielder position. His options seem to be:

1. Can Flamini surprise us all? He is the most similar player to Coquelin in the squad. Unfortunately he is slower, less agile, less powerful, less fit, older, weaker in the air, and less skilful than Coquelin. Apart from that he is fine! (He is a better shouter than Le Coq)

TIM CHARLESWORTH

2. Can Arteta do the job, given he has looked like a player in terminal decline this season? I am really sad about this as he was a stalwart in the difficult years and has been a real lion for us. His injury will presumably keep him out for half the time that Coquelin is out anyway, so he will be of limited replacement value even if he can turn his form around
3. Can Chambers perform in the Defensive Midfielder role? This seems unlikely. Wenger hasn't even tried him in this position for nearly 12 months. He has only had one, horrible match at Defensive Midfield for Arsenal (Southampton, away, last season). He was so bad that he inspired Szczesny to take up smoking immediately!* For the sake of all involved, he has not played in midfield again since. It would be surprising if he was the answer now
4. Will we buy someone in January? This is not likely to be a good solution as it is six weeks until the window opens and even then deals are rarely done at the start of the window. Even if we were lucky enough to get a good player, Coquelin will be nearly ready by the end of January and may even be back. Other clubs might try to hold Wenger to ransom and he nearly always backs out in such circumstances. On the other hand, Wenger may decide that due to the decline of Arteta, he needs better back up even when Coquelin returns. If so, a new player is more likely to pay dividends next season than this
5. Can Wilshere cover the Defensive Midfielder role? This is possible. He doesn't quite have Coquelin's physical strength and certainly not his aerial ability. He has sort of played Defensive Midfield for England, but he is really more of a deep lying playmaker (like Cazorla) than a defensive rock (like Le Coq) when he plays there. He is also still a few weeks away from a return

---

* Szczesny, who also had a stinker in this game, is believed to have been caught smoking in the showers by Wenger and never got his starting place in the team back

IT'S HAPPENED AGAIN

6. Can Bielik play Defensive Midfielder - I doubt it. He has no pedigree or experience at this level. He is young and I understand that he has been playing at Centre Back for the junior teams. It would be wonderful if he could surprise us all, but I am not optimistic. Remember our greatest Defensive Midfielder of recent times, Coquelin, was useless at Bielik's age
7. Can Ramsey do it? This is not impossible. He is probably the most physically powerful of the options. He is naturally a much more attacking player, but could maybe adapt for a short period.

Cazorla is also part of the problem here. He is a wonderful player and brilliant in his new position, but he is not physically powerful. In order for our midfield partnership to work, you need to pair him with a physically imposing player, otherwise we start to suffer from the old problem of looking 'powderpuff in the middle'. I hate to think of the idea of dropping the little genius, but perhaps the answer here is not to replace Coquelin, but to replace the Coq-Caz partnership. Wilshere-Ramsey is the most credible alternative, but is Wilshere still too far away from fitness to make this one viable?

This is my worst nightmare

This type of major injury to Le Coq is the one that I was really scared of and now it has happened. The alternatives listed above look really weak. I'm sorry to be so pessimistic and I really hope I am wrong, but I think that this is a massive blow to our season, against which the defeat to West Brom is but a minor irritation.

The problem with Coquelin:

1. For years we looked desperate for a player like him and never found one, until he emerged triumphant from the wilds of Charlton, around January 2015
2. Sometimes the coincidence of a player's presence and the team's form can be pure fluke (e.g. the Tots never win when

Bale is playing). However, those of us who have watched Arsenal over the last year are in little doubt about the causal link between Coquelin's presence on the field and the tightening of our midfield, defence and physical presence
3. We massively improved when he started playing regularly and it is reasonable to presume that we will decline without him

Looking on the bright side

So it's all doom and gloom. In the name of balance, I have tried to think of some positive points:
1. In an 11-man team and circa 26 man squad can the loss of one player for a third of a season really be that disastrous?
2. I reckon that our game point average has increased by about 0.2 to 0.3 points per game since Coquelin has come into the team. So, if he misses 10 games, that is a loss of 2-3 points; not decisive in a title chase.
3. Wenger is a Managerial genius (although experience suggests that his genius may be slightly lacking when it comes to Defensive Midfield solutions)
4. Where there is Mesut, there is hope

Apology to all Arsenal fans: I wrote a really unfortunate series of articles here. My article entitled 'is this an injury crisis?' argued that the answer was 'no'. It was preceded by an article arguing that our injury record was improving ('What is happening to our players?'). My article arguing that there was no injury crisis was followed by an injury crisis and even this one, admitting the injury crisis, was too optimistic. Cazorla was injured in the next game and missed the rest of the season, Alexis was injured in the same game and took three months to recover his form. Even my analysis of Coquelin was over optimistic. He returned to the field early in 2016, but didn't recover his form for the rest of the season.

IT'S HAPPENED AGAIN

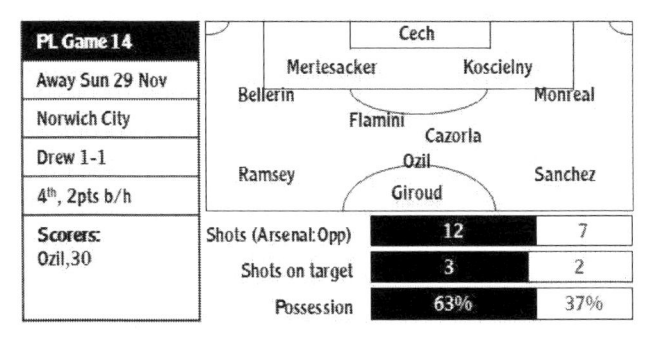

PL Game 14	
Away Sun 29 Nov	
Norwich City	
Drew 1-1	
4th, 2pts b/h	
Scorers: Ozil,30	

Formation:
- Cech
- Mertesacker, Koscielny
- Bellerin, Monreal
- Flamini, Cazorla
- Ramsey, Ozil, Sanchez
- Giroud

	Arsenal	Opp
Shots (Arsenal:Opp)	12	7
Shots on target	3	2
Possession	63%	37%

Oh how I wish we hadn't bothered to turn up for this one and instead just conceded the three points. It was a horrible game played in cold, driving rain. Koscielny (hip) and Sanchez (hamstring) were both taken off with injuries. Cazorla was injured but stayed on as we had used all our substitutes. It turned out he had ruptured his knee ligaments and would miss four months. All this to win one point against an out of form team. The win that we all expected before kick-off would have taken us top.

The team largely picked itself, with Flamini continuing and Campbell being replaced by the return of Ramsey on the right wing. The November curse is nonsense, but this has been one of the worst Novembers ever!

CHAPTER TWENTY SIX
CHRISTMAS IS COMING!

PL Game 15		
Home Sat 5 Dec		
Sunderland		
Won 3-1		
2nd, 2pts b/h		
Scorers: Campbell, 33 Giroud, 64 Ramsey, 90		

Formation:
- Cech
- Mertesacker, Koscielny
- Bellerin, Monreal
- Flamini, Ramsey
- The Ox, Ozil, Campbell
- Giroud

	Arsenal	Opp
Shots (Arsenal:Opp)	16	11
Shots on target	7	4
Possession	73%	29%

Not the most convincing win against weak opponents, but signs that the 'new team' may be bedding in with good performances from Ramsey and Campbell.

Giroud scored at both ends. He deflected in Sunderland's equaliser, but made amends by putting us ahead at 64 minutes. The atmosphere was very tense before Ramsey's 90th minute goal settled it.

Ramsey moved to the centre, replacing the injured Cazorla, with The Ox coming in to replace him on the right and Campbell replacing Alexis on the left. If we are to sustain our title challenge, Ramsey will need a good run of games in Central Midfield alongside Flamini, who had a good game again. It looks like Flamini and possibly Campbell are going to get a run in the team. It feels as if we have limped to the end of November, but is the damage too great?

IT'S HAPPENED AGAIN

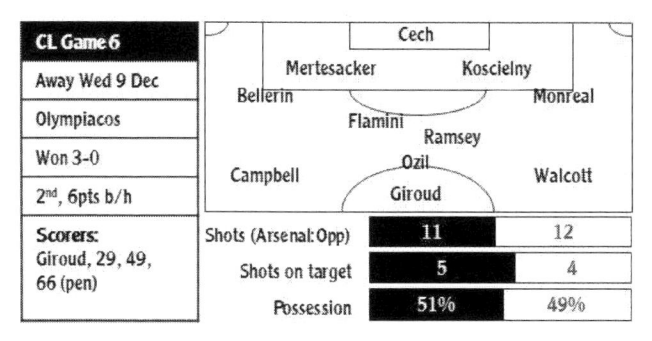

CL Game 6	
Away Wed 9 Dec	
Olympiacos	
Won 3-0	
2nd, 6pts b/h	
Scorers: Giroud, 29, 49, 66 (pen)	

Formation:
- Cech
- Mertesacker, Koscielny
- Bellerin, Monreal
- Flamini, Ramsey
- Campbell, Ozil, Walcott
- Giroud

	Arsenal	Opp
Shots	11	12
Shots on target	5	4
Possession	51%	49%

Wow!!!!

This was really an exceptional result, with a massively weakened team. Maybe Flamini and Campbell aren't so bad after all!

Walcott came into the team and surprisingly played on the left, having only played Centre Forward this season so far. The Ox dropped to the bench. This was a significant step for Campbell, with him being chosen to start ahead of The Ox. Is Wenger starting to trust him? Ramsey and Flamini continued their partnership in the middle.

The game itself went as well as it could have done. We were all terribly nervous at 2-0 as a single Olympiacos goal would put us out. But the third goal (completing Olivier Giroud's first ever hat-trick for Arsenal) ended the contest after 66 minutes, as Olympiacos then needed three unanswered goals to knock us out. The lively crowd went quiet and many went home. The game turned into a procession.

	Team	P	W	D	L	GF	GA	GD	PTS
1	Bayern Munich	6	5	0	1	19	3	16	15
2	**Arsenal**	6	3	0	3	12	10	2	9
3	Olympiacos	6	3	0	3	6	13	-7	9
4	Dinamo Zagreb	6	1	0	5	3	14	-11	3

NB: Arsenal progress via a superior head to head record vs.

Olympiacos. Both teams won one game, but Arsenal won the two fixtures with an aggregate of 5-3

This is a great achievement. We really have come back from the dead here, and our amazing record of qualifying from the knockout stage is extended to 16 years. After Champions League game 2, qualification looked virtually impossible. The wins against Bayern and this one have really been exceptionally good results. Of course, we never should have got into the position in the first place, but the defeats in the first two games were really the result of rotation (and bad luck). In order to get through a season of 60 plus games, Wenger has to rotate (either by plan or by injury). The consequences of those defeats were that rotation has been jettisoned, with our strongest team being played throughout October and November. Are the Coquelin, Sanchez and Cazorla injuries the consequence of no rotation?

WHAT A WEEK

December 11th 2015

Wow again! This is as close to a perfect week as you will get as an Arsenal supporter. We all tend to get carried away with wild optimism after a victory and doom and gloom following a defeat. So let's step back a bit and have a look at what happened:

On Saturday we rode our luck and won a match we could easily have drawn or lost. This seemed to boost the confidence of the team. It also helped their development. Cazorla and Le Coq are irreplaceable players and so we need to learn to play in a completely different way without them. This takes time. Saturday was an important staging post on that learning journey. Ramsey started to show that he can offer something different, but not necessarily inferior, in midfield. The whole team started to learn to cover the enormous Coquelin-shaped-hole in our midfield (no one individual can be expected to do it).

To make this result even better, all our potential rivals lost or drew, which effectively left us top of the table (I am very

IT'S HAPPENED AGAIN

confident that we won't finish behind Leicester). Because no team is dominating, the League position, even at this early stage, is more significant than normal. If we can hang on near the top of the League for the next ten games, I think we have a very good chance of being crowned Champions.

The away trip to Olympiacos was slightly odd in hindsight. In the end we did it comfortably and the third goal totally killed the contest. But let's not underestimate the great achievement that this win represents. Olympiacos are not a first (or even second) rank team in European terms. However, they are no mugs, and winning 2-0 away (let alone 3-0) is always a difficult thing in the Champions League.

To make it even harder, there was a hostile home crowd and Olympiacos had as much interest in the game as Arsenal, as they were also playing for qualification. So this was genuinely a great achievement against the odds. Maintaining our incredible record of 16 consecutive Group qualifications is also significant. The whole thing will be good for team confidence and our status in the European game.

It has been a funny old Group campaign, but in the end our luck evened out and we had two fabulous victories (Bayern home and Olympiacos away). We have also avoided the dreaded Thursday fixtures, which will help our League campaign. Experience suggests we will now only have two more European games this season (I am only half joking) and so the overall fixture burden is considerably reduced compared to the possibility of a Europa Cup campaign. The next Champions League game is now so far away that it's conceivabLe Coquelin will play! Less fixture congestion is important for a team with lots of injuries in the squad facing a tough League campaign.

So what of our future prospects?

There can be no doubt we will miss Coquelin and there is nothing that we can do about this. Before the recent run of injuries, I had as us slight favourites to win the Premier League. Now the odds are slightly against, but I don't think things have changed dramatically. Let's have a look at the 'injury crisis' and see how much damage it has really done to our chances:

1. Coquelin is irreplaceable and we will miss him
2. I am sad for Cazorla, who is a lovely guy. However the Coq - Caz axis was already broken. It is conceivable that we will even see his injury as a blessing if Ramsey comes good (and stays fit)
3. Sanchez's injury is annoying, but it is short-term, and this kind of setback is inevitable for this type of player
4. Walcott and Ramsey have both recovered from their short-term injuries. Bellerin and Koscielny look OK

So overall, it is only the **Coquelin** injury that is a real disaster. And in 11 man games with 26 man squads, I struggle to believe that one bad injury (for about a third of a season) will totally wreck our chances. There are a number of reasons to be cheerful:

Ramsey can offer something different in midfield. His defensive work is also a little better than he is usually given credit for. He is very fit and energetic and uses that energy to get back as well as forward. He is not the same type of player as Cazorla, but he could be equally valuable to the team and is showing signs that this will be the case (please stay fit!). He is certainly adding to our attacking threat.

Flamini is doing well. He is no Coquelin and his defensive discipline looks a little wayward. However, it is not fair to compare him to Coquelin, as few players in the world can do what Coquelin does. Flamini is doing as well as we can expect him to.

If **Wilshere** can return soon, the midfield three of Wilshere, Ramsey and Flamini/Chambers may be good enough to keep us going until Coq - Caz returns. Arteta and Rosicky could also make contributions.

IT'S HAPPENED AGAIN

Campbell's form is very encouraging. It looks like we are going to need him to play well and he is doing so. Being picked over The Ox for Olympiacos is no mean achievement for this player and his performance very much justified it. Expect to see a lot of him in coming weeks.

Ozil's form continues to be good. However gloomy we are about our injury crisis, Ozil on form gives us a good chance in every match we play.

Walcott looks like he is coming back to his best. It is important to have two no. 9s in the squad for rotation and 'bench impact' purposes. It looks like we are getting back to this position.

Koscielny's form is excellent. He looks like he is taking a bit more responsibility for coming out of defence and attacking the areas of the pitch that Coquelin would normally cover.

The longer we go with Petr **Cech** in goal, the better he looks. I don't pretend to be an expert on goalkeeping, but it looks to me as if he is playing very well. Without Coquelin, we will be vulnerable to counter-attacks through the middle and vulnerable in the air (especially if Giroud is not playing). This will undoubtedly lead to more shots for the opposition, as we saw in 2013-14 and the first part of 2014-15 (i.e. before Coquelin got his place in the team). The presence of Cech may mean that a smaller proportion of those shots end up as goals.

Don't expect miracles over the next two months. There will be setbacks, but if we can stay in touch with the top of the league until Coquelin (and Cazorla?) return, I expect us to pull ahead and win in the final 10 games of the season. So far so good. The away game vs. Man City, game 37, scheduled for 7th May 2016, looks like it might be decisive.

Giroud is doing really well. Lots of commentators are reluctant to admit this, having slagged him off in the past. Vardy excepted, he has been the most effective no. 9 in the English game this season.

TIM CHARLESWORTH

There are some minor disappointments to balance against these encouraging signs, but none of them are too concerning:
1. The Ox is still failing to live up to his talent. However, he also looks like he could come good at any time. A run of form in the second half of the season could be very valuable
2. Gabriel has looked a little disappointing (particularly poor mistakes led to goals for Norwich and Bayern). He has failed to dislodge Mertesacker from the team. However, this is more due to Mertesacker playing well than Gabriel playing badly
3. Chambers still looks a bit short of what we can expect from him, but not disastrously so. He may just be short of game time
4. Debuchy continues to disappoint. Is this due to a lack of game time, or is there long-term decline here? Only a significant injury to Bellerin will allow us to find out now. Personally, I would rather not know!
5. I am still looking forward to the first proper cameo from Reine-Adelaide

There is no doubt that November was disappointing. The injuries are serious setbacks, but they are not fatal and our bogey month is over. At the start of the season it looked like one of us, Chelsea or Man City. Now it looks like us or Man City. Every time I look at the league table I think Man U have a chance. Every time I see them play, I am reminded of how awful they really are. The Totts look good, but surely not good enough?

It's a shame that we missed the opportunity to establish a decisive lead over Man City, who are surely our closest rivals, but we are still ahead of them, so let's not be too down-hearted. Above all, let's enjoy a great week. It may not have been our most flamboyant or spectacular period, but in terms of 'much-needed' results it was perfect!

IT'S HAPPENED AGAIN

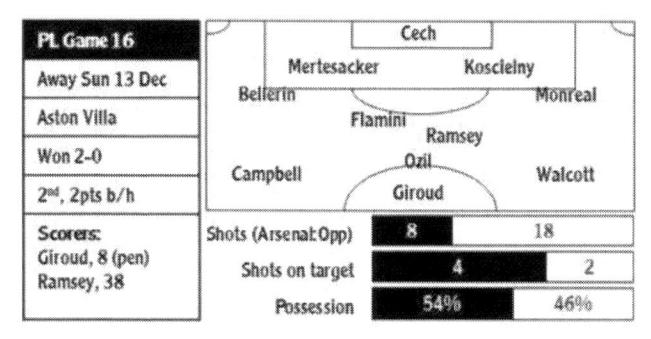

PL Game 16	
Away Sun 13 Dec	
Aston Villa	
Won 2-0	
2nd, 2pts b/h	
Scorers: Giroud, 8 (pen) Ramsey, 38	

Line up: Cech; Bellerin, Mertesacker, Koscielny, Monreal; Flamini, Ramsey; Walcott, Ozil, Campbell; Giroud

Shots (Arsenal:Opp): 8 — 18
Shots on target: 4 — 2
Possession: 54% — 46%

No changes to the line up from Olympiacos (they earnt the right to play again). A good effort. Aston Villa are a poor team, but it is very easy to drop points after a Champions League match, especially an away one. We did exactly what you need to do in these circumstances. We took a decisive lead early in the game, which meant we had a cushion as the fatigue kicked in later in the game. Ramsey had a game in the centre of midfield that reminded us how good he was two seasons ago.

CHELSEA SACK MOURINHO (FOR THE SECOND TIME)
17th December 2015

In an extraordinary season, the demise of Chelsea has been the most extraordinary story of all. The fans at Chelsea saw this coming and tried to support Mourinho by chanting his name in the stadium. They may have had some success in delaying his departure, but results have not just 'spoken louder', they have positively screamed from the rooftops. Chelsea are in 16th place with 15 points after 16 games and nearly half the season has gone. We need to remember that three of those points, against Arsenal in Premier League game 6, were entirely unearned. They have a goal difference of '-8'. They have lost nine games!

There really was no indication at all of this before the season began. Chelsea were favourites to retain their title, Mourinho was spoken of as the most talented Manager of his generation; he was the Special One etc. etc. etc.

Of course Mourinho is fabulously unpopular outside of Chelsea. Nowhere is this truer than at Arsenal. When I wrote earlier in the season suggesting that we shouldn't take this man quite so seriously, I was widely derided by the Arsenal faithful. I suppose this dislike arises from several factors:

1. Lots of people don't like him. He is a wind-up merchant
2. He has achieved very good results against Arsenal
3. He was the man who broke up the Arsenal-Man U duopoly at the top of English football when he arrived in 2004
4. Mourinho and Wenger clearly have a mutual dislike. This may be partly because when Mourinho first arrived in England he stole Arsène's clothes as the 'charming, erudite, enigmatic, foreign' darling of the press. They also have contrasting approaches to football
5. Premier League game 6 was a horrible experience and Mourinho was the obvious scapegoat

So a lot of Arsenal fans will be happy today; and why not?

There is a 'received wisdom' in football, now reinforced, that if you hire Mourinho as Manager, you will get three good years and probably some trophies out of it. You will also get disharmony and discord and you will eventually need to sack him. This sort of pattern has now repeated itself twice at Chelsea and once at Real Madrid. I'm naturally suspicious about 'received wisdom' in football, as it often turns out to be rubbish. I'm not sure that what we have seen with Mourinho is enough of a pattern to demonstrate this fact, but it does at least justify investigation.

Mourinho is a charismatic man with a lively 'latin' temperament who uses these characteristics to help motivate those around him. He is difficult to resist and difficult to ignore. Because he is a passionate man who doesn't have many people with the will or the power to restrain him, he will occasionally go

IT'S HAPPENED AGAIN

too far. His career is littered with incidents when he has overstepped the mark. These are some of the highlights:

- After a 2005 Champions League match, he accused the referee of conspiring with Barcelona coach Frank Rijkaard. Referee Anders Frisk received death threats and promptly retired. Mourinho was not apologetic
- In 2011 he was seen to gouge the eye of Barcelona assistant coach Tito Vilanova during a scuffle between Barcelona and Real Madrid. The fact that Vilanova subsequently became Barcelona Manager and then died of cancer has not helped Mourinho's reputation
- In 2015 he verbally attacked his own team doctor (Eva Carneiro) for going on to the pitch to treat a player (she had been asked to do so by the referee). She left the club and sued Chelsea for constructive dismissal, settling for a rumoured £5 million

So it looks to me as if there is genuinely some substance to the idea that trouble is likely to follow Jose wherever he goes. There is certainly a logic that says that if you constantly upset people, you will eventually upset enough people that they collectively decide they have had enough of you. There are lots of rumours this is the scenario that has unfolded at Chelsea.

Did Mourinho lose the dressing room?

There are claims that he 'lost the dressing room'. This is an odd football phrase. It works on the presumption that football players 'play for the Manager'. There is a kind of implicit contract in football that the Manager takes the credit for success and the blame for failure. This is a bit odd when you think about it, as they don't ever kick a ball. However, it is a way of taking a lot of pressure away from very young men who are not really equipped to handle it. The Manager will deal with the press and divert the scrutiny from the vulnerable young men. It's quite a good deal.

However, this contract breaks down if the players don't like the Manager, or don't trust him to represent their best interests when dealing with the press etc. If this trust breaks down with a large number of players, the Manager is said to have 'lost the dressing room'. As the players are nominally 'playing for the Manager', they are likely to lose motivation at this point and stop putting in 100% effort to training and matches. Obviously this situation cannot go on for long. The players cannot tolerate it because it is bad for their careers and the club cannot tolerate it because it is bad for their results. You might reflect on the remarkable fact that in nearly 20 years, this has never happened to Arsène Wenger at Arsenal.

In Chelsea's case, the implication is that by attacking an insider (Carneiro), Mourinho shocked his players, making them realise that they were not safe in his hands and that they couldn't trust him to look after their interests. It's difficult to know if this is true or not. In football, the truth usually emerges eventually through various post-retirement autobiographies; because as time passes, everyone is less sensitive about breaking the confidentiality of the dressing room. I suspect the truth of what went wrong will emerge eventually, but in this case the idea that he 'lost the dressing room' seems the most likely explanation.

CHAPTER TWENTY SEVEN
CLASH OF THE TITANS

WHY IS FOOTBALL BIASED TOWARDS THE NORTH WEST OF ENGLAND?
December 19th 2015

Football fans are a paranoid bunch. After all we know that our team is the greatest in the world. Given this fact, we need to find explanations for how they keep losing, and this is a subject that exercises the full ingenuity of some fans. I recently read a lovely Arsenal blog that noted that a hugely disproportionate number of Premier League referees hail from the Manchester area. I think he touched on a much wider point. It is not just refereeing that is biased, but the whole of football in England. I'm not sure that there is a conspiracy here though, it's just that the North West is the heartland of English football. If you look at the density of population in England and Wales and compare it to the homes of professional football clubs, you will see that the North West is over-represented and London and the South East are under-represented.

It has ever been thus. If you look at the founder members of the Football League, the North West region of England is massively over-represented and there are no teams from Southern England or London:

- Preston North End (NW)
- Aston Villa
- Wolverhampton Wanderers
- Blackburn Rovers (NW)
- Bolton Wanderers (NW)
- West Bromwich Albion
- Accrington (NW)
- Everton (NW)
- Burnley (NW)

TIM CHARLESWORTH

- Derby County
- Notts. County
- Stoke City

13% of the population of England live in the NW (2011 census), yet half the founder members of the league were from this region. Today, it is home to Man U, Man City, Liverpool, Everton, Blackpool, Burnley, Bolton, Oldham, Wigan and Preston.

There are towns in the South East like Bracknell (pop. 77,000) and Slough (140,000) which have never had professional football teams. Compare these to Bolton (pop. 140,000) and Burnley (73,000). Both of these towns have professional clubs that were not only founder members of the Football League, but have also recently been in the Premier League for extended periods. The distribution of professional football clubs is remarkably hard to change: witness the outcry when Milton Keynes (pop. 230,000) tried to rebalance things a bit by taking over Wimbledon's team.

It is not uncommon for sports to have a regional bias. For example, Rugby League is northern biased and Rugby Union is southern biased. Football is more universal, so the bias is not as obvious, but it does exist. The culture of football in the North West inevitably, subtly invades all sorts of institutions such as the PGMO and the FA.

As a result, matches are refereed in a way which is acceptable to people from the North West, but not to us Londoners, who have a slightly different understanding of how football should be played. When Londoners complain about this, the North West dominated FA looks into it and sees nothing wrong (The Gabriel-Costa incident involved two London clubs).

Interestingly, the comparative lack of professional football clubs in the South East is part of the explanation for Southampton's success with their youth programme. Southampton is the nearest major club for a huge section of

IT'S HAPPENED AGAIN

England's population, so their youth programme can choose the best players from an enormous catchment. 16.3% of England's population live in the South East. For most people there is the choice of going to Southampton, or the difficult journey into London. The development of Reading and Wycombe is slowly changing this (Chelsea also draw young players from the South East), but Southampton still have a good advantage.

So why is there a North West bias in English football? Let's consider a few reasons:

1. **The lack of teams from London and the Southeast in the founder members of the League** is not coincidence. The FA, at the time, was far more regional in nature than today (actually, even today it is more regional than you probably realise)
2. **The early days of football** were dominated by a clash between the northern FAs and the southern ones. Generally the northern FAs were dominated by working men who couldn't afford to take time off work unpaid. The southern FAs were dominated by ex-public school boys and the middle classes who could afford to believe in the Corinthian spirit. The London and South East FA regions resisted professionalism far longer than the Northern ones, so the northern clubs got a big head start in the world of professional football. The game nearly split in the manner of rugby league and rugby union, but disaster was averted when the southerners finally conceded defeat and allowed professionalism
3. **Football is traditionally a working class pursuit.** The industrial towns and factories of northern England were particularly conducive to the formation of the early football clubs. Indeed, Arsenal itself is the product of the Woolwich Arsenal (a munitions factory), a rare example of industrial concentration in late nineteenth century southern England
4. **Success breeds success in football.** Teams that win attract supporters, ambitious players, good Managers etc. All of

these things enable them to perpetuate success. We might note that Arsenal was the first club in southern England to go professional - in 1891 - and is still, over 100 years later, the most successful club south of Birmingham

5. **The northern teams got off to a far better start than the southern ones.** Football is a great respecter of history (history plays a big part in the all-important concept of a 'big club'). However it seems to me that we need a better explanation than just what happened 100 years ago. So here are a few ideas of advantages that the North West clubs still have:

6. **Despite the romantic notions of middle aged men like me**, it is actually very hard for a child to succeed in football. It requires the sacrifice of educational opportunities and a certain mental toughness. This gives an advantage to boys from deprived backgrounds with poor education and employment prospects, of the type more commonly found in northern England. Football, like many other sports, can be an 'escape from the ghetto'. Indeed, a lot of successful English players are from exactly this kind of background

7. **There is something to do with open space.** Football pitches are a problem in southern England. Open space is precious in southern England. The real estate is more valuable and it is difficult to find the space for pitches. Northern English towns are smaller and more compact, so finding space on the edge of towns is not as hard. Real estate is less valuable, so there is less pressure to develop pitches into something else

8. **Southern England is flatter and less well drained than northern England** with more clay based soils. We live in a wet country where football matches are likely to be frequently called off if pitches are not well drained and Southern England is more vulnerable to this than northern England

9. **There is something about large towns and small cities** that is particularly suited to developing children to play football.

IT'S HAPPENED AGAIN

The north of England is particularly rich in these settlements. Living in a town is good for young footballers as the population is concentrated, they have easy access to other players and competitive leagues etc. However, if a city is too big, like London, this can be a problem, because land will become scarce in the city and it is too far to travel out of town to find open spaces to play in. Kids in Islington have less access to 'football spaces' than kids in Stretford (home of Man U). No town illustrates this better than Ashington. Ashington is a mining town in Northumberland (the North East). It has a population of just 27,500 (circa 0.03% of the UK). It is the hometown of a bewildering number of professional footballers, including England internationals Jackie Milburn (second highest all-time scorer for Newcastle, behind Shearer), and World Cup winners Jackie and Bobby Charlton. It also lays claim to Jack Milburn (368 appearances for Leeds, when they were good) and a long list of lesser professionals, including the much-hated Martin Taylor (who played for Birmingham in the match I can never talk about)

10. **The middle class bias towards rugby** is one of my oldest bugbears (I was made to play the beastly game for gentlemen with odd shaped balls as a child). Southern England generally has higher income levels than northern England, and is therefore more 'middle class'. (When I was a teenager in the mid-80s, the North Bank used to sing 'you'll never work again' to the Liverpool fans. To my eternal shame, I found this funny). My feeling is that northern children are not steered towards Rugby League for social reasons. So kids like me and Clive Woodward, who want to play football, are just allowed to do so. I actually cried when I read Woodward's autobiography. He was a keen and talented footballer, but his father sent him to a Rugby playing boarding school in order to get him away from his football friends (Woodward went on to play rugby

for England and then won the World Cup as coach - my sporting achievements are less impressive). I think this kind of thing is less likely to happen in the North West

Actually the balance of power in English football is changing. It is noticeable in recent years that southern based clubs like Reading, Portsmouth, Southampton and Norwich are having the best spells in their history. There are also an unusual number of London clubs in the Premier League at the moment. So perhaps we could argue that the historical benefits of the North West clubs are starting to ebb away:

- The growth of 4G and other astro pitches is starting to make it easier for southern kids to access all weather football spaces
- The English population has continued to drift from north to south over the last 100 years. Southern towns are getting bigger and more able to support professional teams (50 years ago Bracknell was much smaller than Burnley)
- Football is becoming gentrified and so less shunned by the southern middle classes
- The development of local players is becoming less important to clubs as they use less locally developed talent and source youth players from ever further afield. The location of a club is becoming less relevant
- The 'head start' that clubs like Bolton had is less useful the more time drifts on

So English football is dominated by the North West, and this does lead to a certain amount of bias in favour of the clubs from that region. It is likely to remain so for some time to come, but the globalisation of the game and the slow disconnection between clubs and their local communities is slowly undermining the North West bias. It doesn't make it impossible for London clubs to win, but it does make it harder.

IT'S HAPPENED AGAIN

PL Game 17	
Home Mon 21 Dec	
Man City	
Won 2-1	
2nd, 2pts b/h	
Scorers: Walcott, 33; Giroud, 45	

Line-up: Cech; Bellerin, Mertesacker, Koscielny, Monreal; Flamini, Ramsey; Walcott, Ozil, Campbell; Giroud

	Arsenal	Opp
Shots	8	20
Shots on target	5	6
Possession	37%	63%

Happy Christmas Gooners!

This was the big one. The title looks like it is between us and Man City, so this was a classic 'six pointer'.

It felt a bit like a repeat of the match at Man City in January (last season) where we had little possession, but won the game. If anything, we seemed more in control this time, with City looking toothless in possession and Arsenal lethal on the counter attack. Walcott scored a lovely individual goal to put us one up and then Giroud scored again. Giroud and Walcott are both in good goal scoring form, which bodes well for the rest of the season. After going 2-0 up we looked as if we were in complete control. However, the game changed completely when Yaya Touré scored a wonderful goal at 82 minutes. Suddenly the stadium was full of tension and City had a few chances to snatch a draw they hardly deserved.

With Sanchez not quite ready to return from injury there were no changes to the line up from the Villa game.

Unusually, this was the third consecutive game for this eleven. Ozil was irresistible again and is really looking like a player who can deliver in the big games this season. He assisted both goals and now has 15 assists, more than twice the number of any other player in the League! The 'substitutes' Campbell, Flamini and Ramsey also played well.

TIM CHARLESWORTH

We are now four points ahead of City, a useful, but not decisive, lead.

CHAPTER TWENTY EIGHT
THE WORLD'S A LITTLE COLDER

WE LOST A TRUE GENTLEMAN TODAY
23rd December 2015

The Arsenal community is mourning the loss of one of its finest sons, Don Howe. 'The Don' was not just ours, he contributed much to many clubs as a player, Manager, and particularly a coach, but Arsenal will miss him more than most.

Howe's finest hour was undoubtedly Arsenal's double of 1970-71. This season was the highlight of one of the most remarkable 'double acts' ever witnessed in English football. Arsenal's manager, Bertie Mee, had been appointed in 1966, via the unusual route of being the club's physiotherapist. As you might imagine, the appointment shocked everybody, including Mee himself; Mee brought the kind of coaching expertise to the table that you might expect from the club physio. Fortunately, Mee decided to supplement his understanding of the beautiful game by hiring former Arsenal left-back Don Howe (64-66) to assist him; and this was one of the most inspired appointments in Arsenal's long history. Mee acted as the figurehead, whilst Howe took control of the trivial matters such as coaching, tactics and selections. A new group of young players emerged under Howe's tutelage, including Charlie George, John Radford, Pat Rice and Ray Kennedy.

Howe's contribution to Arsenal's success was a badly guarded secret; after the double season he was understandably offered the job as manager of his home town team, West Brom. Unfortunately for everyone involved, he accepted. As happens so often in Arsenal's history, we snatched defeat from the jaws of victory and the wonderful double team slowly faded back into the mediocrity from which Mee and Howe had dragged them.

Eventually, Mee resigned (he was too cherished to sack) and was replaced by Terry Neill. Howe only lasted two seasons at West Brom (a very short tenure by the standards of the day), during which the team was relegated to the Second Division.

Terry Neill realised the historic mistake Arsenal had made in letting Howe go, hiring him as first team coach in 1977. Predictably, The Don's coaching magic struck again and Arsenal reached three consecutive FA Cup finals; from 1978-80. Liam Brady was the finest creation of this period, and that was enough for this writer to fall in love with Arsenal.

From 1981 Howe also worked as England coach with Ron Greenwood and then Bobby Robson. This was a period in which England re-established itself as a major footballing nation after the disasters of the 1970s. Howe succeeded Neill as Arsenal manager in December 1983, replicating his performance as West Brom manager with two fairly disappointing seasons, before resigning and being replaced by George Graham. But wow! What a legacy he left - Tony Adams, Rocky, Micky Thomas and Martin Keown were all products of the coaching regime under Howe's management. Of course we will never know if Howe could have delivered the successes that Graham managed with this group of players. Sadly, my guess is that he wouldn't have, but nonetheless I will always think of the Anfield triumph of 1989 as Howe's triumph, every bit as much as Graham's. The real tragedy is that the two men who had been central to the 70-71 double team didn't work together. The accusation is often made that Graham squandered the talent of the great team that he had, and never delivered its true potential. Perhaps Howe could have counselled Graham to help keep that team together? Perhaps Graham became a man not to accept such counsel?

The Don went on to perform a series of successful coaching roles, helping Wimbledon to a famous victory over Liverpool in the 1988 FA Cup Final. Wimbledon manager Bobby Gould later commented that persuading Howe to coach his team was akin to successfully asking Miss World for a dance. He went on to coach

IT'S HAPPENED AGAIN

England to the semi-finals of Euro 96 with Terry Venables (the last time England have reached a major semi-final). He also had a couple of predictably average spells as a manager with QPR and Coventry. He finally returned to Arsenal for his last football job from 1997 to 2003 as youth team coach, with Ashley Cole his most notable success.

It doesn't take a genius to conclude that Howe was an exceptional coach, but a second rate Manager. The tragedy is that he left a series of successful coaching roles in order to take up managerial appointments – including the two occasions when he left coaching roles at Arsenal. Perhaps it is football more than Howe that is to blame: male environments, in particular, are obsessed with hierarchy and status. The game has always valued managers higher than coaches, and perhaps it was this culture that is truly to blame for Howe's mistakes. Maybe he just lived in the wrong era. Many clubs today are looking for a coach rather than a Manager; this model of managing football clubs would perhaps have better suited Howe than the 'general manager' model which prevailed in the 70s and 80s.

At the end of the day, Howe must be ranked as one of the great Arsenal characters of the 20th Century, and one of the architects of our great club as it is today. He was universally respected in the game for his coaching and analysis skills, and there are very few men, dead or alive, who could make that claim. Of course, when someone dies, everyone tries to find something nice to say about them, so it's not surprising that people only have kind words today. The interesting thing about The Don is that people only had kind words to say while he was alive, too.

Howe was at his happiest and most successful on the training ground with football players: this tells you all you need to know about the man. He was intelligent, kind and nurturing, but above all he was 'a giver' who took pleasure in passing on his knowledge to others. There are far too few like him in our world. He always referred to us as 'The Arsenal', an affectionate habit shared by many fans. In turn, we knew him as 'The Don'. He was always at his best behind closed doors, so his loss will be felt most keenly by Arsenal's playing community rather than its fans, but make no mistake, the world is a colder place this morning without The Don to shine his light onto it.

POSSESSION

24th December 2015

I always listen to Arsène Wenger's press conferences. To be honest, he often talks a lot of rubbish. He says things like 'we will buy a good player if they are available for the right price'. Really?

To be fair to him, he is often responding to inane questions. However, the press conference of 23rd December was a rare gem. He was asked an interesting question about possession statistics. He has obviously been thinking about this, as he noted that in the last round of Premier League matches 8 out of 10 of the winners had enjoyed less than 50% of possession. This is a striking observation and counters common football wisdom.

This is fascinating on two levels. Firstly, Wenger is obviously a very good analyst, and his comments are therefore well worth listening to in their own right. Secondly it gives an insight into our manager's thinking.

We have gone through a lean period in the last six or seven years. The evidence is gathering that these lean years may be coming to an end (FA Cup wins, finishing higher than fourth, title favourites this year, Mesut Ozil, Francis Coquelin, etc. etc.). One of the interesting features of these lean years has been our ability to lose games in which we dominated possession. This was often very frustrating both for the fans and (visibly) for Wenger.

Wenger is a man of principle and belief. This can make him a little obstinate (as his critics like to observe). Generally speaking principles are a good thing. You will not be blown in

IT'S HAPPENED AGAIN

the wind, you will not be constantly changing tactics etc. However, the downside is that if the world changes, it can take you a while to adapt, as your first reaction to a changed world is to stick to your original principles.

Wenger's comments suggest that this may have been what has happened to him. Football has changed. Previously, the team that dominated possession usually won the game. This changed, and it took him a while to realise and to adapt his teams.

After the breakup of the Invincibles and the move to the new stadium, Wenger seemed to go for 'a vision'. The vision was to develop young players and to aim to dominate possession with players like Fabregas, Senderos, Hleb, Nasri, Van Persie and Denilson.

The emergence of the great Barcelona team (particularly under Guardiola), that played a possession based game, possibly reinforced Wenger's belief in the possession model. So Wenger persisted and basically succeeded in realising his vision. He did indeed create a young team that dominated possession in most games, even against the top teams in the league. The problem was that this team didn't win as many games as the possession statistics suggested that they should. This lack of success may have genuinely caught Wenger by surprise. Being a principled and experienced coach, he persisted with his strategy, expecting it to come good, as the team matured. But this didn't happen.

The players maybe lost faith in the project before Wenger did, and started voting with their feet (notably Nasri, Adebayor, Clichy, Van Persie and Fabregas moved elsewhere). The departing players may also have been influenced by the violent tactics that many teams adopted to counter Arsenal's possession dominance (with particularly unpleasant consequences for Abou Diaby, Eduardo and then Ramsey). Remember Gallas accused his teammates of lacking courage in November 2008 (that is nominally why he was removed as captain), and he might have had a point.

TIM CHARLESWORTH

So what has changed? When I were a lad, coaches would often say that the opposition cannot score if they don't have the ball, and this remains true today. It is also generally accepted that it is more tiring to play without the ball than with it. And these are generally held to be the two advantages of possession.

You can't score without the ball, can you?

So let's look at the first advantage of possession (can't score without the ball). Is it possible that the most efficient form of attack today is to allow the opposition to do the work in possession and hit them on the counter? Modern teams (including Arsenal) are good at executing the 'ambush high press'. This is subtly different to the high press that Guardiola teams play. Guardiola teams press instantly when they lose the ball. As a result they can end up with ludicrously high possession statistics - Arsenal had 27% of possession when beating Bayern 2-0 in October, and 31% when losing in Munich.

An ambush press is slightly different. Basically, you let the opposition pass the ball around, but suddenly put collective pressure on them. If the opposition makes a mistake, they are suddenly outnumbered in defence, with too many players high up the pitch, and you are in a very good position to score. Arsenal's second goal against City was of this type. The sudden, unexpected movement of Campbell and Ramsey, then Giroud, put pressure on Mangala. He gave the ball away and their two centre backs were suddenly exposed to the movement of Giroud and Ozil. The second goal against Bayern, our other low-possession-victory this season, was also an ambush press.

Wenger seemed to be referring to this type of attack in his press conference when he talked about the increased 'speed of transition' of modern teams, and offered it as an explanation of why possession had become less important. He also talked about the increased speed of the modern player. Footballers today are given much more explicit training in how to sprint than in days

IT'S HAPPENED AGAIN

gone by, and this was never more evident than in the goal that Ozil scored against Bayern.

Possession tires out the opposition doesn't it?

The second generally understood advantage of possession football is that the opposition gets tired chasing the ball. Wenger talked about players being fitter and not tiring, and offered this as another explanation of why possession football doesn't work anymore. In times gone by, the team chasing the ball would get tired and concede in the last 20 minutes. This is basically what happened in the Champions League final in 2006. Wenger is implying that this doesn't work anymore because the players are fitter, and don't tire at the end. I'm not sure about this, as presumably both sets of players are fitter?

I wonder if it is still true that it is more tiring to play without the ball. The way that modern teams retain the ball, is to give the player in possession lots of options. This means, at least two, usually more, players need to be in motion, giving options and different angles to the man in possession. The diktats of total football and tiki-taka football (as implemented by Barcelona) demand a constant work rate from the team in possession. This is different to the old model of passing the ball around amongst relatively static players, who stay roughly in their positions. Teams that play the modern possession game, are in danger of tiring, reacting slowly when they lose possession, and conceding counter attacking goals. We saw Arsenal lose in this fashion over and over again during the lean years.

Guardiola teams certainly find it more tiring to chase the ball than be in possession. That is because they press high and instantly. Four or five players attack the man in possession and try to cut off all possible passing outlets. However, most teams don't play like this. Against City (and Bayern), Arsenal were dropping back and holding their shape when without the ball, rather than chasing the ball. This requires concentration and discipline, but doesn't look very tiring. If one team is playing possession football with players moving to keep options open, and the other is sitting off and holding position, it looks to me as if the team with the ball is doing the most work.

Conclusions

So possession football is dead right? Wrong. If you look at most of the games that Arsenal win, they do dominate possession. However, it is notable that they are often in the 50%s or 60%s, compared to the 70%s that we used to see during the lean years. Possession is still a valid measure of a team's performance, but I get the feeling that Arsenal are no longer pursuing it as an end in its own right, as perhaps they once were.

Hindsight note: Leicester won the league with an average possession of 47%, the lowest percentage of any Premiership champions. Arsenal recorded the highest average rate of possession in the Premiership with 55%, suggesting that the leopard hasn't entirely changed its spots. At the highest level of football, the two great tiki-taka teams of Europe, Barcelona and Bayern Munich lost in the quarter-finals and semi-finals of the Champions League, suggesting that possession football is still quite effective, if not as irresistible as its proponents might have you believe.

THE BEAUTY OF LEFTIES
December 24th 2015

Amidst the joy of the Man City game, one interesting aspect got slightly overlooked, which was the influence of the left footers.

Left sidedness is an advantage in lots of sports. John McEnroe and Rafael Nadal are the most obvious examples in tennis. Both players benefit from the fact that their shots come from different angles than those expected. Of course the left

IT'S HAPPENED AGAIN

handed player has plenty of opportunities to get used to playing the right handed player and getting used to the angles that result.

The right handed player has less opportunities to get used to playing the left hander.

The sport that we see this effect most obviously is cricket. There are a bizarre number of left handed batsmen in cricket. When we look at this more closely, we find something surprising.

If you go back and watch one of England's most sumptuously talented left handers, David Gower, you might be surprised to see him throw the ball right handed. He is in fact right-handed. The same is true of Graham Thorpe, Alistair Cook, Mark Taylor and Brian Lara. All of these players have found that batting left-handed is sufficiently advantageous to make it worth their while learning to bat the 'wrong way around'.

The same phenomenon is apparent in baseball (a major global game not widely played in the UK). Left handed pitchers are prized and some very talented players teach themselves to be 'switch-hitters', meaning that they bat left handed against a right handed pitcher and right handed against a left handed pitcher.

It's a bit surprising that a simple trick like being left footed or handed is capable of fooling a professional sportsman and conferring a long-term advantage. After all, opponents know that Mesut Ozil is left footed and Raphael Nadal is left handed. It is hardly a surprise.

It seems the advantage for lefties is something to do with angles. All ball sports require phenomenal subconscious mathematics. In order to volley a ball passed through the air, the brain needs to carry out a series of degree level mathematical calculations. We need to do these calculations in a fraction of a second. And yet, a well-coached seven year old can be taught to do exactly that.

The point is that it is subconscious. So however much the conscious brain knows that Mesut is left footed, the subconscious brain, on which players rely to calculate angles, struggles to adapt. Football is a game played with instincts, not the conscious mind.

A surprising number of the current Arsenal team are left footed. This is not easy to spot nowadays, as most modern footballers are good with both feet. However, even the best have a preference.

According to Wikipedia, 81.5% of people are right footed. So with 10 outfield players, we might expect slightly less than two to be left footed (Petr Cech is left footed, but surely this is irrelevant in a goalkeeper?). However in the current team Ozil, Giroud, Monreal and Campbell are all left footers. And this shows us another interesting pattern.

It is usually an advantage for an attacker to be left footed. I see no such advantage for defenders. This is presumably because the 'surprise' element is valuable for an attacker, but not so much for a defender (of course Left Backs are often left footed for different reasons).

It is worth having a look at the goal Giroud scored against City, because the defender got his positioning subtly wrong. Firstly he had the pass from Ozil covered. If Ozil had hit that pass right footed, Otamendi was in a good position to cut it out before it got to Giroud. But Ozil is left footed, so the ball came across Otamendi at an angle he was not really prepared for.

He then allowed Giroud to go outside him in the left channel. This is quite a safe thing to do with a right footed player. The type of shot that Giroud produced is a difficult skill; hitting powerfully across a moving ball at a tight angle to the goal. A right footed player is not very likely to pull this off, so the channel that Otamendi allowed Giroud to run in would normally be a relatively safe one.

Interestingly, Touré's goal was also a left footer goal. If you watch it again, Flamini is perfectly positioned to block the right footed shot. Touré simply allows the ball to drift across him to

IT'S HAPPENED AGAIN

his left foot. Flamini is instinctively positioned to block Touré's right foot, so cannot react quickly enough.

Touré has a clear shot. Only a left footer is likely to get that kind of opportunity. Actually, Touré is right-footed, but enjoys the same benefit as Cazorla; that he is very strong on his wrong foot, which makes him even harder to defend against.

So being left footed is surprisingly advantageous in football. When we look at some of the great all time players, it is surprising how many are left footed. Think of your ten best players of all time.

Remember, statistically, just two of them are likely to be left footers. How many of the following were in your top ten? Lionel Messi; Diego Maradona; Mesut Ozil; Pele; Ferenc Puskas.

If you have any doubt about the advantage of being left footed, have a look at some clips of Diego Maradona. He is actually comically one footed, and goes to ridiculous lengths to 'run around' his right foot. Watch the famous goal that he scored against England in the '86 World Cup (the second one). In that long run, he never touches the ball with his right foot, but the England players constantly position themselves as if they expect him to.

And the best news of all is that my sumptuously talented six year old son (future Arsenal player obviously) is left footed!

CHAPTER TWENTY NINE
ARSENAL ARE CHAMPIONS OF 2015

PL Game 18			
Away Sat 26 Dec			
Southampton			
Lost 0-4			
2nd, 2pts b/h			
Scorers: None	Shots (Arsenal:Opp)	8	14
	Shots on target	5	5
	Possession	65%	35%

Formation:
- Cech
- Mertesacker, Koscielny
- Bellerin, Monreal
- Flamini, Ramsey
- Campbell, Özil, Walcott
- Giroud

For Pete's sake! This is getting silly. Every time it finally seems that everything is going well, it all goes down the toilet again. This looked like a straightforward away game against a team that had got one point from its last five games. We played a poor match with a team that had every right to look fatigued. The score line may have flattered Southampton a bit, but we were definitely second best.

This fixture was played in January last year and was a horrible loss, with Chambers humiliated in midfield and Szczesny caught smoking in the showers, leading to his departure on loan (just when I had finally learnt to spell his name as well!).

An unchanged line up for the fourth game in a row, this is a team that had worked hard and brilliantly (those four games included the Olympiacos and Man City games). But this was a match which showed the limitations of this new team. Koscielny is taking more risks than usual in attacking the ball in front of him. He is trying to close the midfield gap left by the absence of Le Coq, but in doing so he risks exposing Mertesacker's lack of pace. This is what happened here, and Bellerin's pace cannot always save the day.

IT'S HAPPENED AGAIN

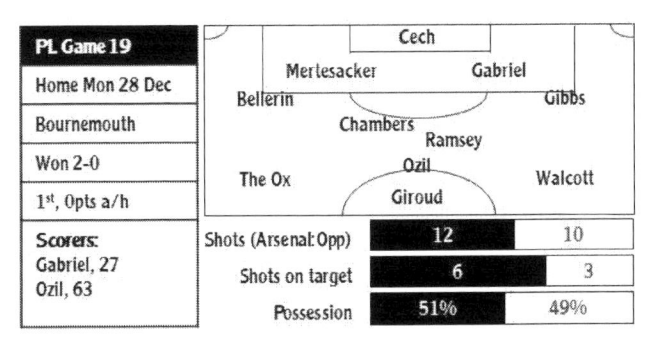

PL Game 19		
Home Mon 28 Dec		
Bournemouth		
Won 2-0		
1st, Opts a/h		
Scorers: Gabriel, 27 Ozil, 63		

Formation:
- Cech
- Bellerin, Mertesacker, Gabriel, Gibbs
- Chambers
- The Ox, Ramsey, Ozil, Walcott
- Giroud

	Arsenal	Opp
Shots	12	10
Shots on target	6	3
Possession	51%	49%

Normal service resumed after the Southampton blip. Half the season played, every team met and Arsenal top of the league. We have been top of the table before, but only when we have played before a rival. This time, after everyone has played game 19, we are still top! Happy New Year!

Four changes made the team look infinitely fresher. This is major rotation by Wenger's standards. Perhaps it was the clear fatigue on show against Southampton, perhaps it was the quick turnaround (kick off only 46 hours after the Southampton start). It's interesting that Wenger picked exactly the same team for four matches in a row until it looked knackered and fell over against Southampton. Then he seems to have remembered that he needed to rotate. A great performance from Ozil, Gabriel came into the side and got his first goal for Arsenal. Gibbs came in at Left Back, Chambers replaced Flamini at the base of midfield and The Ox came in for Campbell on the right. The changes that weren't made were also interesting. Giroud, at Centre Forward, gets no rest and Walcott continues on the left. Ozil was irresistible, with some stunning passes and a beautiful goal.

The team

```
                    GK
                   Cech
          CB                CB
   RB   Gabriel          Koscielny   LB
 Bellerin                            Monreal
              DM
                      B2B
            Flamini
                     Ramsey
   RW                              LW
 Campbell     10                 Walcott
             Ozil
                      9
                    Giroud
```

So our injury ravaged squad has spawned a new team. Interestingly it contains two players (Flamini and Campbell), who were not even considered second choice at the start of the season.

The downside is that we are getting rotation by injury. Wenger's one serious attempt at rotation this season has backfired terribly (Dinamo away) and he seems to have abandoned the concept. Will this hurt us in the end (has it hurt us already with crucial injuries?):

IT'S HAPPENED AGAIN

The table

	Team	P	W	D	L	GF	GA	GD	PTS
1	Arsenal	19	12	3	4	33	18	15	39
2	Leicester City	19	11	6	2	37	25	12	39
3	Manchester City	19	11	3	5	37	20	17	36
4	Tottenham	19	9	8	2	33	15	18	35
5	Crystal Palace	19	9	4	6	23	16	7	31
6	Man United	19	8	6	5	22	16	6	30
7	Liverpool	19	8	6	5	22	22	0	30
8	West Ham	19	7	8	4	28	23	5	29
9	Watford	19	8	5	6	24	20	4	29
10	Stoke City	19	8	5	6	20	19	1	29
11	Everton	19	6	8	5	35	28	7	26
12	Southampton	19	6	6	7	26	23	3	24
13	WBA	19	6	5	8	18	24	-6	23
14	Chelsea	19	5	5	9	23	29	-6	20
15	Norwich City	19	5	5	9	22	32	-10	20
16	Bournemouth	19	5	5	9	22	34	-12	20
17	Swansea City	19	4	7	8	16	24	-8	19
18	Newcastle United	19	4	5	10	19	34	-15	17
19	Sunderland	19	3	3	13	19	38	-19	12
20	Aston Villa	19	1	5	13	15	34	-19	8

At this time of year, I also enjoy looking at the 'calendar year table'.

The next page shows us the table as it would have been if we included all the results since 1st January. It is both meaningful and meaningless. Of course, it is meaningless in the sense that no prizes are awarded or relegations decided. It is meaningful because if gives you a good idea of how teams have performed over 38 games. I particularly enjoyed it this year because it shows a very clear win for Arsenal. The sign of things to come?

TIM CHARLESWORTH

	Team	P	W	D	L	GF	GA	GD	PTS
1	Arsenal	38	25	6	7	70	31	39	81
2	Manchester City	38	22	6	10	79	41	38	72
3	Tottenham	38	19	11	8	67	44	23	68
4	Leicester City	38	19	10	9	66	49	17	67
5	Man United	38	18	10	10	51	34	17	64
6	Liverpool	38	18	10	10	48	45	3	64
7	Crystal Palace	38	19	6	13	50	37	13	63
8	Chelsea	38	17	10	11	55	47	8	61
9	Stoke City	38	16	10	12	47	41	6	58
10	Everton	38	13	13	12	54	47	7	52
11	Southampton	38	14	9	15	48	41	7	51
12	WBA	38	13	11	14	38	47	-9	50
13	Swansea	38	12	11	15	38	50	-12	47
14	West Ham	38	10	15	13	42	47	-5	45
15	Sunderland	38	7	9	22	34	64	-30	30
16	Newcastle	38	7	9	22	37	69	-32	30
17	Watford	19	8	5	6	24	20	4	29
18	Aston Villa	38	6	7	25	35	69	-34	25
19	Norwich	19	5	5	9	22	32	-10	20
20	Bournemouth	19	5	5	9	22	34	-12	20
21	Hull City	19	5	4	10	15	25	-10	19
22	Burnley FC	19	4	5	10	14	24	-10	17
23	QPR	19	3	3	13	21	39	-18	12

DISAPPOINTMENT & DEATH

From a Happy New Year to a miserable spring

January to March 2016

CHAPTER THIRTY
WE ARE TOP OF THE LEAGUE

1st January 2016

This is being widely commented on as an 'exciting' season. The thing I am most excited about is Arsenal's good performance, but others see it differently. Table topping Leicester are obviously making the headlines. Towards the end of last season, the newly promoted Leicester looked certain to be relegated at the first time of asking. They were bottom of the league for four and a half months before an extraordinary run of seven wins in their last nine games earned them a reprieve. They have simply continued this form into the new season.

Chelsea are also making headlines, but for all the wrong reasons. The champions are 14th. Not only do they have no chance of retaining their title, they will also almost certainly miss out on Champions League football next season, being 15 points behind fourth place with only 19 games to go. The much reviled Mourinho has been sacked amidst much acrimony and the club are facing an employment tribunal complaint from a female doctor that Mourinho verbally abused her during and after the first game of the season. Chelsea and Leicester are the two biggest stories of the first half of the season. These situations are overshadowing surprisingly good performances from Watford, Bournemouth and Crystal Palace and a poor one from Liverpool, where new Manager Jurgen Klopp is struggling to improve matters after the sacking of Brendan Rogers.

It really looks as if only Arsenal or Man City can triumph, hence why we were all so happy after the City win. Man United look worse than their league position suggests; following a Champions League exit and a turgid playing style, their Manager, Louis van Gaal, is under pressure for his job, with rumours that Mourinho might replace him.

TIM CHARLESWORTH

Who is going to win the League?

Of course we are all desperately interested in 'who is going to win the League?'. I am always quite interested in the views of various football pundits on this question. However, their views should always be taken with a pinch of salt. Obviously they have a good understanding of the game, but many ex-pros are second rate analysts, often with an agenda of preferences for one club or another.

My own opinion on the matter is also fairly unreliable. Although I know a lot about Arsenal, my knowledge of the other teams is patchy at best, so even if I have good insight into how Arsenal might perform, my assessment of the performances of everyone else is based only on a smattering of knowledge. On top of this, I consistently overestimate Arsenal's likely performance. After all, like many fans, I know for a fact that Arsenal are: 'by far the greatest team......the world has ever seen'

Most of all, I always feel that this question should be answered as a probability. There are lots of unknowns in a football season, even if you have all the relevant facts to hand. In particular, transfers, injuries and the form of opponents are all unknown at this point in the season. So the real question should be 'who is most likely to win the league?'. For this reason, I am always interested in bookmakers' odds. Bookies have no agenda and in fact will pay a very heavy financial price if they get these probabilities wrong. The odds are effectively the product of a 'market', with bookmakers adjusting the prices depending on how many bets they receive. As such, they are the product of the 'wisdom of the crowd', the most expert opinion there can be.

So if you want an honest and reliable assessment of how likely Arsenal are to win the League, you can't do better than look at the bookmakers odds. Even though I rarely bet, I am always interested in bookmakers' odds, as they tell me how likely various events are. Interestingly, we have not been favourites to win the league since early in the 2004-5 season (the year after

IT'S HAPPENED AGAIN

the Invincibles). Even during our long spells at the top of the league in 2007-8 and 2013-14, we were never favourites. On both occasions, the bookies thought we were likely to be caught and they were right. But this season is different. Finally we are favourites to win again; and have been since the Man City game. Of course the bookies can be wrong, but more often than not they are right. There is now a widespread view that the team which scored most points in 2015 will also score most points in 2015-16. Let's hope they're right!

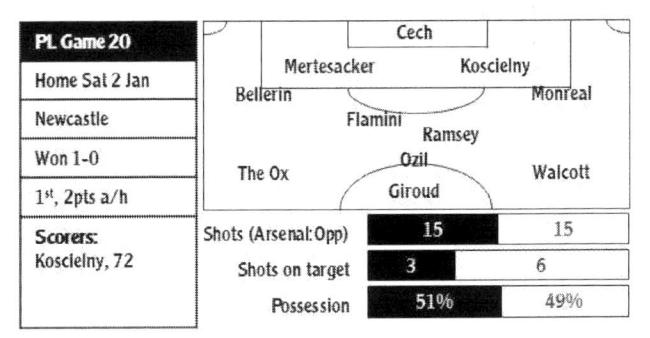

PL Game 20		
Home Sat 2 Jan		
Newcastle		
Won 1-0		
1st, 2pts a/h		
Scorers: Koscielny, 72		
	Arsenal	Opp
Shots (Arsenal:Opp)	15	15
Shots on target	3	6
Possession	51%	49%

Formation: Cech; Bellerin, Mertesacker, Koscielny, Monreal; Flamini, Ramsey; The Ox, Ozil, Walcott; Giroud

Koscielny, Flamini and Monreal came back in for Gabriel, Chambers and Gibbs, after being rested for the last game. The Ox kept his place at the expense of Campbell. The team instantly looked tired again and this was a very unconvincing display. A scrappy Koscielny winner was harsh on Newcastle.

TIM CHARLESWORTH

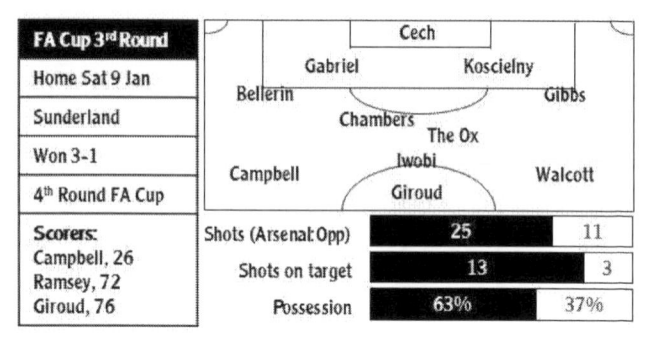

FA Cup 3rd Round
Home Sat 9 Jan
Sunderland
Won 3-1
4th Round FA Cup

Scorers:
Campbell, 26
Ramsey, 72
Giroud, 76

Formation: Cech; Bellerin, Gabriel, Koscielny, Gibbs; Chambers, The Ox; Campbell, Iwobi, Walcott; Giroud

	Arsenal	Opp
Shots	25	11
Shots on target	13	3
Possession	63%	37%

We went behind, but then quickly took control to record our 13th consecutive win in the FA Cup. It was a strong team and still no rest for Giroud. Iwobi impressed at no 10. Bellerin registered two impressive assists and is looking like a very good player.

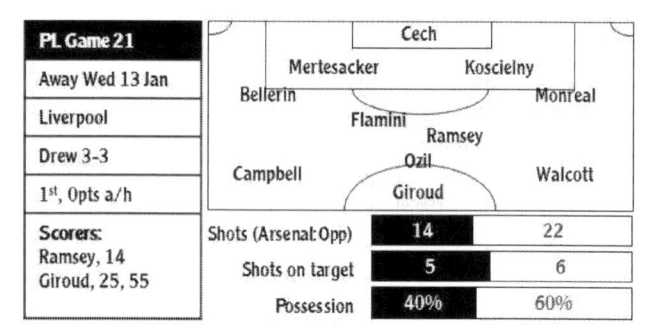

PL Game 21
Away Wed 13 Jan
Liverpool
Drew 3-3
1st, 0pts a/h

Scorers:
Ramsey, 14
Giroud, 25, 55

Formation: Cech; Bellerin, Mertesacker, Koscielny, Monreal; Flamini, Ramsey; Campbell, Özil, Walcott; Giroud

	Arsenal	Opp
Shots	14	22
Shots on target	5	6
Possession	40%	60%

This was really heart-breaking. We were just moments away from something great here. After a tough game, we led 3-2 as the final whistle approached. We were poised to go four clear of Leicester and five clear of Man City. But then Liverpool equalised and Leicester got a last minute winner. Suddenly we were only ahead of Leicester on goal difference. Oh cruel and fickle game!

The team reverted to the team that played Newcastle, but with Campbell getting his place back on the right at the expense of The Ox.

IT'S HAPPENED AGAIN

ARSENAL SIGN ELNENY
14th January 2016

Mohamed Elneny will become Arsenal's first Egyptian player. He is a Central Midfielder who can play box to box and more defensively. Reports suggest that he has outstanding stamina and a fierce shot. The signing surely signals the end for Mikel Arteta, captain and honest servant of the club, for whom we all have great affection. Elneny has been signed for approximately £5m from Swiss club FC Basel.

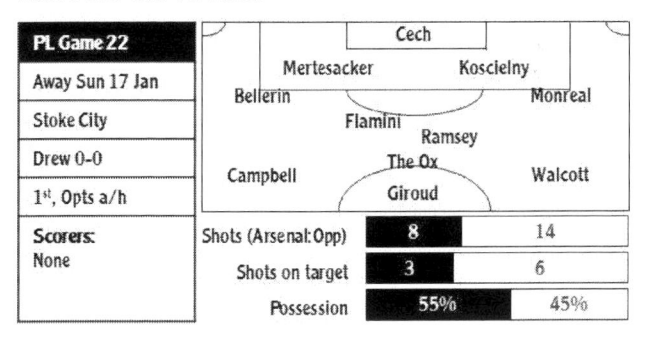

PL Game 22		
Away Sun 17 Jan		
Stoke City		
Drew 0-0		
1st, Opts a/h		
Scorers: None		

Formation:
- Cech
- Mertesacker, Koscielny
- Bellerin, Monreal
- Flamini, Ramsey
- Campbell, The Ox, Walcott
- Giroud

	Arsenal	Opp
Shots	8	14
Shots on target	3	6
Possession	55%	45%

Our bogey fixture.

This was disappointing as it would have been lovely to slay the bogey with a win. However this was a hard fought draw by a team that looked ready for the fight for the title and prepared to do whatever it took. The Ox came in for the injured Ozil, but we were otherwise unchanged. We looked short of creativity without our German wizard. A good display from Cech kept us in it, and we stayed top on goal difference. It's not often that a title chasing team is happy with a point, but this might just be such an occasion.

HOW TO BECOME AN ARSENAL LEGEND
January 22nd 2016

I must confess, I am a little over-excited at the news that Coquelin is 'back in training'. Of course, it is never quite clear what is meant by this sort of thing. Wenger can be a bit of tease and it may well be that Coquelin is not ready to play for a few weeks yet. I shall certainly have cold sweats every time I hear the 'setback' word for a while. Even so, his absence seems shorter than first thought and I suspect we won't be far into February before we see him back in the team.

The Coquelin injury was my worst nightmare, not necessarily because he is our most important player, but because there was such a big difference between his quality and the quality of his replacements (Arteta and Flamini).

Actually we have missed Coquelin a little less than I feared. I think the injury has cost us points, but not many. This is largely thanks to some excellent performances from Matthieu Flamini; most notably in the Olympiacos and Man City games, where he got the absolute best out of himself and produced priceless performances.

What I rather hope will happen from now onwards is that Coquelin will come back into the team, stay in it, and the team will win the League. Should this happen, I will always look back on Flamini's period in the team with affection and recognise a major contribution made to a title winning side. I expect Flamini will probably leave the club at the end of the season, realising that with the development of Elneny, Chambers and others, his future chances will be very limited.

And if all this happens, it will change my perception of Flamini forever. He will then be a bloke who played a heroic part in a title winning team. I love all the Arsenal title winning teams - and if this one wins, it might just be my favourite of all time, due to the redemptive effect it would have on Wenger's reputation.

Up until recently, I thought of Flamini as one of those traitors who abandoned the club, damaging both the team and his own

IT'S HAPPENED AGAIN

career, during the lean years (which I define as the ones between Henry's departure and Ozil's arrival).

In Flamini's defence, the club wasn't very loyal to him either in 2007-8. Arsenal seemed quite happy to let his contract run down until he unexpectedly displaced Giberto from the team at the start of the season when, suddenly, they were keen to sign him up to a new contract. But football fans are a bit harsh. Our affection depends on all sorts of things, which are beyond a player's control.

I remember Manninger, for example, with more affection than, say, Hleb. This is a little unfair on Hleb (a lovely player with stick legs, who suffered from the same shooting allergy as Ozil). In many ways Hleb made more of a contribution to our club than Manninger.

Manninger however, was loyal and crucially, made a great contribution to a winning cause. For those who don't recall, Manninger was the reserve goalkeeper who kept six consecutive clean sheets deputising for the injured Seaman in the 1997-8 double-winning team. This run of games came at a crucial point in the season and included a 1-0 victory at Old Trafford. At the end of the season, Manninger only had seven appearances and therefore didn't qualify for a Premier League winners medal (10 appearances were required). He was however, granted special dispensation by the FA in recognition of his contribution and so did receive a medal. His six consecutive clean sheets remains a joint club record. Overall, Manninger made 64 appearances for Arsenal over four seasons, without ever becoming first choice.

Hleb, by contrast, appeared 129 times and was first choice during his entire Arsenal career. He made an important contribution to the fourth place trophy wins in 2005-6, 2006-7 and 2007-8 (third). I can accept that fourth place is important enough to qualify as a trophy, but not that it confers legendary status on its winners. Hleb's biggest problem however, is the selfish manner in which he left to join Barcelona.

TIM CHARLESWORTH

A legend needs not only to contribute to a winning team, but also so show some loyalty. Flamini was a bit disloyal when he left the first time, but in my book he has now done his penance with a tough professional stint as a squad player. His namesake, Debuchy, has shown us just how hard it is to do a good job of being a squad player when you don't get many games!

So with just a handful of good games at the back end of his career, Flamini may have transferred himself from the 'slightly disloyal, also-ran' group with Hleb, to the legendary hero group with Manninger. Well done Matthieu. Congratulations, you have done your job exceptionally well. Now it's over to your teammates. If they get it right, you will be a legend!

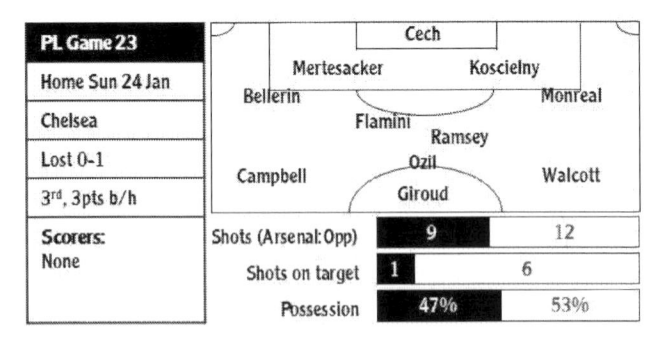

PL Game 23			
Home Sun 24 Jan	Cech		
Chelsea	Mertesacker Koscielny		
Lost 0-1	Bellerin Monreal		
3rd, 3pts b/h	Flamini Ramsey		
Scorers:	Campbell Ozil Walcott		
None	Giroud		
	Shots (Arsenal:Opp)	9	12
	Shots on target	1	6
	Possession	47%	53%

This was one to watch with your hands over your eyes, peering through the gaps in our fingers. Chelsea owed us one after the disgraceful refereeing performance in the PL4 fixture but life doesn't always work out that way. In minute 18, Willian played the ball through to pantomime villain Diego Costa, who was making an intelligent diagonal run across and past Mertesacker.

Mertesacker's actions were a bit odd. He seemed intent on looking around him rather than at the ball or Costa. Was he looking for an offside flag, or trying to assess what cover there was, knowing he was beaten? Whatever he was thinking, he stuck out a long leg, way short of the ball, with the apparent intention of tripping Costa. Costa is not a man to decline such

IT'S HAPPENED AGAIN

opportunities and duly fell over. Mertesacker was deemed 'last man' and given a red card. This time we had no real complaints, but the match was over.

If you go a man down with 72 minutes to go, the best you can hope for is a streaky draw. As it was, Costa delivered the coup de grace with a goal four minutes later. Gabriel (and Flamini) looked at fault for losing him when he scored. Chelsea then set out to defend their lead. We made a good fist of trying to equalise, but it was an uphill struggle. Massive frustration all round. Almost worse than the first Chelsea game, as this time we couldn't really take the moral high ground.

For what it's worth, the team was unchanged apart from Ozil returning from injury and The Ox dropping back to the bench.

CHAPTER THIRTY ONE
THE LOVE THAT DARE NOT SPEAK ITS NAME

January 28th 2016

I recently saw a film about Charles Darwin, author of 'Origin of Species'. This has a legitimate claim to being the most influential book of all time. One of the themes of the film was Darwin's moral struggle with his theory of evolution. He realised it would undermine the church, by suggesting that animals were not created by God. The church was a formidable presence in 19th Century England and Darwin delayed publication by nearly 20 years. Rarely has the epithet: 'publish and be damned' seemed so appropriate. The dilemma reminded me of an article that I wrote for Untold and then didn't have the courage to submit for publication. Inspired by Darwin, here it is!

I have managed to get myself a bit of a reputation for writing articles that are not very popular. My article suggesting that Arsenal might not be the victim of a refereeing conspiracy was rightly greeted with derision by all true Arsenal fans (objectivity is not a proper attribute for a fan after all). Later, I suspect that the 'abuse filters' on Untold protected me from the full reaction to my pieces in defence of Mourinho and Piers Morgan. One lovely commenter managed to ensure that every article I wrote after the Mourinho piece was accompanied by a comment rejecting all my work on the grounds that I was a 'Mourinho-apologist'. I rather admired the determination and consistency of these comments, but sadly he (I presume) has now desisted.

In order to truly cement my status as public enemy no. 1, I have now decided to confess my dirtiest of secrets. My awful secret is that I rather like Tottenham Hotspur. This affliction arises from a number of sources and if you haven't stopped reading in disgust yet, I would like to explain myself.

IT'S HAPPENED AGAIN

The first point to note is that I have never lived in North London, so I have never had to deal with large groups of 'baiting' Spurs fans. Defeats in North London derbies are only mildly painful to me and I am usually only really worried about the points lost.

My second defence is that it's all to do with my childhood and therefore I can't be blamed for it. I grew up in the era of the post-Brady, pre-Graham Arsenal. I loved Arsenal, but we were a dour and not very successful team under the rather disappointing Terry Neill and then the lovely, late Don Howe. The brief hope attached to the Charlie Nicholas coup soon eroded in a whiff of alcohol and general high living. The Spuds, meanwhile, delivered FA Cups with swashbuckling teams containing Hoddle, Villa and Ardilles. Even Steve Perryman had a certain panache. They were hard not to like.

The third source of my affection is my love of the name 'Hotspur'. My other great love in life, besides Arsenal, is history. I particularly enjoy late medieval English history; a time of chivalry, knights and valour, the Wars of the Roses, plots and dynastic intrigue.

The tale of Harry Hotspur

One of the most irresistible characters from this period is Harry Hotspur. Properly known as Sir Henry Percy KG (1364-1403), he comes from an incredible family. The Percies came to England with William the Conqueror and were awarded land in England in gratitude for their contribution to the battle of Hastings. Being a medieval nobleman was a hazardous business. Eventually every family would join the wrong side of a rebellion/civil war, or fail to produce children, so the family name would die out. Incredibly, nearly 1,000 years later, the Percies are still going. The current Duke of Northumberland, Ralph Percy, is the ultimate blueblood and even still lives in a castle (Alnwick, widely used in the Harry Potter films). He also sat in the House of Lords until the abolition of hereditary peers in 1999. His eldest son George, Earl Percy (heir apparent to the Dukedom), shared a house with the ravishing Pippa Middleton (star of the 2010 Royal Wedding) at university and they remain good friends. The Duke's daughter Melissa is a close friend of Princes William and Harry and his son-in-law is the godfather of Princess Charlotte of Cambridge.

Shakespeare immortalised Harry Hotspur in my favourite Shakespeare play Richard II. (Hotspur also appears in Henry IV Part I, although this is not such a good play). Hotspur is one of the rebels who overthrows the tragic old King Richard II and places Henry IV on the throne.

The real Hotspur was a true hero of the battlefield, in an age of knightly legend. He was the eldest son of the Earl of Northumberland, but never became Earl, as he predeceased his father. Like James Dean, Marilyn Monroe, David Rocastle and Princess Diana, the passing years never eroded his youthful dash. From Northumberland, Hotspur led the troops that defended England against the constant Scottish menace during the reign of Richard II. He was one of the leading nobles who sided with Henry Bolingbroke (later Henry IV) in his rebellion against Richard II. After Henry became king, Hotspur's various deeds established him as the leading soldier of his generation. Eventually, he fell out with the new king, the dour and dull Henry IV, leading a rebellion to overthrow him. The rebellion culminated at the Battle of Shrewsbury where Hotspur died a hero's death at the age of 39.

King Henry, upon being brought Percy's body after the battle, is said to have wept over the loss of his deadliest enemy. However, when rumours circulated that Hotspur was still alive, the king 'had the corpse exhumed and displayed it, propped upright between two millstones, in the market place at Shrewsbury'. The king then dispatched Percy's head to York, where it was displayed on the Micklegate Bar, whereas his four-quarters were sent to London, Newcastle upon Tyne, Bristol, and Chester before they were finally delivered to his widow. She

IT'S HAPPENED AGAIN

reunited the bits and had him buried in York Minster (his memorial can still be seen there). Percy was posthumously declared a traitor, and his lands were forfeited to the Crown. But the Percies survived and the title and lands were restored to Hotspur's son by the next king, Henry V (of Agincourt fame).

By the late 19th Century, the Percy family owned land all over England, including some marshes north of London, known as Tottenham. The legend of the Hotspur still burned bright, five hundred years after his death. When some locals formed a cricket team, it was perfectly natural for it to be called Hotspur CC. The cricket team then morphed into a football club, Hotspur FC.

Today, there is even a Spurs blogger who calls himself 'Harry Hotspur' (www.theboyhotspur.com). It's actually quite a good blog as well!

The representatives of an ancient and noble religion

I am not Jewish myself but I am, for various reasons, a great admirer of Judaism (which lies at the heart of the three great monotheistic religions). Although Tottenham is traditionally identified as the 'Jewish club', our own Jewish followers are a very important part of our support base. In particular, the club has benefitted enormously in recent times from the services of two Jewish men, David Dein and Danny Fiszman. I always see Arsenal and Tottenham as the Jewish clubs, and I can't help admiring both sides on this basis.

We Gooners are fast building a reputation as the leading online supporters. The interweb is alive with Arsenal slang (Le Coq, BFG, 'the 50th game', 'the Boss', etc. etc. etc.). My favourite piece of Arsenal slang is a written one. Many writers refer to Tottenham as 'Sp*rs'. I don't really know the origin of this habit, but it does wonderfully echo the Jewish tradition of writing Yahweh as Y*HW*H. The ancient Jewish god was a far more terrifying and vengeful deity than the one recognised by modern Islam, Christianity and Judaism. He was so terrifying that it was sacrilege to speak his name. Ancient writers wrote YHWH, but as the name was not spoken, its pronunciation is lost. It is often presumed to be Yahweh, but in recognition of the uncertainty, and out of respect, some modern Jewish writers use Y*HW*H. Of course, Yahweh, Allah and God are all the same entity, Allah being the Arabic word for God, and modern Jews having largely abandoned the alternative words used for their god (Yahweh, Jehovah, Adoni, etc.).

I suspect that the writing of 'Sp*rs' is not intended to convey respect to the club, or to Judaism, but I like to interpret it that way.

So in part one of my article, I have managed to almost totally avoid the subject of football! After Sunday's game, I hope I have managed to get you thinking about something else. Please read part two of the article before sending me abuse.

Part the second

Many thanks to those of you who resisted the temptation to abuse me after part one of my homage to Tottenham Hotspur. For those who didn't resist, I remind you of Arsène's post-Stoke words: 'Maybe when you go home and watch it on television, you are less proud'*. Here's part two:

The thing I most love about Tottenham is the pleasure that they have given to Arsenal down the years. After all, they are the club that gives us St Totteringham's Day every year and we all enjoy that. The use of a spindly cock as the club motif is also a generous gift to satirically-minded rivals, and it's not even the best bird logo in the Premiership (Liverpool). Quite why the cock

---

* In 2010, Arsenal midfielder Aron Ramsey was the victim of a horror double leg break in a match against Stoke. The incident is described earlier in this book. During the Arsenal Stoke match on 17th January, the Stoke fans had chanted 'Aaron Ramsey, he walks with a limp'. This chant was audible throughout the match. This comment, questioning whether the Stoke fans would really be proud of their behaviour, was Arsène Wenger's erudite and understated response.

IT'S HAPPENED AGAIN

perches improbably on top of a ball (another gift) is a mystery, as the ball in question is clearly a basketball.

Although I rather like the Tots myself, I obviously have lots of Arsenal friends who enjoy seeing things go wrong for them. I like to see my friends and indeed the whole Arsenal community, enjoy themselves. And the Tots have been a particularly rich source of enjoyment in recent years.

The Champions League era has been particularly kind to Arsenal fans. On top of our wonderful qualification record, bettered only by Real Madrid across the whole of Europe, the Tots have had a true nightmare. An endless succession of fifth place finishes has been statistically improbable in its own right. However, the pain of the Tots has been increased immeasurably by the fact that they keep losing out (often by ridiculously narrow margins) to us. This has been the kind of story that you simply couldn't make up. The highlights have been:

Lasagnegate was at the end of our final season at Highbury. We had reached the Champions League final, but it looked like our new ground would be christened by a season without Champions League football. Going into the final game, the Tots were one point ahead of us in fourth, with a relatively simple game at West Ham. The Hammers were safely mid-table and had an FA Cup Final to look forward to. They had no stake in the game and would surely roll over meekly, allowing the Tots to confirm themselves in fourth place. That's what should have happened.

What did happen was that ten of the Spurs team came down with a tummy upset (a common complaint of my infant daughter). Spurs Manager Martin Jol tried to get the game postponed. However it is important that all games are played simultaneously on the last day of the season and so the League would not agree. Poor Martin didn't know what to do. Should he play a team of invalids or a team of reserves? In the end he just decided to send out his first choice eleven and cross his fingers.

TIM CHARLESWORTH

At one point in the first half, the Tots were drawing 1-1 and we were losing 2-1 at home to Wigan. It looked like the Tots would be OK after all. But then Thierry Henry (who was then considering leaving Arsenal for Barcelona) scored a hat-trick to help us win 4-2. The Spurs players visibly wilted as the match wore on with the pivotal Michael Carrick looking like he was about to fall over. West Ham scored with 10 minutes left, to complete Spurs' misery.

The fun just kept on coming for Arsenal fans. Tottenham called the Police. An investigation by health inspectors showed no irregularities in the food samples, or the way that the food had been prepared. Jol then tried to persuade the Premier League to replay the match. All to no avail.

2011-12. An absurd sequence of events even better than Lasagnegate. It's so ridiculous that I can hardly write about it for giggling. The Tots were in third place for most of the season. On 26th February 2012 they took a ten point advantage over Arsenal to the Ems after 25 games. They went 2-0 up against a lacklustre Arsenal team after 34 minutes (Adebayor, of all people, scoring for the Tots). This was one of the great low points in modern times for Arsenal supporters and caused genuine despair. Surely even the Tots couldn't screw this one up?

Arsenal woke up and scored five goals. A demoralised Spurs team then managed to throw points away in the ensuing weeks whilst Arsenal hit a purple patch of form. After 37 games the Tots trailed Arsenal by a single point. Both teams won on the final day (Arsenal with a very scrappy win at West Brom, Koscielny scoring the winner) and we finished in third place, one point ahead of the Tots again!

But it was all OK. Despite a humiliating capitulation and a failure to beat the Arsenal, everything was fine, the Tots had still finished fourth; in a Champions League position. There was one little problem. Chelsea, in the midst of their worst season of the Abramovich era (soon to be exceeded, surely), had finished in a disappointing sixth place, five points below the Tots. However,

IT'S HAPPENED AGAIN

they had also completed an improbable run (featuring a truly absurd victory over Barcelona) to the Champions League final where they faced Bayern Munich.

After Liverpool's Champions League win in 2005, UEFA had introduced a new rule, that if a club won the Champions League but failed to qualify for the next year's competition, they would take the place of the lowest finishing qualifier from that country. This meant that, in the unlikely event that Chelsea were to win the Champions League final, the Tots would lose their place. But Chelsea were no match for Bayern, surely?

Chelsea were completely outplayed in the final, which was co-incidentally played at Bayern's home stadium. Bayern finally scored after 80 minutes and Chelsea's freakishly lucky run seemed to have finally come to an end. The Tots were safe after all. But two minutes from the end, Drogba equalised for Chelsea with a header from a corner, and then Chelsea held on for penalties, which they won. Spurs remain, to this day, the only club in Europe to lose a Champions League place in this manner.

The end of Bale. The sale of Gareth Bale to Real Madrid has been a great source of fun for Gooners the world over, particularly as it facilitated the signing of Mesut Ozil. The Tots behaved like kids in a sweetie shop and managed to blow the £80m proceeds (and more) on a series of remarkably bad signings. This all came on top of a wonderful piece of last day drama on the final day of the 2012-13 season.

Yet again, Arsenal had slowly reeled in the Tots' lead over the final few weeks of the season (you really couldn't make this up). After 37 games, Arsenal again led by a single point from fifth placed Tottenham. But this time the odds were a bit more heavily stacked in Tottenham's favour. Arsenal had a tricky away fixture at Newcastle, whilst Spurs were at home to a weak Sunderland team.

Spurs endured a tense afternoon. They couldn't find a way to turn their dominance into goals, even after Sunderland went down to ten men. Over the previous few weeks Gareth Bale had kept them in Champions League contention by rescuing them with spectacular, late, individual goals. After 88 minutes he did it again.

But up in Newcastle, Arsenal were scraping through with an unconvincing performance. Laurent Koscielny scored a priceless scrambled winner that was remarkably similar to the one he had scored on the last day of the previous season (also to break Tottenham hearts). In injury time, Walcott missed a practically open goal to seal it. The final whistle blew at White Hart Lane, with Arsenal still playing. The Tots could only wait and hope, but we hung on.

The whole thing was topped off by a wonderful moment (lovingly recorded by Match of the Day). As hope ebbed away for the Tots, a rumour floated around White Hart Lane that Newcastle had equalised. The ground erupted in celebration, and looks of pure joy flashed across the faces of the Spurs fans. Of course, the rumour was untrue and the Tots were desolate again. Star player Bale, deprived of the chance to play in the Champions League, was so disgusted that he agitated for a move to Real Madrid. Happy days!

Anyway, there it is, I've said it now. I have 'come-out', confessed my Tottenham love, and my soul is cleansed. I am braced for the abuse* from all proper Spurs-hating Arsenal fans.

---

* Actually I received no abuse; the way this article was received genuinely warmed my heart. I was particularly happy not to receive any of the anti-Semitic comments that I feared. The humorous and generous comments on the article reassured me that the Arsenal-Tottenham rivalry really is good natured and comradely at heart (it doesn't always come across that way). It also reminded me of the essential humanity of Arsenal fans in particular and football fans in general. Football supporters are easy to vilify. One of the things that often worries me is the 'hatred of the other'. It can sometimes look as if this is the same sentiment that underlies racism. The response to this article reassured me that the fierce tribal rivalries of football fans are actually more akin to light-hearted banter than the 'hatred of the other' which does so much harm in our world

IT'S HAPPENED AGAIN

I am delighted to give you an outlet for your frustration after the horrible game on Sunday.

My final observation is that I am a bit of a jinx. Just before Flamini's terrible game against Chelsea, I praised his contribution in the absence of Coquelin. Tottenham are now only two points behind us in the League. Their team looks good and they seem to be genuine title contenders. Spurs sympathy is all very forgivable and funny, as long as we beat them. But one day we won't beat them...*

---

* I had nightmares about this paragraph for the rest of the season. As Tottenham overtook us in the League, I began to worry that I really had jinxed dear old St Totteringham. As they pulled away from us, my fears began to crystallise. As they pulled out of sight, our defeat turned inexorably from probability to fact. I decided that I had to learn to live with what I had done. But Oh! - I should have had more faith in the lovely Totts

CHAPTER THIRTY TWO
FRUSTRATION & ANGER

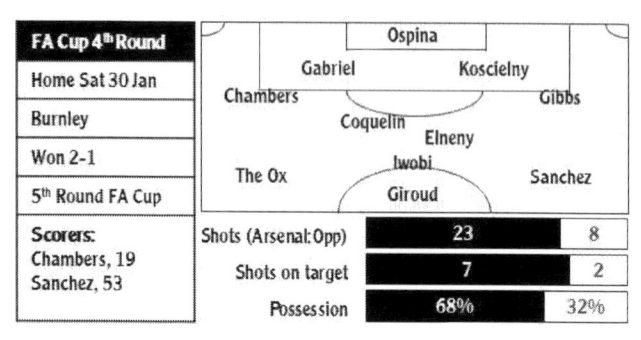

FA Cup 4th Round		
Home Sat 30 Jan		
Burnley		
Won 2-1		
5th Round FA Cup		
Scorers: Chambers, 19 Sanchez, 53		

Formation:
- Ospina
- Chambers, Gabriel, Koscielny, Gibbs
- Coquelin, Elneny
- The Ox, Iwobi, Sanchez
- Giroud

	Arsenal	Opp
Shots (Arsenal:Opp)	23	8
Shots on target	7	2
Possession	68%	32%

Although this was a fairly routine match against mediocre opposition, there were some things to celebrate in the team sheet. Sanchez finally returned following his injury in late November. He scored and looked his old self, busy and hard to handle. We have really looked like we were missing his stardust and never-say-die attitude in recent weeks. New signing Elneny finally made his debut in midfield and looked good, full of energy and passing. Most excitingly, Coquelin returned ahead of schedule, following his knee injury. He could well be the key player for the remainder of the season. What a timely boost as we approach the final 14 Premier League games.

Walcott dropped to the bench after 11 straight games on the left of the front three. It was also a run out for some squad players. Chambers really grabbed his opportunity with an eye-catching curler of a goal. Life is good when your second choice Right Back/utility Defender can do that!

IT'S HAPPENED AGAIN

GUARDIOLA COMES TO MANCHESTER

1st February 2016

Manchester City announced that their Manager, Manuel Pellegrini, will be leaving at the end of the season, to be replaced by Pep Guardiola. Guardiola, the Bayern Munich Manager, is widely regarded as the best in the world. I have to say that I think this is rather overstated. He has had two Managerial jobs. The first was at Barcelona where he had to manage a team full of the best players in the world, including Lionel Messi. Now to be fair, he did a good job of it, but hardly had the cards stacked against him. His second job was to take over the reins at Bundesliga and European Champions Bayern Munich; not exactly a poisoned chalice either.

Having said all that, I must admit that he coaches teams to play the most wonderful possession game, which I find simply mesmerising to watch. It will be interesting to see whether it is possible to play such a game in the Premier League, where a more robust form of tackling is generally allowed. It certainly seems that when Arsenal teams tried to play a Guardiola style game five or so years ago, they were dissuaded from doing so by a violent reaction. But, if anyone can carry it off, Guardiola can; and if he does so successfully I will be both pleased and impressed.

The team he will inherit at Manchester City will not be as good as those that he took over at Barcelona and Munich, and its best players are ageing. This role will test his teambuilding skills in a way that his previous jobs have not. I get the feeling that he and Wenger don't really like each other. Wenger's teams have inflicted a surprising number of defeats on Guardiola in Champions League play and the Spaniard seems to take defeat every bit as badly as Wenger (the latest incident came in game Champions League game 3, back in October) . Although he is over-hyped, I cannot help liking this man and I am glad he is coming to England. Of course, I hope he is not too successful.

Meanwhile, Pellegrini and Manchester City are left in an odd position. It is clear that this deal was finalised some time ago, and it is only being announced now because the speculation about it was starting to become distracting. Nonetheless, there is a feeling that Pellegrini's authority is undermined and it will be interesting to see if this affects City's title challenge. As they are the main threat to an Arsenal victory, I rather hope it does.

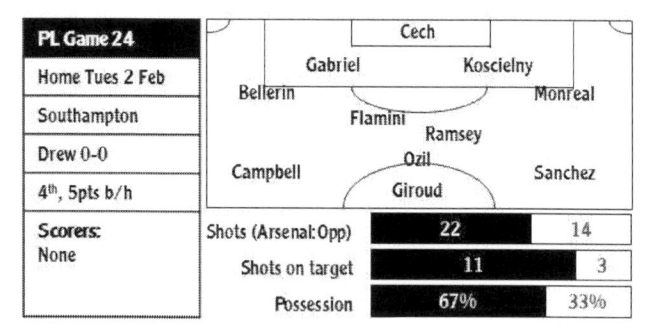

PL Game 24			
Home Tues 2 Feb			
Southampton			
Drew 0-0			
4th, 5pts b/h			
Scorers: None			
	Shots (Arsenal:Opp)	22	14
	Shots on target	11	3
	Possession	67%	33%

Lineup: Cech; Bellerin, Gabriel, Koscielny, Monreal; Flamini, Ramsey; Campbell, Ozil, Sanchez; Giroud

Southampton are living up to their billing as our new bogey team. Having dished out our worst thrashing of the season on Boxing Day, they gave us a hard time again.

The team largely reverted to those picked for the last Premier League game, bar two survivals from the weekend. Gabriel stayed in for the suspended Mertesacker and Sanchez kept his place at the expense of Walcott. Interestingly, Flamini kept his place ahead of Coquelin, who is obviously not deemed fit enough for two starts in four days.

Wenger looks genuinely riled by Southampton Manager, Koeman. In many ways Koeman represents the coming generation of Managers, with the emphasis on a furious pressing game, whilst Wenger is obviously the leading light of the 'old guard', with a more measured approach to football. There is something of the ageing Lion King about Wenger, knowing that the young cubs will get him eventually. Koeman looks like one of the candidates. A brilliant goalkeeping performance by Fraser

IT'S HAPPENED AGAIN

Forster, and Spurs went above us on goal difference. Despite many good chances this was the first time since 2009 that we had failed to score in three consecutive league games. It all added up to a very frustrating evening.

THE ANGRY PROFESSOR?
6th February 2016

There was much gnashing of teeth at the Ems last Tuesday. Of course general disappointment and frustration were the cause of much of it. But some unhappiness emerged even before the kick-off. Some Gooners were both surprised and disappointed to see Flamini start ahead of Coquelin and Elneny. I wasn't surprised. It is normal Wenger practice to ease in players who are returning from injury, or new to the country. Two games in four days for either would have been a surprise to me.

What seemed to get less attention was Gabriel taking Mertesacker's place in defence on Tuesday and then again against Bournemouth. This was both surprising and predictable. It was surprising because Mertesacker has seemed to be preferred to Gabriel for most of the season.

It was predictable because this was the third time this season that Wenger has rewarded a player for being sent off by dropping them. Wenger was keen to verbally defend Mertesacker after his dismissal against Chelsea, but it seems that actions speak louder than words. It has ever been thus with Wenger. At one point his ability to defend dismissed players was legendary and the source of some mirth (we all fondly remember the 'I didn't see it' period).

Wenger has always been massively reluctant to criticise players in public, so we sometimes confuse this with his real feelings. 'Le Prof' may be good at internalising his anger and frustration, but that doesn't mean he is immune from those emotions. For example, last season following the Southampton game (new bogey team), Wenger was clearly absolutely livid with

Szczesny. He came as close to saying 'you will never play for Arsenal again, son' as Wenger will ever get. And this threat has basically been carried out. Wenger's public criticism of Szczesny was relatively mild, but I'm prepared to bet that behind the scenes it was a different matter.

There have been four red cards this season. Two straight reds and two double yellows. Let's have a look at them in chronological order:

Giroud (Dinamo Zagreb away, Champions League game 1, 16th September 2015, two yellows). This was a bad one. The second yellow was for an over-exuberant challenge. This is forgivable in a competitive player, but the first one was for dissent, and entirely unnecessary. This is the sort of thing that winds Managers up, and the circumstances were particularly unfortunate.

Wenger is not very good at rotation, which often creates a problem for Arsenal. During the first part of the season Arsenal players are effectively playing more games than the teams they are playing against, which is a disadvantage in terms of fatigue and injuries.

During the first three months of the season, we play Premier League teams who do not have to fit in an extra six Champions League games to the autumn (or eight if we finished fourth the previous season and had to play the qualifying round). We also play Champions League games against teams (like Bayern) who play in less competitive domestic leagues than us and can therefore afford to rotate their teams in League games.

Our traditional November blip is at least partly attributable to this problem. November marks the end of the Champions League Group Stage and, by then, we are playing teams that have significantly fewer games 'in their legs' than we do. The obvious answer to this problem is to have a deep squad (as we did before all the injuries) and to rotate the team.

IT'S HAPPENED AGAIN

For the Dinamo game, Wenger had the courage to overcome his natural shyness with regard to rotation. It was a risk, and it didn't pay off. Giroud got sent off against Dinamo and we lost. As a result of this failure (and Olympiacos at home), we had to play first choice teams and expend 100% effort for the rest of the Champions League group games. The inevitable result was a run of bad injuries and defeats in November. Arguably, these problems were all a direct result of Olivier Giroud's stupidity in Zagreb.

Following the Zagreb game Walcott was picked ahead of Giroud at no. 9 consistently, until Walcott was injured. Giroud then came back in and kept his place by dint of form (good for him, poor for Walcott) and goal scoring.

In this context, it is worth noting that Ospina was pretty harshly treated following his mistake against Olympiacos, which also contributed to the same problem. It seems pretty clear that Ospina had been promised a start in all our Champions League games. This was presumably part of the deal under which he agreed to stay following the Cech signing. This use of the reserve keeper in Champions League games is becoming increasingly common (Real Madrid won the Champion League in 2014 while following this policy). Again, Wenger defended him in public, but Ospina was dropped after Olympiacos and hasn't appeared in a either a Champions League, or Premier League game since.

Gabriel (Chelsea, away, Premier League game 6, 19th September 2015, straight red, rescinded on review). It looks to me as if the 'Gabriel vs. Mertesacker' decision has been on a knife edge all season. Mertesacker has had the better of it, probably due to his established partnership with Koscielny. Mertesacker also brings other qualities of leadership, height etc. However, Gabriel has often looked the more accomplished defender on the pitch.

Mertesacker had the nod for the early games. He then got the 'flu and missed Premier League game 3 against Liverpool. Gabriel came in, played well and seemed to keep his place (it wasn't clear exactly when Mertesacker regained fitness). But then Gabriel got sent off against Chelsea. This cost us again; losing a match we should have won. Gabriel was certainly culpable for his sending off (even if Costa was more culpable).

It was very upsetting due to Wenger's dislike of Chelsea and Mourinho; and particularly frustrating on top of Giroud's dismissal three days earlier. You can see why Wenger was upset and despite Gabriel's exoneration by the FA, Wenger didn't appear to forgive Gabriel for letting the team down. Mertesacker certainly seemed to return to his starting berth after the Chelsea game.

Cazorla (Chelsea, away, PL6, 19th September 2015, second yellow). This was a pretty innocuous dismissal for a second yellow. Cazorla was chasing a lost cause a little over enthusiastically. His tackle actually showed a bit of character. I don't think anyone was really annoyed with him.

Mertesacker (Chelsea, home, PL23, 24th January 2016, straight red). If Mertesacker got his place back from Gabriel following the latter's red card against Chelsea, has the opposite now happened? Has Mertesacker's red card against Chelsea tipped the balance back in Gabriel's favour? Certainly the player was culpable. The tackle on Costa was a mistake.

Wenger didn't appear angry with Mertesacker immediately afterwards, but then as we know, you cannot rely on what Wenger says in public on such occasions. If this is the case, Gabriel didn't seem to have his best game against Southampton (albeit a clean sheet kept). If the decision is on a knife edge, it will be interesting to see if Mertesacker gets his place back against Bournemouth.

CHAPTER THIRTY THREE
IT'S GOING TO BE ALL RIGHT

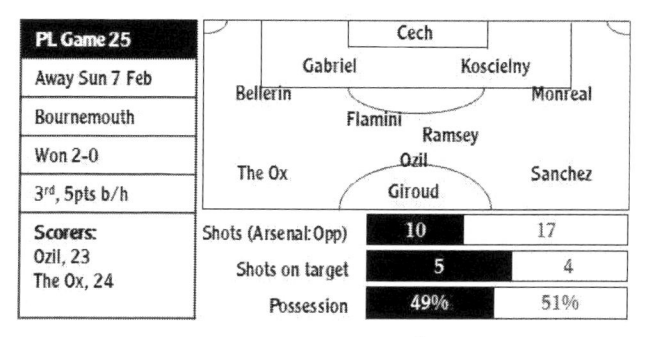

PL Game 25			
Away Sun 7 Feb			
Bournemouth			
Won 2-0			
3rd, 5pts b/h			
Scorers: Ozil, 23; The Ox, 24	Shots (Arsenal:Opp)	10	17
	Shots on target	5	4
	Possession	49%	51%

Formation: Cech; Bellerin, Gabriel, Koscielny, Monreal; Flamini, Ramsey; The Ox, Ozil, Sanchez; Giroud

Our first league victory since January 3rd. It was not our most convincing performance, but the three points were much needed to keep in touch with Leicester, who really are looking like serious contenders now.

The team was unchanged except for The Ox replacing Joel Campbell on the right, a decision that looked rather justified by a strong, goal scoring performance from The Ox. I was surprised that Flamini kept his place ahead of Coquelin. Flamini was then a bit fortunate not to be sent off for an agricultural, two footed challenge in the ninth minute. The referee had a good look at it, did a double take almost as if to say 'I didn't really see that did I?' and decided to give a yellow card. Ramsey played well and got two assists. Is he finally settling into the Central Midfield role?

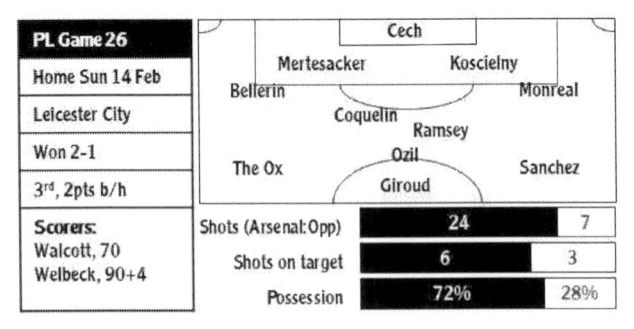

PL Game 26	
Home Sun 14 Feb	
Leicester City	
Won 2-1	
3rd, 2pts b/h	
Scorers: Walcott, 70; Welbeck, 90+4	

Formation: Cech; Bellerin, Mertesacker, Koscielny, Monreal; Coquelin, Ramsey; The Ox, Ozil, Sanchez; Giroud

	Arsenal	Opp
Shots	24	7
Shots on target	6	3
Possession	72%	28%

Mertesacker returned for the injured Gabriel and Coquelin finally made his first league start, in the only two changes from the Bournemouth game. There was a surreal air about this match. No-one could quite believe that rag-tag Leicester really were potential Premier League winners. But if they could beat us today, they would be eight points ahead of us with only 12 to go. And that started to look all the more possible when they took the lead in the first half.

The penalty with which Leicester took the lead was debatable - Monreal made an unwise challenge and missed, Vardy took full advantage of the opportunity to run into Monreal's leg and fall over. What was not debateable was the blatant foul on Mesut Ozil at the start of Leicester's move. All the officials can only have been looking the wrong direction, as no intelligent person who saw the foul could imagine it didn't merit a free kick. This doesn't feel like the first time I have had to explain an occurrence in a big match by saying 'all of the officials must have been looking elsewhere'. The referee was rightly booed off at half time.

At the start of the second half, the referee gave a second yellow to Danny Simpson. It was a harsh decision, and Leicester fans were understandably aggrieved. Was the referee trying to even it out?

Leicester started to really struggle with only ten men and Walcott got one back, but we just couldn't find the winner. As

IT'S HAPPENED AGAIN

the sands of time ebbed away, a clumsy and unnecessary Leicester challenge gave Arsenal a free kick from 35 yards. It was one of those awkward off centre free kicks. A left footer could curl the ball in as a cross for the onrushing players to head in. However, the angle meant that if the ball was not touched, it might just creep in anyway. There is no better free-kick taker in the world than Mesut Ozil for this situation. The cameras closed in on Ozil as he prepared to hit the free kick. His face was a picture of concentrated serenity as he controlled his breathing and focused on the ball to the exclusion of all else (and there was a lot to exclude). He curled it in and Danny Welbeck, on as a substitute for his first appearance after a year out with injury, glanced it in with his head.

Wow! What a spectacle. The players leapt into the crowd en masse. One of Arsenal's truly magic moments. It made me think of Michael Thomas. We had suffered a blip, but this puts us right back in it, with Sanchez and Coquelin back and momentum on our side! Nothing could stop us now.

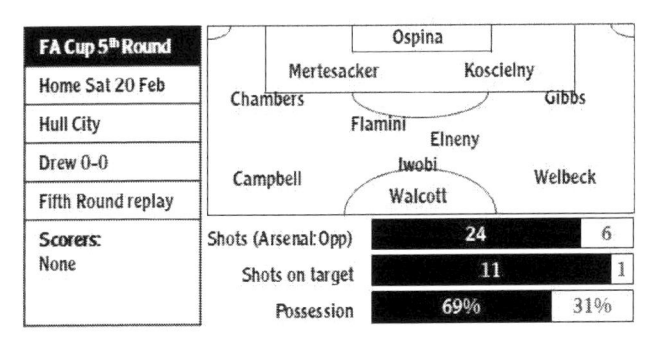

FA Cup 5th Round		
Home Sat 20 Feb		
Hull City	Shots (Arsenal:Opp)	24 / 6
Drew 0-0	Shots on target	11 / 1
Fifth Round replay	Possession	69% / 31%
Scorers: None		

Lineup: Ospina; Chambers, Mertesacker, Koscielny, Gibbs; Flamini, Elneny; Campbell, Iwobi, Walcott; Welbeck

Anything would be a comedown after the magical Welbeck moment. This game certainly fitted the bill. Hull played a reserve team, focussed on promotion from the Championship[*]. We were

---

[*] Hull would eventually finish fourth in the Championship, but gain promotion via the play-offs. It was reckoned that the play-off final was worth a minimum of £170m to the winner, as a result of the payments they would attract for being in

more interested in the midweek game to come against Barcelona. Only Mertesacker and Koscielny survived from the team that played the previous weekend.

Our line-up was difficult to read. There was a lot of interchange between the front three, but it seemed to be essentially Walcott in the middle with Campbell on the right and Welbeck on the left.

Shockingly, Mike Dean (see Premier League game 6) was selected as referee for the match. This was incredible. This is a referee that many Arsenal fans believe routinely cheats against them and has been doing so for years. There is a surprising amount of evidence to support this theory. Now you might think that all this evidence is just 'circumstantial', but there comes a point when common sense tells one to avoid further trouble.

After the Chelsea debacle, you might remember that over 100,000 people signed a petition demanding that he never referee another Arsenal game. You might dismiss all this as paranoia, but why send him to referee an Arsenal match again? There are plenty of other referees. At the very least, this shows contempt for the fans, who were undeniably cheated in game 6. It also provides 'conclusive evidence' to those who are convinced of Dean's bias, that not only Mike Dean, but also the PMGO, who manage the referees, are biased against Arsenal. I am not one for conspiracy theories myself, but this was a genuinely crass and stupid decision.

BARCELONA: THINGS TO LOOK OUT FOR
February 23rd 2016
We're all rather wracked with anxiety about tonight's game. I find a nice way to deal with football tension is to think about some aspects of the game to look out for (other than the 'who

---

the Premier League, even if they were relegated straight away. I'm not surprised that Hull weren't very interested in trying to beat Arsenal in the FA Cup!

IT'S HAPPENED AGAIN

scores the most goals' question). Matches like this define teams, and the consequences may be far reaching, so let's focus on a few of the sub-plots:

Mertesacker and Koscielny. This has been a great partnership, without ever quite being world class. There are question marks about them as they age, particularly Mertesacker (and his leg speed). If they can handle the 'Barca three' (Messi, Neymar and Jaws Suarez), it would suggest that there is life in the old dogs yet. If they are overrun, Wenger may consider his options.

The defensive shield. Defending is about more than the two Centre Backs. Barca have (to put it mildly) a wealth of attacking options. Monreal, Bellerin, Coquelin and others have roles to play in resisting them. Of course, Cech has put in more than one excellent display against Barcelona whilst at Chelsea. This is particularly a test for Coquelin. He will be under great pressure and hasn't yet convinced us that he is fully back up to speed following his knee injury. He has proved his worth in the Premier League, but is yet to do so on the European stage. A good performance may put him in the frame to play for France in Euro 16. Ramsey will also have to show defensive skill. Against Bayern at home, Ozil got pulled deep, and we may see this again.

Ozil. If he wants to be recognised as the best in the world (and I think that is well within his grasp), he needs to start performing in this kind of match. This season, we are starting to see the kind of 'big match' performances which he is capable of (Bayern, Man U). This is his biggest test. He played in matches like this for Madrid, but always as Ronaldo's wing man. Now the expectations are on him.

Giroud. Presuming that he - and not Walcott - starts, this will be an interesting game for him. Barca are vulnerable in the air, but can he see enough of the ball to do any damage? His goal scoring form is a 'little short', as Arsène might say. He doesn't have the pace to expose Barca's vulnerability to counter attack. Opportunities for 'hold up play' are limited against a team that presses as well as Barca do. He will be 30 in September and is towards the back end of a striker's peak years. He won't get many more chances to impress on the biggest stage.

The Barca boys. Bellerin and Sanchez will both be desperate to impress. It was the experience of playing against Barca that seemed to finally turn Fabregas' head. Let's hope the same doesn't happen to Bellerin. Sanchez was basically dumped to accommodate Jaws Suarez at Barca. He will be even more desperate to impress than normal (if such a thing is possible). We badly need him to return to form and this would be a great game for it.

The referee. It is not only Arsenal who have been the victims of sendings off against Barca. The dismissal of RVP in 2011 remains the most perplexingly stupid refereeing decision I have seen. The decision gifted the tie to Barca and whenever I see Barca's European triumphs listed, I mentally chalk 2011 off, as it was not a trophy honestly won. If a refereeing bribery scandal is ever uncovered, I expect that game to feature. Man City have had three players dismissed in their last four games with Barca, and even Real Madrid have been the victims on a surprising number of occasions. Barca have had nearly twice as many red cards in their favour as the second highest team in Champions League history. This is suspicious. Bribery is the obvious explanation for this phenomenon, but there are others:

- Barca are almost universally admired. They are seen not only as winners, but also beautiful in their style. Even referees may not be immune from this and have a tendency to see 'roughing' of Barca players as morally outrageous. Barca seem to get exactly the same protection that Arsenal have needed, but not got, in recent years
- Barca's stadium and their crowd are the most intimidating in the world. Players are reasonably immune to this. They have each other. The referee is on his own, literally in the middle of it all. Can any human being be reasonably expected to defy 100,000 baying Barca fans? Can there be a lonelier place to be in the entire world?

IT'S HAPPENED AGAIN

- Barca's playing style naturally draws fouls. They play the ball late, inviting men to commit themselves. The players are small and quick, and they are in possession of the ball for most of the game. Because they are small and light on their feet, they are easily knocked over. This is a perfect recipe for red and yellow cards

The crowd. I touched on this above, but a home crowd can make a big difference to a key match. We have seen as much twice this season. In the Chelsea away match (Premier League game 4), the crowd intimidated Mike Dean into mistakes which handed the match to Chelsea. At the Ems against Leicester, our crowd intimidated the referee into 'righting the wrong' of the Leicester goal, by sending a Leicester player off. The crowd reaction also possibly forced him into awarding the last minute free kick and then allowing the time for it to be played out. We can be a bit 'Anglo-Saxon' about this, but it is part of the game. The 'latin' view of the world sees football as a kind of audience participation theatre. No-one embodies this more than Portuguese Mourinho, who seems to see it as a major part of his job to 'play' the referee. If you are there tonight, remember that the Barca crowd will not hold back, so neither should you!

Flat track bullies? Any statistical analysis suggests that Barcelona are a phenomenally successful team. But are they only beating weak La Liga opposition? There may be a little truth to this, but not really. Remember they are European Champions, after all. However, the kind of dominance that Barca have shown is difficult to sustain. It will probably come to an end soon (remember how the Invincibles finally ground to a halt). Will Arsenal be the turning point?

Weak Defence? Barca are certainly stronger in attack than defence. However, Centre Backs Mascherano and Pique are fine players by any standards. They keep Vermaalen out of the side (although to be fair, that is no more than Koscielny and the BFG did). Busquets is also a world class Defensive Midfielder and the Full Backs are very good - albeit more attacking than defensive.

TIM CHARLESWORTH

They are a bit weak in the air and probably vulnerable to Giroud. They also press high, and this makes them vulnerable to counter attacks at pace. Of course, if they do have a defensive weakness, we need the ball to expose it!

Just enjoy it. This is one of the highest quality games that will be played in world football this year. Players come to Arsenal because they want to play in games like this. I realise that in picking out the crucial issues, I have picked out almost everything. This reflects the intensity that we can expect to see, all over the pitch. For one evening, the title race will be forgotten and everyone will be 100% motivated. Remember that you love football, as well as loving Arsenal, as we will see some very good football. This is a genuine test for a Barcelona team that knows that no club has ever successfully defended a Champions League title. The odds may be against us over two legs, but we have a good chance of victory at home.

CHAPTER THIRTY FOUR
THE ANATOMY OF COLLAPSE

CL R16 1st Leg			
Home Tues 23 Feb			
Barcelona			
Lost 0-2			
agg. 0-2			
Scorers: None			
	Shots (Arsenal:Opp)	8	15
	Shots on target	3	4
	Possession	34%	66%

Line-up: Cech; Bellerin, Mertesacker, Koscielny, Monreal; Coquelin, Ramsey; The Ox, Özil, Sanchez; Giroud.

This was a tough one to take. It was the biggest test of the season; a chance to measure ourselves against the team widely viewed as Europe's best.

The starting line-up was much as expected, with The Ox keeping his place on the right. Unfortunately he picked up an injury during the match that would rule him out of the rest of the season (and the subsequent European Championships).

We perhaps knew that we needed a clean sheet at home to have a realistic chance of getting to the quarter finals. We sat deep, conceding possession and a certain amount of territory. It looked like the team was remembering how it had beaten Bayern. The game was unspectacular, but fascinating for those of us who like to see technical skills executed at a fast pace all over the pitch. As the game wore on, our confidence visibly grew. It was almost as if the team realised there was nothing to be afraid of. They were not outclassed and they began to sniff an opportunity for a famous victory. We started to go forward in greater numbers.

Unfortunately there was something to be afraid of. The Barcelona goal was a thing of beauty. For the first time in the match they had a three on two against the Arsenal defence and were absolutely clinical. With pace, power and accuracy, the most feared front three in the world simply ran at us and passed the ball into our net.

Our team wilted, apparently aware that it had blown its only real chance. Flamini came on to shore things up and gave away a penalty 47 seconds after arriving. His haymaker kick into the shins of Messi was a moment of genuine footballing comedy (it looked like he hadn't even noticed that Messi was there) and suddenly, having been competitive all night, we looked second best. The result was harsh, but the efficiency with which Barcelona pounced on our mistakes could only be admired.

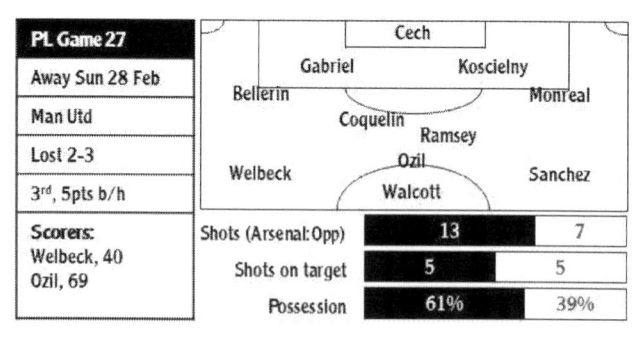

PL Game 27		
Away Sun 28 Feb		
Man Utd		
Lost 2-3		
3rd, 5pts b/h		
Scorers: Welbeck, 40 Ozil, 69	Shots (Arsenal:Opp)	13 / 7
	Shots on target	5 / 5
	Possession	61% / 39%

Formation: Cech; Bellerin, Gabriel, Koscielny, Monreal; Coquelin, Ramsey; Welbeck, Ozil, Sanchez; Walcott

Tuesday was a big disappointment. This is not what we needed five days later. The team lacked energy: it was an insipid performance against an injury ravaged Manchester United team. There was a feeling after this game that maybe this was 'one too many' bad days for a title winning side. The Goonersphere reaction, however, was near hysterical, with universal doom and gloom even from experienced commentators. It was certainly a very disappointing defeat, but the post-game, doom-laden analyses seemed to miss the following points:
- It is always difficult to win after a Champions League fixture
- This is doubly true if the ensuing fixture is an 'away'
- This is triply true if you have had a tough match against Barcelona

IT'S HAPPENED AGAIN

- This is quadruply true if you have suffered a demoralising defeat
- Old Trafford is never an easy place to go
- Arsenal had 61% of possession, 13 shots to Man U's 7 and both teams had 5 shots on target. Man U's winning goal was deflected. This is hardly a thrashing

A little bit of the hysteria can perhaps be put down to the fact that we fell behind Tottenham for the first time this season.

Walcott started, as did Welbeck, with Giroud dropping to the bench (due to lack of goals?). It was a fluid front three with Walcott and Welbeck interchanging a lot. Gabriel returned from injury and replaced Mertesacker at Centre Back.

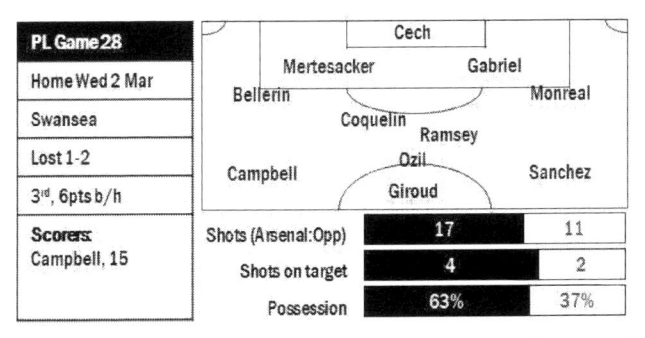

PL Game 28	
Home Wed 2 Mar	
Swansea	
Lost 1-2	
3rd, 6pts b/h	
Scorers: Campbell, 15	

Lineup: Cech; Bellerin, Mertesacker, Gabriel, Monreal; Coquelin, Ramsey; Campbell, Özil, Sanchez; Giroud

	Arsenal	Opp
Shots	17	11
Shots on target	4	2
Possession	63%	37%

After the hysterical reaction to the Man U game, I expected outright warfare and a general spike in suicides after this one. But it didn't happen; the fans' response was relatively mild, as if this result was almost expected. There are two possible explanations for this:

1. The rest of the Goonersphere (not me) genuinely expected this one. They could see how rubbish/gutless we were in the Man U game and they were right to expect this result
2. The general hysteria following the Man U game had stoked up the fans into a frenzy of negativity. This contributed to a poisonous atmosphere at the following home game (this

one) which made it a very difficult environment for the players and contributed to a very unusual defeat (it is extremely rare for Arsenal to lose a home game in which they have led). It should be noted that Arsenal dominated possession and shots in this game, hitting the post three times (post strikes are statistically rarer than goals in the Premier League)

I generally favour the second explanation, but doubt that I have the guts to say this to the 60,000 angry faces.

Mertesacker returned to the team with Koscielny injured. Campbell and Giroud replaced Welbeck and Walcott. Campbell scored and was the best player on the pitch. Was his selection a sign of 'patience running out' with Walcott, or simply the start of a rotation policy going into a period of two games per week?

If the Man U game was the one that bought the WOB (Wenger Out Brigade) back to life, this was the one that allowed them to say 'told you so'.

CHAPTER THIRTY FIVE
I CAN'T WATCH ANY MORE

PL Game 29			
Away Sat 5 Mar			
Tottenham			
Drew 2-2			
3rd, 8pts b/h			
Scorers: Ramsey, 39 Sanchez, 76	Shots (Arsenal:Opp)	10	26
	Shots on target	4	11
	Possession	48%	52%

Team: Ospina; Bellerin, Mertesacker, Gabriel, Gibbs; Coquelin, Elneny; Ramsey, Ozil, Sanchez; Welbeck

I have now started too many game write ups with 'this was horrible' or 'this was awful'. The problem with blowing your major adjectives early in the season is that you have nowhere to go when further bad things happen. We took the lead just before half time in a very hard fought game (Tottenham really do look good). We were holding our own and starting to control the game. Then Coquelin, who seemed to have grown out of his 'walking red card' phase, made an unwise challenge on Kane, earned a second yellow and within 10 minutes we were 2-1 down and without any further hope in a critical game. In the interests of objectivity, it should be recorded that Kane's goal was one of the best you will see all season (grudging harumphs).

The fat lady had been warming up to sing her final sorrowful tune, but once again Arsenal drew back from the brink. Sanchez scored his first league goal since October (a very depressing fact for our superstar). Ramsey even had a good chance to score the winner, but it wasn't to be and the game finished in a draw.

The team selection was interesting. Elneny replaced Ramsey in Central Midfield and had a good game. This was his first outing as a 'first choice' player. Ramsey has been looking out of sorts in his favoured position for a while now. He moved to the right side of midfield and looked more effective. Welbeck got a first start of the season at Centre Forward and did well. It looks like Olivier Giroud's goal scoring drought might have finally cost him his place. After a couple of unsuccessful outings for Walcott, Welbeck got the start this time. Ospina and Gibbs replaced the injured Cech and Monreal.

IT'S THE HOPE THAT KILLS YOU
March 8th 2016

I am starting to reflect on how lucky I am in life. I am blessed with a wonderful family, have my health, the privilege of education, live in a world without war, pestilence, famine etc. (my bit of it anyway).

This is not usually a good sign. I am reminding myself of these things because I am sad about the performance of my football team. And it all seems so daft. When there are so many things in this world to be happy about, I am sad. I'm sad because a bunch of men, who I don't really know (however much I think I do) are not doing very well playing for their football team. Just for the sake of clarity, this is a football team that I have never played for myself and with whom my connection is largely imagined in my own mind.

Wouldn't it be better just to walk away? I don't need to suffer like this. Most seasons, we don't win and of course this is true of all teams (even Bayern Munich have won less than half of the Bundesligas they have participated in). The whole thing is pointless and even if we win, I can only gain by someone else's similar misery. My pain and nervous energy makes no difference to the team. They will do just as well without me and I would be letting no-one down if I left.

And I think I am not the only one who feels this way. I hear talk of people who won't renew their season ticket, people who want to 'resign' or even 'switch to another team' (the ultimate crime for a football supporter). Of course they won't. I have

IT'S HAPPENED AGAIN

wanted to resign on a number of occasions (particularly in recent years), but I have given up trying now. I know I never will. The next win just sucks me back in. I just have to enjoy the good times and suffer the bad ones. There is simply no other option. I don't know why I can't walk away, but I have given up wondering.

We've suffered before. 2007-8 was taken away from us in a truly cruel manner. 2013-14 was hard and really frustrating. But this is worse. This team is stronger, the opposition is weaker. I really think we are the best team in this League. The sudden run of bad results is both perplexing and surprising. It came from nowhere and was accompanied by some bizarre losses of form (Walcott, Sanchez, Giroud, Gabriel).

And the prize seems greater too. It may be silly, but I genuinely care about Arsène Wenger. He is an amazing man. He suffers with us, he hurts even more than we do in defeat. He is a genius of football. If he could pull off just one more title, it would be one of the great achievements of all time. Has any Manager ever gone 12 seasons between triumphs - I don't think so.

And there is something magical, in life, about the 'old dog' proving that they still have it. Sport is littered with people who were unpopular in their pomp, but we came to love them towards the end. Jimmy Connors, Martina Navratilova, Stuart Pearce, Greg Norman, Tom Watson, Brian Clough, Teddy Sheringham, Bobby Robson, to name but a few. We came to support all these people because they reminded us of times gone by, of happy days with friends and family lost, because they gave us all hope that we're 'not done yet'.

But also, there is a darker side. We know that if these older characters lose, they won't get another chance. When a youngster is vanquished, the hope lives on. They will get another shot. A victory for Wenger would be one of the great comeback stories and might finally earn him the universal affection that he deserves. But it seems we may be denied that uplifting story. And we start to wonder how many more chances he will get.

TIM CHARLESWORTH

Worse than that, I fear for the club too. Arsenal looks like it is corporately over-reliant on Wenger, and under-prepared for the next chapter. His departure will leave a lot of holes which won't easily be filled. This is the era of the internet, when every setback is accompanied by gaggles of baying fans, feeling sorry for themselves and working themselves up into a self-fuelled feeding frenzy of anger and outrage. Many boards of football clubs have made mistakes in the face of such provocation. Arsenal's board has resisted so far, but will they hold out forever? It only takes one mistake after all. The Man U-Fergie experience is not a good precedent. The fans may be unhappy now, they may be angry, but I'm afraid that won't stop things from getting worse.

Barcelona was disappointing, the Man U game was upsetting, but the Swansea game was a genuine disaster. By the time of the Tottenham game, I had gone apathetic. Like many of us, my pre-match feeling was one of dread and gloom. I knew we had to win to stay in the race. I knew an away win against the second placed team was unlikely. I expected us to lose and for the final hope to be extinguished. I didn't dare to hope any more. (Out of interest, all the Spurs and Arsenal fans I know were implacably convinced that their team would lose this match. How ironic that they were all wrong!) I couldn't watch, but just kept an eye on my phone amidst the Mother's Day festivities. I inwardly groaned when we took the lead. It was the first time this season I have failed to greet a goal with joy. Not more hope, I thought. Not now, please.

Of course I couldn't ignore the siren call of the North London derby. I had to watch the second half, Mothering Sunday or not. I arrived in a pub full of Spurs fans just in time to see Coquelin making a slightly silly tackle. "Oh, you'll get booked for that", I thought, not realising he already had a yellow - because I hadn't watched the first half. Of course, I had arrived just in time to watch the worst ten minutes of the whole season (there is some pretty stiff competition for this title). I sat there and just wanted

IT'S HAPPENED AGAIN

to cry (being an Englishman, of course I didn't - especially as I was the only Arsenal fan in a sea of Spurs). I thought I had got rid of all the hope, but I clearly hadn't, there was still enough to hurt me on its way out.

Sanchez's goal barely caused a flicker of a smile. It was too little too late and anyway I expected Tottenham to score the winner (a Kane rabona from his own half seeming the most likely option). The Tottenham fans around me were charming by the way, full of sympathy and equally convinced that their team was about to concede the winner.

But neither team did concede, and both derbies end in draws that could end up expensive for either team. The draw keeps us in touch with Spurs and still hoping for St Totteringham to visit. And if you can still beat the second placed team, then it's got to be possible to catch the leaders. Leicester are not out of sight. If they slip up, they are still catchable. And if ever you thought a team leading at this point in the season had a chance of slipping up, then surely Leicester would be the most likely candidate.

And that's even worse. If Leicester do it this season, it will be one of the great sporting stories of all time. Surely their supporters deserve it, for all the years of loyal support without hope, suffering the privations of the Championship. Surely, a Leicester win would be a good outcome for most fans and for the game overall? And here's me, wishing misfortune upon them, for my own petty selfish reasons.

My heart tells me that something, which I don't really understand, has gone wrong with this talented team. My head tells me that I shouldn't believe in mumbo-jumbo, and this is a high-quality team that can still do it. Of course, as observed above, my own assessment of the situation is now highly unreliable. And you can't get around this problem by talking to fellow fans right now. We are all emotional wrecks who have lost the power of reason and objective analysis. I listen - even to respected commentators - and they are talking nonsense. Bookmakers seem to think there is something around a one in five, or 20%, chance of Arsenal winning the Premier League. This is actually quite similar to the odds at the start of the season. (And I wasn't depressed then!)

So there is a chance in the Premier League. I struggle to see it myself, but that's an emotional reaction, not a logical one. The objective bookies evidence suggests there is enough of a chance to keep me interested, but also that I am very likely to suffer more disappointment. This is exactly what I don't want now. I don't know how much more I can take. And I think that's why I really didn't enjoy the Sanchez goal. It restored a glimmer of hope, in a hopeless situation; and that was the worst thing about it.

The truth is that, in the unlikely event of us winning the title this year, I will be delighted with everything that has happened (including - and especially - the Sanchez goal). I will say things like 'what a ride' and 'I wouldn't have it any other way'. It's all ridiculous, isn't it? I quit. Only, I don't of course; and I won't.

So now it's back to the FA Cup. And it's really difficult to keep the hope away. Even the most pessimistic analysis has to conclude that we have a good chance in this one. Hull are surely beatable (albeit another Swanseaesque opportunity for unexpected heartbreak). And if we win, then it's Watford at home, a good draw and a good chance to make the Semi Final. Even if the Champions League and the Premier League chances are gone, the FA Cup dream lives on.

The irrational side of me still thinks that somehow we are destined to meet Chelsea in the final and finally prove that we can beat them in an 11 vs. 11 match. And what a story that would be: three in a row, Wenger winning more Cups than any other Manager, Arsenal setting a new high watermark in FA Cups won. All on a happy, sunny May afternoon, with spring turning to summer and Spurs to come in the Charity Shield...

IT'S HAPPENED AGAIN

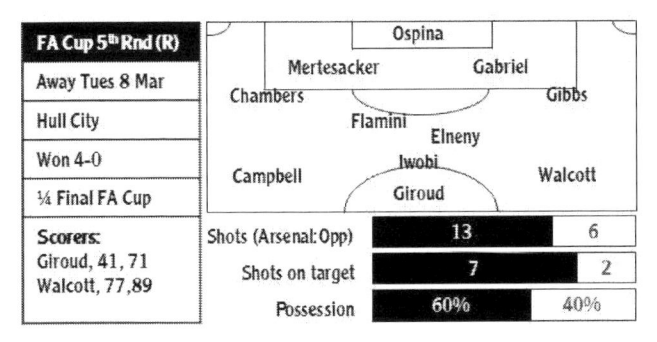

FA Cup 5th Rnd (R)	
Away Tues 8 Mar	
Hull City	
Won 4-0	
¼ Final FA Cup	
Scorers: Giroud, 41, 71 Walcott, 77, 89	

Formation:
- Ospina
- Mertesacker, Gabriel
- Chambers, Gibbs
- Flamini, Elneny
- Campbell, Iwobi, Walcott
- Giroud

	Arsenal	Opp
Shots	13	6
Shots on target	7	2
Possession	60%	40%

Hull played the reserves again. Arsenal did what they should have done the first time, delivering a firm spanking. A comfortable win was balm for sore Arsenal sensitivities. After all the tension and disappointment in the Premier League, it was nice to get back to a competition that felt homely and safe. Most of the other big teams had been knocked out of the Cup, and the 'three-peat' was really looking possible. Wenger rotated as much as injury would allow. Interestingly, both Walcott and Giroud played in this game. Are both now relegated to being squad players?

CHAPTER THIRTY SIX
THE DEATH BLOWS

NONSENSE, IMAGINATION, FORM, THEO, FRAGILITY & HOPE
11th March 2016

Human beings talk a lot of nonsense. And nowhere is this truer than football (hello Robbie Savage). We are basically 'pattern seeking-apes'. We are genetically programmed to look for causes and effects. This is actually our finest feature. It drives things like curiosity, reflection, imagination, and ambition. These are the things that make us unique and have enabled humans to develop technologies allowing us to dominate our planet.

Wonderful though they are, our pattern-seeking instincts are a little crude and impatient. They occasionally misfire. In our hunger to understand, we naturally reject 'random chance' as an explanation for anything. When we can't explain things we use our imagination to make an explanation up. We are quite good at this. This phenomenon can be seen most clearly in the case of religion. Early human societies imagined gods who controlled natural elements such as rain, sun, the moon and the seasons. These things are crucial to primitive farming groups. More sophisticated societies crafted more sophisticated gods who concern themselves with love, justice, death, and other imponderables. These ideas feed the illusion that everything in our world can be explained and that allows us to continue in our amazing quest for eternal truth.

Things imagined by Arsenal fans

In football, as in every other walk of life, we seek patterns that aren't really there. Arsenal fans are prone to the idea that the club is deliberately seeking 'top four finishes and nothing else'. This is patently ridiculous - such an ambition would be idiotic, as well as virtually impossible to achieve.

IT'S HAPPENED AGAIN

What we are actually trying to do is to win the League; we just happen to keep falling short. Of course, finishing in the top four is a valuable objective, but it is not the starting point. The reason we keep falling short is actually not the same every season: there is not a single cause. Of course there are similarities; after all it would be surprising if some things didn't stay the same from one season to the next. But the idea that we don't 'want' to win is clearly silly - even if you are very cynical, coming first is worth a lot of money!

Recently I have heard people speculate that we are 'bottlers'. This is possible, but serial bottling is actually quite rare in sport. I find it hard to buy the idea that both our current team and the 2008-9 team are ='bottlers'. Only Theo and Wenger have featured in both teams, and if you think Wenger is a 'bottler', I don't know what to say to you.

The suspicion that we are deliberately aiming for fourth place arises because we keep finishing in the top four without winning the League, which is a statistically improbable outcome. It is too important a phenomenon to ignore and simply put down to chance, so we need to imagine an explanation. This is really no different to ancient humans imagining a god who made sure that the sun rose every day to keep them alive, having abandoned them the night before. We are pattern-seeking apes and we are pre-programmed to seek explanation for what we see. If you are in any doubt about Arsenal's strategic intentions, just look at Arsène's face when he is questioned on this subject (top four, not sun-gods) - he can barely disguise his contempt for the question.

The fallacy of form

The most common fallacy that arises in football is the 'fallacy of form'. Daniel Finkelstein writes an excellent series of articles for The Times (called the Fink Tank). His basic proposition is that football is a game of statistics. The more shooting chances you create, the more you will score. The more chances you deny your opponents, the less they will score. Better Strikers and better Goalkeepers will slightly alter the 'conversion rates' both for your shots and for your opponents'. The more you score and less you concede goals, the more games you will win.

He suggests that over-analysis of an individual shot or save is pointless and that it is important to look at a bigger data set. Messi does not score with every shot and Giroud doesn't miss every time. However, Messi's average is better. You cannot necessarily tell this from one game. It is quite feasible that next week Giroud will score from a single chance and Messi will score none of three. That doesn't make Giroud the better player.

In fact, there are a number of statistically based football betting systems that can beat the bookies consistently. This is interesting because 'experts' like Mark Lawrenson consistently fail to beat the bookies if you follow their tips. The systems in question slavishly follow statistical principles and ignore considerations of 'form' or other similar ideas. These statistical systems almost always outperform 'expert' analysis. Football is not a game of certainties, but one of statistical probabilities, and this is much truer than we think it is.

NB Before you get excited, these systems are not a route to easy riches and require degree level statistical knowledge to operate them properly. Your return will only be slightly better than 100%, so you will need to lay a lot of bets and have big stakes to make any kind of money. Oh, and by the way, if you see someone selling such a system on the internet, be very suspicious - if it really works, how could the seller gain more by selling it than by using it? Modern bookies are also quite capable of monitoring online accounts and are not shy of banning players who consistently make money at their expense, so you might spend as much time setting up new accounts as laying your bets.

IT'S HAPPENED AGAIN

How is the form illusion created?

If you take a coin and flip it 38 times, you will get a few runs of consecutive heads and consecutive tails (I tried this and got one run of five consecutive heads). The coin will appear to have 'form'. Of course it doesn't, but we humans look for patterns, even when they are not there. Runs of wins and defeats will take place in football as a result of exactly the same effect. Finkelstein says: "Form is an illusion caused by randomness. If - if - you have class you will win clusters as well as lose them." You can improve the odds of victory with better players, good teamwork, fitness, training etc. But all you do is improve the probability of victory. You simply cannot draw reliable conclusions from a single game, or even a run of games.

A football match is a highly complex, probabilistic phenomenon. Its outcome is dependent on all sorts of random variables. One obvious variable is the referee. Single mistakes can easily change the outcome of a game. Football is a low scoring game, so a single kick like Martina's Boxing Day goal for Southampton can completely change a match. This sort of shot will succeed one time in 100, but the fact that it succeeded that day made all the difference.

Luck is a major consideration. Does your shot hit the woodwork and go in (Kane in the NLD) or bounce out (us three times vs. Swansea). Post strikes are rarer than goals; the bounce off the post depends on considerations of millimetres, way beyond the direct control of even the very best players. A pass can hit a divot in the grass that puts it the way of the Striker, or just out of reach. The random elements in a football match are huge and affect the game all the time. That is partly what makes it worth watching. Every Swansea has a chance to get a lucky win, even if they are outclassed.

Of course, not all variations in performance are random. A player may be carrying a niggling injury, which may cause a dip in performance that lasts for a few games. Fatigue may have a similar effect. Players returning from injury will lack full match fitness for a number of games. A personal mental state may affect performance. Footballers rarely suffer from depression because the constant exercise that they do protects them from mental illness. Nonetheless, they will have ups and downs, affecting them for a number of games.

So is Theo going to hit form?

As a result of all this, I generally ignore discussions of 'form' or 'confidence', either of players or the team as a whole. However, I couldn't help thinking about form when I watched Walcott playing against Hull. Theo is one of the great enigmas of English football. After an incredibly inconsistent and injury ravaged career, I got really excited about him earlier this season. Very briefly, he looked like the best no. 9 in England, fulfilling a long-held promise. Then it all went wrong. He picked up a bizarre hamstring injury in the Carling Cup against Sheffield Wednesday and has not recovered his 'form' since.

I think Wenger understands better than most that the concept of form is really nonsense. This is why he sometimes sticks with players that everyone else has lost patience with. Of course, this strategy doesn't always come up trumps (Denilson, Eboue), but is also one of the things that marks him out as superior to his peers (Coquelin, Ramsey and many others owe their careers to this approach).

The interesting thing about Theo is that he had another poor game against Hull, right up to the point that he assisted Giroud's second goal. The assist seemed to bring him to life. In fact the transformation was almost miraculous. Suddenly he was a menace to the opposition defence, making runs and making the Defenders nervous. At one point, he went on a mazy run into the box that nearly ended in a penalty or a goal.

I can't remember the last time I saw Theo run at Defenders like this. And they hate it - he is a walking invitation for them to make fools of themselves. His particular combination of pace, skill and finishing is absolutely terrifying for them.

His first goal was stunning. It was a great run, into an imaginative position. He then controlled the ball and beat the keeper. It all looked so easy. It reminded me of two things: This is the kind of thing that Messi does (also making it look easy) and this is what he looked like during the brief 'best no. 9 in England' phase earlier in the season.

So even an arch-cynic like me found it difficult to avoid the conclusion that 'confidence' had made a difference to Theo's play and even to hope that he might be 'coming into form'. And it's not just Walcott. I had the same thought when Sanchez scored against Tottenham.

Do we have vulnerable players?

Wenger has talked a lot about Sanchez's 'risk-taking' and his need to be successful. The finish against Tottenham was a great example of exactly this. It has been commented that he didn't hit it very truly and that the Goalkeeper should have saved it. This is true, but what Sanchez did was take a risk. Contrast his finish to Ramsey's miss (tackled) at the death of the NLD. Ramsey took an extra touch and allowed the Defender to make the tackle. Sanchez didn't. He hit the ball early. As a result, he wasn't quite ready. His weight distribution wasn't right as he was sprinting on to the ball and he slightly mis-hit it. However, the Goalkeeper also wasn't quite ready to make the save and the Defenders weren't quite ready to make the tackle and that's why he scored.

Sanchez and Walcott are both players who take risks on the field. They both lose the ball quite a lot because they take players on, they try flicks and dribbles and they try to do the unexpected. This is quite different to a Defender. A Defender is risk averse and tries to execute his skills simply and reliably (Midfielders are somewhere in-between). Risk taking does require a certain level of confidence, which is difficult to sustain when your risks keep failing to come off and the crowd gets on your back.

So is there something in the 'form fallacy' after all?

Maybe 'form' is real for attacking players; particularly ones who take lots of risks. If Walcott and Sanchez don't take risks, they are both quite ordinary players. Their passing ability is not exceptional and they are not very physically imposing. Walcott is 5'9" and 10st 7lb, Sanchez is 5'6" and 9st 8lb. They may be quick, but you wouldn't be very perturbed if you bumped into them in a dark alley.

Sanchez and Walcott are particularly significant players because we have lost both of them for the best part of four months. They were lost to injury, but when they returned were both useless for a further two months. The loss of these two players has played a major part in our poor performance in recent games.

Mesut Ozil is also a notable risk-taker on the football field, albeit one who tends to try risky passes rather than risky one-on-one movements. The battle with Ozil seems to be to get him to try the risky passes. When he plays poorly, we will often observe he has high 'pass completion' statistics, suggesting that he hasn't tried the difficult passes.

Are Arsenal mentally fragile?

All this makes me wonder if Arsenal, with Walcott, Sanchez and Ozil, are unusually vulnerable to 'confidence' issues. The atmosphere for the Swansea game was incredibly difficult for the players and I find it hard to believe they were not affected by the environment in which they had to perform.

It's difficult to imagine mental fragility in Sanchez, who seems to have endless reserves of determination. But actually, determination like that usually masks some kind of 'need'. Ozil

IT'S HAPPENED AGAIN

and Walcott are less mysterious. Both are clearly sensitive and gentle characters, verging on shyness. They seem anxious to please. They are natural team players, who want to help their team mates and seem to care deeply what people think of them.

It is not difficult to imagine that both could be affected by criticism. In particular, they might become more risk averse. The home crowd can be very harsh on players who lose the ball. The 'Emirates groan' is a peculiarly vicious rebuke and it is not difficult to imagine that risk-taking players might become risk-averse in the face of it.

So usually when people comment after games like the Hull match that 'so-and-so player has played themselves into form' or 'that will help their confidence', I ignore the comment. In this case, I wonder if there is some truth to it. Walcott visibly grew after his assist. Bellerin might gain some confidence from his assists against Spurs and Sanchez should gain confidence from his risk-taking goal. Giroud may be more relaxed now he has scored a couple of goals and his baby has arrived. Truly great sportsmen will tell you that you need to be 'in the zone' to get the best out of yourself. And part of this skill is being relaxed. Our players don't need to 'try harder', 'run harder' or use more adrenalin, they need to relax (especially our attackers).

So maybe, as winter gives way to spring, our players and our fans will relax a bit. Maybe we really are about to hit 'form' and put together a wonderful run to the end of the season. Maybe the 'players meeting' that Theo described after the Hull game will be a bit like the famous 'Sopwell House meeting' that galvanized the 1997-8 double team. I might be clutching at straws, but there's always hope.

TIM CHARLESWORTH

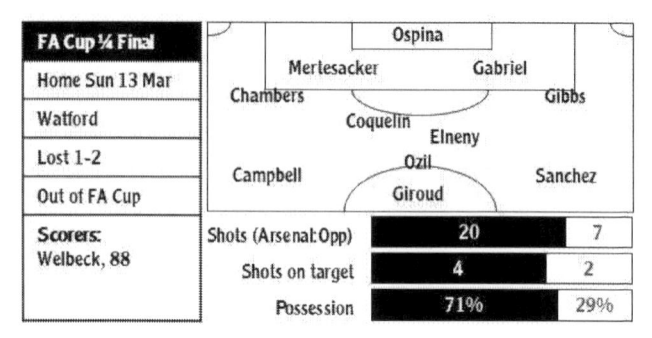

FA Cup ¼ Final		
Home Sun 13 Mar		
Watford		
Lost 1-2		
Out of FA Cup		

Formation:
- Ospina
- Chambers, Mertesacker, Gabriel, Gibbs
- Coquelin, Elneny
- Campbell, Ozil, Sanchez
- Giroud

Scorers: Welbeck, 88		Arsenal	Opp
	Shots (Arsenal:Opp)	20	7
	Shots on target	4	2
	Possession	71%	29%

No-one saw this one coming. Our first defeat in an FA Cup match in over three years (756 days since we lost to Blackburn).

We dominated the game with 71% possession and 20 shots to seven. Watford scored two goals from two shots on target; we scored one from four. On 50 minutes, Watford scored from their first real attack. Our defence looked weak in failing to clear a throw in. The ball came to Ighalo who seemed to turn Gabriel too easily and scored. If the first goal was soft, the second was hard not to admire. As the ball was laid off to Watford midfielder Guedioura, the Arsenal defenders failed to close him down. The momentary hesitation was fatal, as the midfielder unleashed a shot reminiscent of an exocet missile and we were two down. It looked hopeless at that point, but Welbeck came on and got an equaliser two minutes from the end. He then missed a bit of a sitter after Iwobi hit the post and it was all over.

Chambers and Gibbs played at full back with Gabriel (a bit lucky not to be red carded for a two footed challenge) and Mertesacker continuing in the middle. Coquelin and Elneny played together in midfield for the first time. Giroud came in up front for Welbeck (is Welbeck first choice now?).

There is very little discussion of it amongst the general hysteria surrounding this game, but Wenger did not pick his best 11, almost certainly with an eye on the Barcelona match. Was this wise, given the impossibility of the task in Barcelona, but the realistic prospect of winning a third FA Cup. Man City,

IT'S HAPPENED AGAIN

Tottenham, Chelsea, Liverpool and Leicester are all out of the Cup. The historic FA Cup treble was there for the taking!

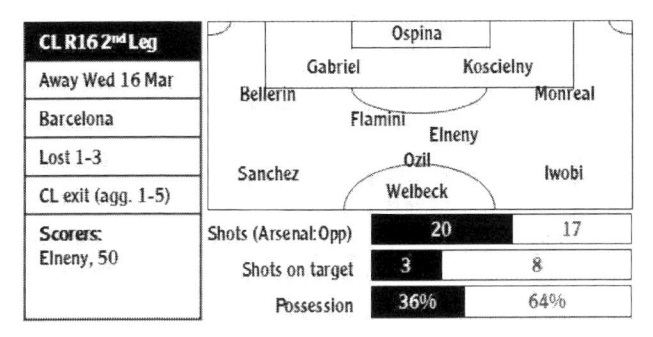

CL R16 2nd Leg	
Away Wed 16 Mar	
Barcelona	
Lost 1-3	
CL exit (agg. 1-5)	
Scorers: Elneny, 50	

Lineup: Ospina; Bellerin, Gabriel, Koscielny, Monreal; Flamini, Elneny; Sanchez, Ozil, Iwobi; Welbeck

	Arsenal	Opp
Shots	20	17
Shots on target	3	8
Possession	36%	64%

The inevitable result. Arsenal played OK, without ever looking like we might win. We needed to win by two goals, but Barcelona were on the end of a club record 37-game unbeaten streak and they hadn't been beaten at home since February 2015.

The selection was interesting. Iwobi, Flamini and Welbeck played with Giroud, Walcott, Coquelin and Mertesacker on the bench. Were players being rested for the Everton game at the weekend? Koscielny finally returned from injury and Mertesacker made way. The front three were Iwobi, Alexis and Welbeck, with Welbeck in the middle and Alexis shifted to the right. 'Front threes' are becoming the 'in thing' in football. Nowhere is this more obvious than in Barcelona, with the almost legendary Messi, Neymar and 'Jaws' Suarez. It looked here a bit like Wenger was trying to create his own front three.

Although this was a fluid front three, Alexis played on the right after playing on the left all season. This was an interesting change. Lots of fans have been complaining that Alexis looked predictable on the left. Every time he gets the ball, he cuts in from the left touchline and tries to dribble across the pitch, looking for a shooting opportunity or an assist. He is very good at this move, but it has started to look stale in recent months. It's not clear whether this is because he is no longer executing this move well, or because he has done it so many times that teams are expecting it and setting up to defend it? Has Wenger finally decided that Alexis needs to try something new?

Iwobi and Elneny played surprisingly well, and everyone was pleased to see Elneny get his first goal for Arsenal. The tie that looked so exciting before kick-off at the Emirates ended in a whimper. Overall, Arsenal didn't look outclassed (apart from in the 'clinical finishing' department) over two fixtures, but Barcelona certainly deserved the win, and 5-1 was not overly flattering.

CHAPTER THIRTY SEVEN
FAREWELL JOHANNES

JOHANN CRUYFF DIES
24th March 2016

Soon after we played Barca they lost their greatest icon, Johann Cruyff, the man who turned everything he touched to gold.

Hendrik Johannes Cruyff was born in 1947 to a humble working class family in Holland, near the De Meer stadium of Ajax Amsterdam. Inspired by the stadium and his football-loving father, the young Johan grew up, like many small boys, spending all his free time playing football. When Johan was twelve his father died of a heart attack. Johan thereafter saw a career in professional football as a way of honouring his father's memory. He joined Ajax's Academy.

Ajax were developing a revolutionary brand of football, inspired by two football visionaries from Lancashire called Jimmy Hogan and John Reynolds. Hogan and Reynolds both wanted their players to constantly interchange positions as the game demanded. When one player was dragged out of position, another player would simply slot in, thereby maintaining the shape of the team as the play unfolded. Hogan managed across Europe and was more influential there than in his home country. He inspired the famous Hungary team that beat England 6-3 at Wembley in 1953, a game that changed European football forever. After the match, Gusztáv Sebes, the Hungarian footballer and coach, said of Hogan *"We played football as Jimmy Hogan taught us. When our football history is told, his name should be written in gold letters".*

John Reynolds managed Ajax from 1915 to 1947, making even Arsène Wenger look flighty and impermanent. Ajax won their first eight Eredivisie Championships under his management, and he designed the whole club around the interchangeability concept, which fast became known as 'totaalvoetbal', or 'total football'. Rinus Michels played for Reynolds at Ajax and later became Manager, refining the system into a deadly combination of pace and fluidity. Cruyff was the greatest exponent of the total football system. By the time he was 20, Cruyff was the division's leading scorer in Michels' championship winning Ajax team. Cruyff, Michels, Ajax and total football were suddenly irresistible. In the 1971-2 and 1972-3 seasons, they won every single home game (46 in total). Ajax won the European Cup for the first time in 1971 and retained it for the following two seasons*. The second and third European Cup Finals were played against Inter Milan and Juventus. The Ajax total football system contrasted starkly with the dour, defensive, Catenaccio system which was widely employed by the Italian teams. Suddenly, football was fresh and exciting and the rest of Europe was in awe.

Cruyff left Ajax in the summer of 1973 for a world record fee paid by Barcelona and he spent most of the rest of his life in the city. In his first season, he helped Barcelona to their first La Liga championship since 1960. When Barca beat deadly rivals Real Madrid 5-0 at the Bernebeu, Barcelona fans watching on televisions spontaneously flooded onto the streets. Cruyff was crowned European Footballer of the Year (Ballon D'Or) in 1974, for the third time.

Cruyff's most celebrated hour was at the 1974 World Cup. Holland, an international minnow before Cruyff's appearance, dazzled the world with their total football style and were the stars of the tournament. In an early match against Sweden, Cruyff executed a trick where he shaped to cross and then dragged the ball inside his planted foot with his crossing foot. The Defender was sent completely in the wrong direction and left with a rather perplexed expression. The move is today practiced by aspiring

---

* Ajax and Real Madrid are the only two clubs ever to have won three consecutive European Cups

IT'S HAPPENED AGAIN

trainee footballers throughout the world and is known as the 'Cruyff turn'.

Holland progressed to the final where they played hosts West Germany. The opening of that final is one of football's magic moments. Cruyff kicked off and the ball was moved rapidly around the Dutch team. After thirteen passes, the ball came back to Cruyff, just inside the West German half. Cruyff took the ball and embarked on a slaloming run, driving into the penalty area, where he was tripped. The referee awarded a penalty, which Holland scored. After 88 seconds Holland were 1-0 up and Germany still hadn't touched the ball. To football's eternal regret, Holland went on to lose 2-1 and have still never won the World Cup.

Cruyff's greatest days were now behind him, but he played another three seasons with Barcelona. Towards the end of his time with Barcelona, he persuaded the Club President to establish an academy in the image of the one he had come from at Ajax. La Masia became world famous, perhaps even eclipsing the fame of the Ajax Academy on which it was based. Pep Guardiola, Lionel Messi, Xavi Hernandez, Cesc Fabregas, Mikel Arteta and Hector Bellerin are all graduates. In 2010, six of the Spanish staring line up that won the World Cup Final were alumni of La Masia.

In 1978 Cruyff moved to play in the US for two years, having retired from international football in 1977, following a kidnap scare. He finally returned to Ajax, who had never really recovered from his departure, at the age of 33. Such nostalgic returns are rarely successful in football, but Cruyff delivered two more Eredivisie titles at Ajax. The club then annoyed him in a dispute about his playing time, so he moved to arch-rivals Feyenoord. Outrageously, Feyenoord won the title in his only season before his final retirement. 37 year-old Cruyff missed only one match all season and was voted Dutch Footballer of the Year for the fifth time!

TIM CHARLESWORTH

There can be no doubt that Cruyff is one of the greatest ever to play the game. It wasn't just his skill, but his intelligence and elegance that marked him out. Dutch journalist Hubert Smeets wrote: *"Cruyff was the first player who understood that he was an artist, and the first who was able and willing to collectivise the art of sports."* Sweden defender Jan Olsson, victim of that first Cruyff turn at the 1974 World Cup, said *"I played 18 years in top football and 17 times for Sweden but that moment against Cruyff was the proudest moment of my career. I thought I'd win the ball for sure, but he tricked me. I was not humiliated. I had no chance. Cruyff was a genius."*

Cruyff could never walk away from football. He became Ajax Manager in 1985 and won the Cup Winners Cup in 1987 (with Denis Bergkamp in the team). He, inevitably, went on to manage Barcelona in 1988.

Cruyff lasted an incredible eight seasons as Barcelona Manager. He put together a team known as 'the dream team', including Pep Guardiola and Ronald Koeman. He took on the mantle of total football and gave it a new angle: the style he developed became known as 'tiki-taka', which involves a lot of short, fast, one or two touch passing combined with dynamic movement off the ball. It is designed to monopolise the ball and disorientate the opposition players. It was usually combined with a high defensive line and often a 'high press', where the attacking players put pressure on the opposition when they don't have the ball, in the hope that they will force an error high up the pitch. Tiki-taka is extremely difficult to execute, requiring high levels of skill throughout the team. But when it is executed well, it is an incredible thing to watch. The team playing a tiki-taka style will tend to have the ball most of the time. When they lose the ball, they pounce on their opponents and invariably get the ball back, condemning their opponents to another long period chasing the ball. It is visibly demoralising to the opposition.

With Cruyff at the helm, Barcelona won four consecutive La Liga titles and their first ever European Cup. Altogether he won

IT'S HAPPENED AGAIN

11 trophies, making him the most successful Barcelona Manager of all time. He never took another full-time coaching job, but was a constant presence behind the scenes at Barcelona, both involving himself in club politics and providing technical advice.

Cruyff's affection for Barcelona was more than skin deep. Barcelona is the capital of the Catalan region of Spain, and Catalans identify with their region in a way that has some similarities with a Scottish identity within the UK. Many Catalans believe that Catalonia should secede from Spain and FC Barcelona is a proud symbol of Catalan nationalism. This is the sentiment behind the Barcelona epithet *'mes que un club'* (more than just a club). Madrid is the symbol of the repression of Catalan nationalism, and the home of Spanish dictator General Franco, who ruled Spain from 1939 to 1975. Franco was particularly violent and deadly in his repression of Catalan nationalism and this is the political backdrop to the rivalry between Real Madrid and Barcelona (known as the *el classico* rivalry).

When Cruyff joined Barcelona, he was an outspoken critic of Franco at a time when it was still not entirely safe to be so. He claimed to have rejected the chance to join Real Madrid because he could never join a club 'associated with Franco'. In order to understand the impact of this statement you have to remember that at the time, Real Madrid was a hugely more successful club than Barcelona and that it is largely thanks to the efforts of Cruyff that this is no longer true. Cruyff named his third child Jordi, after the patron saint of Catalonia, St Jordi. He actually had to fly the baby to the Netherlands to register its name, as Franco had outlawed the use of the name in Spain. Jordi Cruyff inevitably became a professional footballer, even playing for Barcelona, albeit without the elan of his father.

Like every genius, Johan was flawed. He smoked cigarettes. In 1991 he required double heart bypass surgery (a procedure that might have saved his father all those years ago) as the cigarettes had damaged his arteries. He stopped smoking and became an outspoken anti-smoking campaigner. In 2015 he was diagnosed with lung cancer. On the morning of 24th March 2016, the disease killed him at the age of 68. He left a wife and three children.

On the day after his death a match between France and the Netherlands was halted in the 14th minute for a minute's applause. 14 had been Cruyff's number. On the 2nd April, Barcelona played Real Madrid. The Barcelona team had the words 'Gràcies Johan' printed on their shirts.

Manchester City-bound Manager Pep Guardiola said of his former Manager: "He painted the chapel and Barcelona coaches since have merely restored or improved it". This is a particularly generous comment when you reflect that Guardiola's own period as Barcelona coach is arguably the most successful period that any coach has ever had in the history of world football; winning 15 trophies to eclipse Cruyff's record.

Wenger said *"He was the kind of exceptional personality that marked me and all my generation".* The two men moved in similar circles later in life, but don't seem to have been particularly close. Wenger doesn't form many close relationships with his peers in football, and perhaps the tersity between Arsenal and Barcelona in the last decade prevented them from becoming friends.

Like all great Managers, Cruyff himself was the master of the pithy one liner. These are my favourites:

"If I wanted you to understand it all, I would have explained it better."

"I don't believe in God. In Spain, all 22 players cross themselves. If it works, the game is always going to be a tie."

"Why couldn't you beat a richer club? I've never seen a bag of money score a goal."

"Playing football is very simple, but playing simple football is the hardest thing there is."

IT'S HAPPENED AGAIN

Pele and Diego Maradona are often ranked above Cruyff in the canon of all-time great players, perhaps because they were World Cup winners and Cruyff was not. And other legends are spoken of in the same breath as Cruyff, such as Best, Puskas, Messi and Zidane. However, none of these can claim to have had anything like the success as a Manager that Cruyff enjoyed. So for his influence as a Manager as well as a player, I rank Cruyff as the greatest football man of all time.

He was more than just a football player.

GRINDING TO A HALT

The long march home
April & May 2016

CHAPTER THIRTY EIGHT
HANGING ON TO HOPE

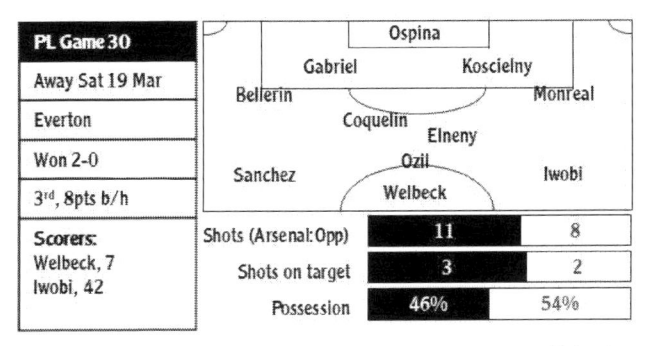

PL Game 30		
Away Sat 19 Mar		
Everton		
Won 2-0		
3rd, 8pts b/h		
Scorers: Welbeck, 7 Iwobi, 42	Shots (Arsenal:Opp)	11 / 8
	Shots on target	3 / 2
	Possession	46% / 54%

Lineup: Ospina; Bellerin, Gabriel, Koscielny, Monreal; Coquelin, Elneny; Sanchez, Ozil, Iwobi; Welbeck

This was a solid away win that just about keeps our flickering title hopes alive going into the last Interlull of the season. We only have one competition to play in now, but in order to have a chance, we really need to win all our games. Even then Leicester, and to a lesser extent, Tottenham need to slip up. There is still hope, but not much.

CAN LEICESTER HANG ON?
March 25th 2016

One of the (many) things that winds me up when I am listening to people talk about football is the accusation that the team is not 'motivated', nor 'trying hard enough'. The observation that players should be trying harder is generally up there with the idea that people with a mental illness should 'snap out of it', or bereaved people should 'move on'.

This is professional sport, not park football, so there are very few occasions on which it makes any sense for a professional footballer to take their foot off the gas. They are always playing for something. Even if they want to leave, better performances will lead to higher wages at the next club.

Very occasionally you get a player who realises that they cannot cut it any more, or decides not to work so hard. They know they will never get another contract; the only option open to them is to collect their money until the end of their contract and retire, or drop down the leagues.

A recent example of this was Sebastien Squillaci, who seemed to lose any hope after about six months at Arsenal and simply let his career slide away. Faced with deteriorating effectiveness, most players desperately seek first team football as an alternative to 'seeing out' the contract in the reserves. Even Squillaci has been a regular for Ligue 1 Bastia for three seasons since leaving Arsenal.

Another example of this is Emmanuel Adebayor (bless him!), who is truly raging against the dying of the light with his latest (apparently futile) move to Crystal Palace. Adebayor got his big pay day when he moved to City. All his subsequent moves seem to be motivated more by a genuine desire to play, than to gather cash. The fact is that most professional footballers love the game. They love playing and they enjoy training. These are not average individuals.

A Premier League football career requires massive dedication and sacrifice. It is difficult to spend endless hours on football drills if you don't enjoy it. There are the odd occasions when outrageous talent, combined with pushy parents and coaches, can get a player through, but this is rare. Most players who appear to be 'effortless' are conning you. They actually spend hours and hours practising to look like they are not trying. They tend not to mention this, as it suits their marketing image for people to believe that they are 'naturally gifted'.

Believe me, any player that you see playing for Arsenal has worked very hard to get there. If you ever could detect a reduction in effort, it would probably be on the training ground (which fans don't see), not during a match. A player's default setting is to give 100%, especially during a match and it takes quite a lot to stop them from doing so.

IT'S HAPPENED AGAIN

Can effort levels dip during a match?

Of course, there are occasions in a match where the effort levels will drop. This usually occurs when the outcome of a match is decided, either in the case of a victory or a defeat.

This was recently noticeable towards the end of the Barcelona and Everton matches. In such circumstances, both teams can drop into a sort of implicit 'conspiracy truce' where the 'snappiness' of the tackling declines and everyone drops a little deeper position-wise. Players are quite used to playing like this, because it is similar to what they do in training. It is a way of playing that avoids injury and excessive fatigue. It is perfectly sensible to do this in circumstances where the outcome of the match is very unlikely to change. Effectively, the players are saving their limited energy for a game in which their effort might actually change the result.

There are also rare occasions in which the subconscious efforts made by players may reduce. This can happen if players are upset with each other or with the Manager (or maybe even the fans). This may have happened to Chelsea earlier this season (but see alternative explanation below). However, I don't think that Arsenal have been affected by any of these scenarios in recent weeks. I don't think there was any lack of effort or motivation against Watford or Swansea. If you look at the statistics from these games such as distance run, they suggest no diminution of effort. There may be occasions on which the team ran out of ideas a little bit, but not when they ran out of motivation.

And that brings me to an interesting observation about Leicester City. They do appear to be getting a little bit in excess of 100% out of their players. The movement of the players on the pitch seems slightly manic, the determination is palpable. They look like an irresistible force.

TIM CHARLESWORTH

The way they are playing, with hard fought 1-0 victories, reminds me of Blackburn Rovers during their run in to the 1994-5 title, and even Leeds in 1991-2. Both of these teams seemed to be winning by sheer force of will towards the end of the season. They seemed to draw on deep reserves of energy and determination that are not usually available to players. Interestingly, in both cases, the teams did not recover from their gargantuan efforts. Both teams failed to put up any sort of defence to their titles; and never recovered their competitiveness.

Can a team exhaust itself & did Chelsea do it?

I am beginning to wonder if the same thing happened to Chelsea last season. We haven't seen such a poor title defence for a while in the Premier League. All the teams that have won recently have not needed to go into deficit in order to do so. Manchester United, Chelsea and Manchester City have had deep and talented squads. But maybe this is changing as the Premier League becomes more competitive. Maybe the Premier League is now so tough to win, that it is becoming very difficult to repeat. There are now seven consecutive seasons where the Champions have failed to defend their title.

2014-15 Chelsea had a wonderful start to the season, based on brilliant runs of form from two newly signed players, Fabregas and Costa. Basically Fabregas passed it to Costa, who scored. This is a neat trick and Chelsea built up a large lead in the Premier League off the back of it.

As Fabregas and Costa inevitably faded, Chelsea hung on for grim death, relying on defensive solidity and Eden Hazard. I remember thinking the way that Chelsea celebrated their 0-0 draw at the Emirates in April 2015 was a bit strange. Arsenal's late run was impressive, but Chelsea still looked pretty secure at the top.

IT'S HAPPENED AGAIN

With the benefit of hindsight, I suspect that Chelsea were hanging on more than anyone realised at the time (possibly deceived by the cunning Mourinho). Chelsea were, perhaps, a lot more worried by Arsenal's late charge than anyone really appreciated, hence the celebrations.

Hazard's loss of form is one of the great mysteries of this season. I don't accept that he has lost motivation because he wants to move. Hazard is doing himself no good at all and his previously high stock is plummeting fast. This looks involuntary to me and will affect any kind of deal he can get for himself, if and when he leaves Chelsea. Mourinho put a lot of pressure on him to perform towards the end of last season, and he rose to the challenge, but it's beginning to look as if he may have done so by dipping into irrecoverable reserves.

The parable of Petit

Hazard's travails remind me a bit of Emmanuel Petit. By any standards, Petit had the most incredible season in 1997-8. He moved to Arsenal in the summer, played brilliantly in the double team (after a slow start), established himself in the French team and won the World Cup (scoring in the final from a Patrick Vieira assist).

After the World Cup, he was a 27 year old with the world at his feet. Unfortunately, he had played over 50 games that season, many of them very competitive and he would never be the same again. He remained a dominant player on the pitch, but niggling knee injuries made those performances increasingly rare. Our failure (by one point) to defend the title in 1998-9 was very much the story of a failure of Vieira and Petit to reproduce their form of the second half of 1997-8, and Petit's absences were the most obvious symptom.

I think Petit had just given too much in the previous season. He had taken his body beyond the point of natural endurance in the joyful euphoria of Arsenal's winning run at the end of the season, and then France's similar run in the World Cup. And this kind of phenomenon has been observable in other periods of Arsenal's history.

The run of ten consecutive victories from March to May 1998 was incredible and the team made it look easy, but as soon as the title was won, they lost the next game 4-0. The failure of the Invincibles to defend their title in 2004-5 is also a bit strange in the context of their dominance the previous season. The achievement of the 49 games may have come at a price.

What is long-term fatigue?

Long-term tiredness is a curious phenomenon in human beings, and is not well understood by science. We understand short-term tiredness. We understand that running a marathon will cause micro-damage to muscles and tendons that require rest to heal and various chemical imbalances in the body that need to be restored by the body's metabolic processes. Similarly, we understand the relationship between sleep deprivation and tiredness. We even understand some of the mechanisms in the brain that cause this. However we have very little understanding of long-term fatigue.

We will all be familiar with periods in our life when we have worked very hard and as a result feel exhausted in a way that a long weekend with plenty of sleep cannot get rid of. We are mysteriously able to avoid injury or illness during these periods, but such things often catch up with us soon afterwards.

Major events like moving house, or having a new child, can elicit this response and sportsmen seem to suffer from a similar kind of fatigue. Tennis players lose energy if they play too many tournaments and footballers pay a price if they do too much in a season.

It seems that humans have the ability to draw on some kind of reserve of energy, both mentally and physically. We almost seem to be able to 'borrow' future energy. Presented with a prize

IT'S HAPPENED AGAIN

in front of our noses, such as a Premier League title, a World Cup, a new house, or a new baby, we may not even be aware that we are operating at over 100%. But if we do so, there is a consequence and the payback period can be long.

Arsène Wenger sometimes talks about being in the 'red zone' to describe this scenario, almost as if a player is building up an overdraft. Alexis Sanchez is an example of this. His feats last season were superhuman and he seemed to be able to draw on deep wells of energy. He appeared to defy commonly understood rules about fatigue, but there may be a consequence to this extraordinary spell of energy and we may be seeing it now. So if you want Arsenal players to 'try harder', be careful what you wish for.

So what of Leicester?

It seems to me that, with the winning post in sight, Leicester are drawing on deep reserves of energy, which are not really available to other teams or players. Their performances represent a rare collective phenomenon and are worth watching in that light. Their closing down, concentration, tackling and defensive agility are exceptional.

My suspicion is that they will probably find enough resources to hang on to the end of the season. This may make you happy (because they beat Tottenham) or sad (because they hold off a late charge from Arsenal). Either way, I expect them to suffer the consequences of dipping into the red zone at the start of next season. I am not at all optimistic about their Champions League campaign in 2016-17.

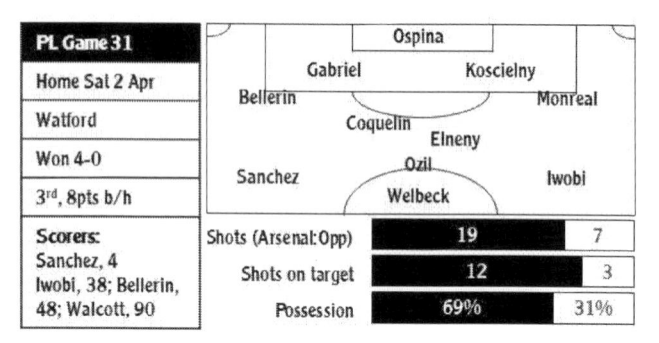

PL Game 31	
Home Sat 2 Apr	
Watford	
Won 4-0	
3rd, 8pts b/h	
Scorers: Sanchez, 4 Iwobi, 38; Bellerin, 48; Walcott, 90	

Formation:
- Ospina
- Gabriel, Koscielny
- Bellerin, Monreal
- Coquelin, Elneny
- Sanchez, Ozil, Iwobi
- Welbeck

	Arsenal	Opp
Shots	19	7
Shots on target	12	3
Possession	69%	31%

So the FA Cup defeat to Watford is duly avenged. The revenge feels a little flat.

Everything went right on a sunny day. We got the early goal that makes matches like this much more comfortable for players and fans alike. Our favourite young players, Bellerin and Iwobi, scored, as did the widely admired Alexis Sanchez.

The same team that played Everton played again. Looking strong and balanced, this was our biggest Premier League win of the season. But were we brilliant, or were mid-table Watford, with an FA Cup Semi Final to come, disinterested? Difficult to know, but time will tell. This bright new team looks good, but still needs to prove itself in sterner tests than this.

CHAPTER THIRTY NINE
THE LAST KNOCKINGS

WHAT IS WENGER SAYING TO US THROUGH HIS TEAM SELECTIONS?

April 6th 2016

It is always wise to take the words of football Managers with a pinch of salt. When they talk to the press, they know that players and opponents are listening to what they say. Passing on accurate information may not be their top priority.

I always feel it's worth listening to what Arsène says. He is not particularly Machiavellian, there is usually some truth in his words and we can often find some deep wisdom. However, like lots of Managers in the modern squad game, he is reluctant to opine on his 'first choice' players. For this reason, if I want to know what he really thinks of his players (and I value his opinion very highly), it pays to look at his team selections.

Although he doesn't like to discuss the subject, presumably in order to maintain the confidence of non-first-choice players, it is absolutely clear that Wenger does have first choice players. Ozil is a blatant example of this. Ozil does not play every game, but the games for which he is dropped are always lesser games where Wenger feels he can win with a weaker team.

The same is true of Koscielny and Sanchez. These are obviously our strongest players, and you could probably add Bellerin, Monreal, Cech, Cazorla and Coquelin to the list of names who will always play in a big game if available. However, Wenger is never explicit about this, so if we want to work out his 'first choice' team, we have to do it by deduction. His words may deceive us, but his team selections speak a clear truth. When he chooses a team he is not trying to influence anyone, he is trying to win a match (or maximise season performance in the case of rotation).

TIM CHARLESWORTH

In the matches leading up to the Interlull, it was particularly difficult to interpret what Wenger was telling us through his selections. We had a series of four matches in 11 days in three different competitions and Wenger's priorities were not clear. With the benefit now of hindsight, following the Watford game (the Premier League one), I am reasonably sure I understand what Wenger was doing. So here it is:

Hull away (FA Cup 6th round replay), 4-0 victory, 8th March

This was basically a rotation team. Wenger saw this as an easy game in the midst of a tough run of fixtures (the result suggests he was right). In the centre of defence were Mertesacker and Gabriel, with Gibbs getting another game after his surprise selection against Tottenham. Was Wenger trying him out, or resting a niggle for Monreal (who was on the bench for both matches, so not badly injured)? Subsequent events have suggested that Monreal was just getting a rest.

It is also interesting that Bellerin was not rotated for this match. Is this because Wenger doesn't trust Chambers at right back, or because he feels Bellerin can physically withstand a heavy match schedule? If the latter, this is a bit worrying, as Bellerin has just turned 21 and we have seen players apparently harmed by playing too much at this age. Bellerin's extreme pace makes me wonder if he is particularly vulnerable in this respect (see Michael Owen).

In midfield, Coquelin was suspended, but may have been rotated in favour of Flamini anyway. Elneny played. It was already looking like Elneny had replaced Ramsey in the middle at this point and subsequent events have confirmed this suspicion.

Rotation was particularly evident up front. The two wide players, Ramsey and Sanchez, rotated to the bench, giving Walcott and Campbell a game. Welbeck, recently returned from injury, was rested altogether, giving Giroud a chance. Ozil was

IT'S HAPPENED AGAIN

also rotated to the bench, giving Iwobi a match at no. 10. Welbeck is the interesting one here, as it seems he had now become the first choice Centre Forward. Giroud's run out against Hull was a case of rotation. It was obvious that both Giroud and - particularly - Walcott, were falling short of the mark at Centre Forward, but not obvious that Welbeck had moved ahead of them.

Of course, we don't see what happens in training. Hindsight seems to suggest that Welbeck had become first choice at Centre Forward as far back as the Tottenham match on 5th March (or even the Man U game on 28th Feb). It was not at all obvious at the time that merit, rather than rotation, was behind his selection. Welbeck's promotion is particularly surprising because he seemed to have fallen behind both Giroud and Walcott prior to his injury last season.

Indeed, Welbeck's priority may not have been 100% clear to Wenger when he selected him for the Man U game. He may have felt that Welbeck was his best option, but this could have perhaps changed if Welbeck had performed badly in the Man U or Tottenham games. After all, the Man U game was his first Premier League start for 10 months. Nonetheless, Wenger's selection pattern shows us that by the time of the Hull game, Welbeck had clearly become first choice.

Watford home (FA Cup Quarter Final), 2-1 defeat, 13th March

For this game, Chambers and Gibbs played at Full Back. This was clearly rotation, although it looked at the time as if Gibbs might be making a play to regain his previous priority at Left Back. The Centre Backs were Gabriel and Mertesacker again; the two senior available Centre Halves. Wenger doesn't usually believe in rotating his Centre Backs very much, and he knew he had Koscielny to return in the near future. Coquelin and Elneny looked like first choice Midfielders with Ozil at 10. Sanchez and Campbell played wide with Giroud up front. With the possible exception of Chambers at right back, this looked like a first choice team.

Hindsight suggests that four players: Chambers, Campbell, Gibbs and Giroud were all in the team due to rotation, with the Barcelona game (four days later) in mind. Koscielny was injured, but given that he was available to play a tough game four days later in Barcelona, we must wonder if he could have played this match.

Barcelona away (Champions League, R16, 2nd Leg), 3-1 defeat (lost 5-1 on aggregate), 16th March

For this game Monreal and Bellerin came back to Full Back, Koscielny replaced Mertesacker and Gabriel kept his place. This looks like the first choice back four that has played all season, with doubt around only the Mertesacker/Gabriel selection. In midfield, Coquelin dropped to the bench in favour of Flamini with Elneny.

This was clearly rotation, with Coquelin only recently returned (early) from a long injury. Ozil played 10 and Iwobi and Welbeck joined Sanchez in the 'front three'. The Iwobi and Welbeck selections looked like rotations at the time, but in hindsight look like first choice picks. This is interesting. Clearly some rotation took place in both the Watford and Barcelona games, but it looks like the Watford game took the brunt of it, not the Barcelona game.

Everton away (Premier League, game 30), 2-0 victory, 19th March

For the Everton game, the same team that played in Barcelona came out again, with the exception that Coquelin started instead of Flamini. This was starting to look like a first choice team. The team played well in Barcelona, albeit in a hopeless situation. The

IT'S HAPPENED AGAIN

same team played well again against Everton and achieved a very creditable 2-0 win.

Watford (Premier League, game 31), 4-0 victory, 2nd April

Now Wenger's choices were beginning to become clearer. With no game for another seven days, there was no need to rotate this time. Wenger picked exactly the same team that beat Everton. This suggests that the teams that played at Everton and Barcelona (Flamini excepted) were first choice teams. As we enter a period of seven games in six weeks, there will be very little need to rotate and we can look forward to seeing first choice teams for the rest of the season.

So what does it all mean?

If this analysis is correct, it raises some interesting questions about the Watford Cup tie. This game cost us our best remaining chance of silverware. Four rotated players is nearly half the outfield team. Did Wenger gamble here and make an error? He looked very upset after the match.

If he did gamble, was it for the benefit of the Barcelona game? It can't have been for the benefit of the Everton game because he played the same players who played in Barcelona again at Everton. If he was gambling in order to improve performance in the Nou Camp, did he really think he could win? Was he worried about the effect on morale (and negative fans) of a thrashing in the Nou Camp if he prioritised the Watford game and rotated players in Spain? Was he worried about damaging the prestige of the club if we were thrashed in Barcelona? In the end, we put up a reasonable show, but did we sacrifice the Watford Cup tie in order to do so; and if we did, was it worth it?

The changes to the team pose a few more interesting questions:

- Can Welbeck maintain his selection as first choice Centre Forward for the rest of the season? Both Walcott and Giroud have occupied this position at various times in the season, but neither have been able to sustain performance. What implications does this have for the question of whether or not we need to buy a new Centre Forward over the summer?
- Can Elneny cement his place in midfield? He seems to be preferred to Ramsey in this position. What happens when Wilshere (don't giggle) and Cazorla return? Can he hold them off?
- Is Iwobi going to keep his place? At the moment it seems to work with him on the left and Sanchez on the right. Will this change when Ramsey returns? Ramsey surely can't play on the left, and Iwobi looks undroppable on form. Sanchez looks like he is finally getting back to form playing on the right and surely he can't be dropped?
- Is the repositioning of Sanchez, to the right, permanent or just an experiment to accommodate Iwobi? Sanchez looks rejuvenated by the change
- Will Gabriel continue to be selected ahead of Mertesacker? Gabriel appeared to be ahead earlier in the season, but then Mertesacker looked to return to first choice after Gabriel's dismissal against Chelsea. Gabriel seems to have been preferred since Mertesacker's dismissal against Chelsea, but has looked unconvincing at times. He might be the long-term answer in this position, but he still needs to prove the point
- Will Cech get his place back? I presume he will, but Ospina has done well and Cech was on the bench for the Watford game, so clearly fit. I presume that Cech was 'fit enough for the bench', but we can't be sure about this. Wenger sometimes likes to leave a successful team unchanged, and with only seven games in six weeks for the rest of the season, there is no need to rotate

IT'S HAPPENED AGAIN

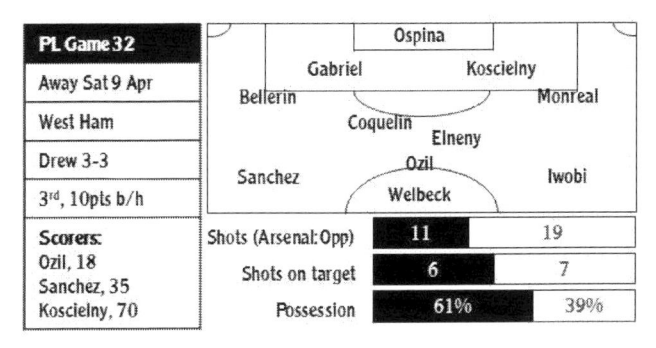

PL Game 32	
Away Sat 9 Apr	
West Ham	
Drew 3-3	
3rd, 10pts b/h	
Scorers: Ozil, 18; Sanchez, 35; Koscielny, 70	

Formation: Ospina; Bellerin, Gabriel, Koscielny, Monreal; Coquelin, Elneny; Sanchez, Ozil, Iwobi; Welbeck

	Arsenal	Opp
Shots	11	19
Shots on target	6	7
Possession	61%	39%

After we went 2-0 up, hope was really starting to glimmer. The chase for the title was almost back on. But it was all a trick; we conceded two quick goals before half-time. Both were scored by Andy Carroll, a huge, perpetually injured striker. For a 20 minute spell either side of half time, Carroll was unplayable (for our defence at least), and he reminded us why back in 2011, Liverpool paid £35m for him on the same day they bought Luis Suarez for £20m. Carroll completed his hat-trick just after half time. West Ham ran out of steam a bit after that and we scored a well worked equaliser. In the end it was a classic Premier League game with examples of breath-taking skill, teamwork and power from both teams. If it hadn't spelt the death knell of our title hopes, I might even have enjoyed the game on its merits!

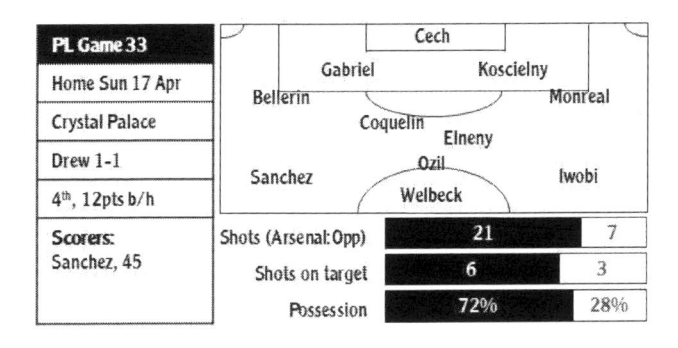

PL Game 33	
Home Sun 17 Apr	
Crystal Palace	
Drew 1-1	
4th, 12pts b/h	
Scorers: Sanchez, 45	

Formation: Cech; Bellerin, Gabriel, Koscielny, Monreal; Coquelin, Elneny; Sanchez, Ozil, Iwobi; Welbeck

	Arsenal	Opp
Shots	21	7
Shots on target	6	3
Possession	72%	28%

We totally dominated this match, but couldn't find the second goal we needed to put the game to bed. In such circumstances, you are always vulnerable to a well taken goal, and this is exactly what we got in the 82nd minute, with a well taken finish from Palace's Bolasie. Suddenly, even Champions League qualification is looking in doubt.

The team was unchanged, except for the return of Cech in place of Ospina. Wenger got some criticism for playing Ospina in the last game with Cech on the subs bench. This latest team is starting to look less impressive now after its initial triumphs over Everton and Watford.

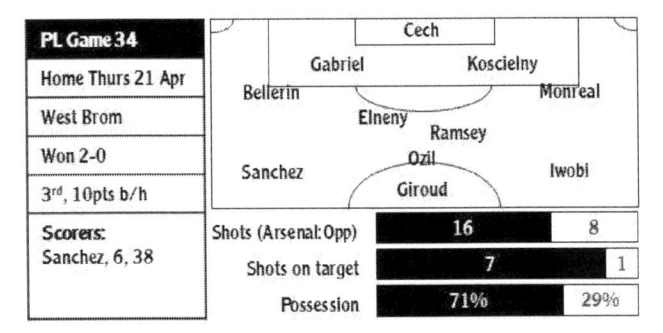

PL Game 34		
Home Thurs 21 Apr		
West Brom		
Won 2-0		
3rd, 10pts b/h		
Scorers: Sanchez, 6, 38	Shots (Arsenal:Opp)	16 / 8
	Shots on target	7 / 1
	Possession	71% / 29%

Formation:
- Cech
- Gabriel, Koscielny
- Bellerin, Monreal
- Elneny, Ramsey
- Sanchez, Ozil, Iwobi
- Giroud

This is as close to an unhappy win as you can really get. Although sold out, The Emirates was shockingly empty. This was maybe more about apathy on a Thursday night than the 'fan protest' alleged by the media. Certainly latecomers were also partly responsible; the stadium did fill up a bit as the evening progressed. However, the number of empty seats was greater than I have ever seen for a League game at the Ems.

Wenger made some changes. This was the last week in the season with more than one game. Were we seeing some rotation, or did the changes reflect Wenger's frustration with the last two games? Mertesacker came in for Gabriel, who has really failed to grab his chance during an extended run in the team. Giroud got a chance, replacing Welbeck up front. Ramsey came back into

IT'S HAPPENED AGAIN

the team, with Coquelin rather than Elneny making way. Even if this was a rotation, this reflects both how well Elneny has done, and how disappointing Coquelin has been since his return from injury. Coquelin hasn't done much wrong (red card against Spurs excepted), but hasn't looked like the player who dominated midfield with his athleticism before his injury.

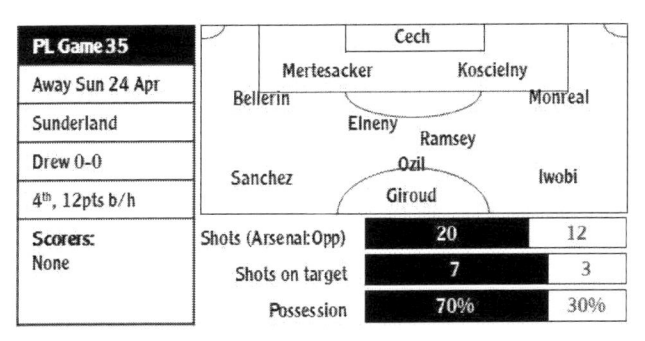

PL Game 35			
Away Sun 24 Apr	\multicolumn{3}{l	}{Cech}
Sunderland	\multicolumn{3}{l	}{Mertesacker Koscielny}
Drew 0-0	\multicolumn{3}{l	}{Bellerin Monreal}
4th, 12pts b/h	\multicolumn{3}{l	}{Elneny Ramsey}
Scorers:	\multicolumn{3}{l	}{Sanchez Ozil Iwobi}
None	\multicolumn{3}{l	}{Giroud}
	Shots (Arsenal:Opp)	20	12
	Shots on target	7	3
	Possession	70%	30%

A sorry game that was as poor as the score line suggests. This was the match that finally ended our mathematical chance of winning. With Leicester twelve points ahead of us after match day 35, even a win wouldn't have done us any good. Funnily enough, match 35 looked like the end for Tottenham too. They drew with West Brom at home (hitting the woodwork three times), to leave them seven points behind Leicester with three games to go. St Totteringham's day still looks a forlorn hope though, with Spurs five points ahead of us. Indeed we are now more worried about staying in the top four.

Wenger surprisingly started the same team as the West Brom game. So it looks like Welbeck and Gabriel were genuinely dropped, not rotated. Similarly it seems that the disappointing Coquelin has genuinely lost his place to Ramsey. What a sad situation for the player that did so incredibly well last season.

CHAPTER FORTY
MEMORIES OF A TRUE TRAGEDY

April 29th 2016, shortly following the findings of the second inquests into the Hillsborough deaths, on 26th April 2016. The verdict was 'unlawful killing' and many of the victims' families saw this as final vindication of a 27 year battle for justice against 'the establishment'; and in particular the Police, who had dishonestly tried to evade their own guilt for the disaster by blaming others, including the dead

The world of football is full of talk of 'the good of the game' and other meaningless epithets. Football is mostly, however, what economists describe as a 'zero sum game'. Every winner creates a loser. If you get together a group of Arsenal devotees and a group of Tottenham devotees and put them in a room, they will tend to focus on their differences rather than the numerous things that they have in common. It's a curious thing to overhear a conversation between rival fans. An undertone of teasing contempt is never far away.

As a result, it is not really true to speak of a 'community' of football supporters. It is not often that football fans can find it in their hearts to admire each other. However, I like to think that most of us have the humanity to empathise with - and admire - the Liverpool fans and the way they have handled the tragedy of Hillsborough.

The Liverpool supporters were the victims of one of the most shameful attempted Police cover-ups the nation has ever witnessed. The actions of the South Yorkshire Police would have been outrageous in a banana republic. In a democratic nation, they are unforgivable. I can understand people who make mistakes in their professional lives, even if those mistakes have terrible consequences. But the attempt to cover it up and blame

IT'S HAPPENED AGAIN

the Liverpool supporters can only be seen as criminal and I hope the perpetrators feel the full force of British justice, even at this late stage.

The survivors and their families, despite the terrible effects of trauma, maintained a dignified, persistent, civilised and noble campaign to reveal the truth. The finding of 'unlawful killing' at the inquest this week was the final vindication of that battle. I take my hat off to each and every person involved. The 96 people who lost their lives were fans who went to a football match to cheer on their team. It was a different world to the football of today, a world in which something as elegant, efficient and modern as the Emirates Stadium couldn't even be imagined.

As a teenager in the 1980s I stood on the bleak North Bank terraces of Highbury with my schoolmates. Those terraces were similar to the Hillsborough terraces in many ways (although, to their eternal credit, the Arsenal directors refused to install fences between the terraces and the pitch). Those games were amongst the most memorably thrilling experiences of my young life. They are experiences which future generations will never share.

When the crowd surged forward, you went forward, carried in a wave of irresistible humanity. You were acutely conscious that if you lost your footing (on the poorly surfaced concrete, complete with the occasional steps that gave the terraces their name), you were dead. The people behind you were as helpless as you were, and couldn't stop surging forward any more than you could. If you fell to the floor you would be mercilessly trampled.

Trying to stay on your feet, whilst having no idea what direction you are going to move next, is a disconcerting experience. Of course, most of the time falling was not an option, because we were too tightly packed. But every now and then, fleeting holes would open up in the swirling crowd, a bit like an eddy in a swollen river. If you were on the edge of such a gap, falling suddenly became a real possibility and you needed to keep your wits about you.

TIM CHARLESWORTH

As the crowd surged, it would be compressed and breathing would become momentarily impossible, but the moment would soon pass and the sensation just added to the thrill. The overall effect was a thrilling one for teenage boys like me and my friends. The excitement of football was combined with the raw masculinity of the terrace community and its inherent dangers.

Deaths on football terraces were not unknown, but they were almost always as a result of people falling and being trampled. As far as I can recall, we never seriously considered the possibility of being crushed to death whilst still standing. The real risk of trampling accidents was on the way in and out of the ground. When a crowd was moving purposefully, such as at the beginning or end of a match, sudden gaps could open, allowing one to fall to the ground if tripped or pushed. The entry and exits were genuine moments of danger, especially when cramped staircases or tunnels were added into the mix.

I suspect the Liverpool fans at Hillsborough felt much the same. Once they were in the ground, they probably felt safe. The story is sometimes told that the problem started as a result of a Peter Beardsley shot striking the bar. It was perfectly normal for a surge to accompany such an event. As the victims felt the first pressure of the crush which would kill them, they probably weren't overly concerned and may not even have been particularly distracted from watching the game. As the problem persisted, they would presumably have become aware that this was not a normal incident.

The Police have come in for much criticism for the way that they failed to respond to the danger; it is a frequent complaint of the fans there that day that the Police ignored the tragedy developing around them. I think the Police were guilty of many failings that day, but the callousness of the pitch side officers, in the face of this disaster, is curiously understandable. The Police would have been just as accustomed to crushes on football terraces as fans were. They were probably no more sensitive to the real risk of death or injury from crushes than the fans.

IT'S HAPPENED AGAIN

Before Hillsborough, such things were virtually unheard of during a match. Whilst it quickly became clear to fans that this was not an ordinary crush, this turn of events would have been less obvious to the attending Police officers. It isn't possible to see that someone is not breathing just by looking at them, especially not in the context of a noisy, packed football stadium.

And so, a tragedy of unimaginable proportions unfolded. As a father of two girls, I will be forever haunted by the idea of Trevor Hicks watching, from one of the lateral stands, the disaster that killed his two beautiful daughters.

And after Hillsborough, the season continued.

After a break of 21 days, Liverpool played football again. They won the replay of the fateful FA Cup Semi Final, and fittingly went on to win the FA Cup Final, during which the Everton fans showed a touching solidarity with their opponents.

In the League Liverpool, the leviathans of the English game, put together a fabulous run, slowly reeling in the runaway leaders, George Graham's young Arsenal team. Because of the delay to the League fixtures resulting from the Hillsborough disaster, Liverpool's final league game - to seal the double - was against Arsenal and was played after the FA Cup Final. It had been obvious for a while that the outcome of the League would hinge on this fixture and my friends and I planned to go. As the game approached, Liverpool seemed like a dark, distant and dangerous place to visit on a late Friday night. Our courage was further dampened by the fact that we felt that this was mission impossible. We resolved [sighs] to watch it on television. Interestingly, even at this point, the danger of being crushed to death on a football terrace didn't play any part in our decision.

For many of us the moment of Michael Thomas' winning goal is our dearest footballing memory. At the time, I thought of nothing but the pure joy it bought us. I was a young man consumed by the narcissism of teenagehood. My mind was full of the sense of a title thrown away and then rescued at the very last moment. Our hopes were strangled, only to be reborn, and our 18 year wait for a title was ended (I was 16 at the time).

But when I look back, with the wisdom of years and the bitter tinge of grey hair, I reflect more and more on the vanquished. The numbing disappointment that the Liverpool fans must have felt was, at once, both cruel and irrelevant. It wasn't even the worst thing that happened to them that season and yet it seems pitiless to have heaped another source of sadness on to the Liverpool fans that day. This was a time when the 'double' still held legendary status. 96 fans would have gone to Hillsborough dreaming of another step towards the Liverpool double of 1989. I can't help but feel sad that those dreams were not posthumously realised, snatched away in a single moment*.

Despite all our tribal differences, there will always be a place in my heart for the lost Liverpool 96. And in that sense, at least, they never will walk alone.

---

*Interestingly, the iconic baseball team, the New York Yankees suffered a similar fate to Liverpool in the 2001 World Series, following the 9/11 attacks. Many baseball fans consider this the greatest World Series of all time. After a freakish run to the final, with numerous last minute heroic wins, the Yankees seemed destined to be World Champions for an incredible fourth consecutive year. It would have been a fitting sporting tribute to the thousands of murdered New Yorkers. Like 1989, the baseball season had been postponed to accommodate a period of mourning, so was finishing late. With the series tied at 3-3, the Yankees led 2-1 late in the seventh, deciding match. They brought on Mariano Rivera, the greatest 'closing pitcher' of all time. Rivera had to close out two innings. He predictably closed out the first, but in the bottom of the ninth and final innings, with national emotional pandemonium about to break out, the unthinkable happened. Rivera conceded two runs to lose 3-2. If you aren't a baseball fan and hadn't followed Rivera's career, it is difficult to understand what a bizarre occurrence this was. It was the equivalent of a Gus Caesar clean sheet or an Alan Hansen hat-trick of own goals. Just like Michael Thomas' goal, you could never get away with making this stuff up. Like Liverpool, the Yankees have never recovered their dominance of the sport

IT'S HAPPENED AGAIN

JUSTICE FOR THE 96

This article was written in April 2016, but not published at the time

The recent findings of 'unlawful killing' in the Hillsborough case has brought the events of April 1989 to our minds once again.

A question that has often been asked is: 'Is it really worth it?' Enormous sums (at least tens of millions) of public money and legal resources have been tied up in this two year inquest, which concerns events of 27 years ago. Many of the people involved and affected have died in the intervening period. Not a single life has been saved by the inquest. The 96 are still dead, the families still bereaved. We have learnt a little about how the world worked 27 years ago, but does this really get us anywhere?

It's a good question, and one which deserves a thorough answer. My answer is "yes, it is worth it". In order to explain why, I hope you will indulge me as I take a little trip down memory lane to the late 1980s.

As a 15 year old, I was inquisitive, persistent, headstrong and argumentative with a strong sense of natural justice. Naturally, it was suggested that I might make a good barrister, and it sounded like an interesting idea to me.

A friend of my parents', who was then a QC and is now a judge, took me to Marylebone Magistrates Court to see young barristers in action. I watched the trial of a young man who was being prosecuted for assaulting a Police officer, a serious offence. Two Police officers had arrested him when they found him urinating in public, a little the worse for drink. They had put him in the back of a van and driven him away. That much was agreed. What happened next was disputed. The Police officers said that the defendant had hit one of them. The defendant said that he had been thrown into one of them as the van went round the corner and/or hit a bump. There were no serious injuries to the Police officer, and the case very much turned on the word of the Police officers against that of the (admittedly tipsy) defendant.

The defence barrister seemed to me to have done a good job. He got the Police officers to admit that they had got together to write their notes, several hours after the incident, with a particular eye to consistency. This undermined the prosecution, who made a great play on the fact that the two officers recalled exactly the same facts (of course they did, they wrote it together, knowing that their notes would be evidence in a court case).

Now, this was a tricky case. The officers seemed to have no good explanation as to why the defendant would hit them. He was way past the point of being able to meaningfully resist arrest, and appeared to have nothing to gain by his actions. The possible explanations for the scuffle put forward by the defence barrister seemed plausible (if a little unlikely). At the very least, it seemed possible that some sort of misunderstanding had led to a scuffle. At worst, I suspected the Police officers had roughed the defendant up, or deliberately provoked him. I expected the magistrate to retire and consider the case in depth in his chambers. With the naivety of youth, I expected him to question himself on the subject of 'reasonable doubt'.

Instead, the moment the defence barrister finished his last sentence, the magistrate said 'I have no hesitation in finding you guilty. We will reconvene in ten days for sentencing'

I was shocked and devastated. The law died for me that day, and I lost all interest in pursuing a career in it.

What really shocked me was that the Police officers got away with it. I'm not sure if they got away with a bit of malpractice in recording evidence, or they got away with outright lies. But the lesson they would have walked away with was that it was perfectly acceptable for them to 'collaborate' when writing their account of an incident; that it was perfectly OK for them to write notes designed to secure a conviction, rather than to describe what happened. Worst of all, the message was that the magistrate would believe whatever they said, regardless of the quality of their evidence. They knew that in future, they could concoct any story they liked, regardless of truth, and that the

IT'S HAPPENED AGAIN

magistrate presiding that day (and others I suspect) would believe them without question.

Funnily enough, I can even tell you the date of this case, because I remember watching Sandy Lyle win the US Masters Golf the night before. It was 11th April 1988, 369 days before the Hillsborough disaster. The late 80s were a strange time in Britain. We were living in a period where the government had recently taken on the miners and won. The Police had been instrumental in that victory, and the government was grateful. The government had been re-elected in 1983 on a 'law and order' ticket (and nothing makes governments grateful like a re-election)*. British Police had put their safety on the line dealing with rioting youths in the early 1980s (one of them having been killed during the Tottenham riots). Throughout the 1980s, their lives were under a very real threat, as they were considered a legitimate military target by Northern Irish republicans. There were very good reasons why 'the establishment' was keen to defend the Police, and a socially authoritarian, self-confident government was fully behind them.

But I wonder if the Police began to take advantage of this situation. After all, it is only human to succumb to temptation.

---

* For the historically minded amongst you, Margaret Thatcher was the first Prime Minister since Lord Liverpool to win three consecutive elections. Lord Liverpool's government presided over the Peterloo massacre. At St Peter's Field in 1819, perhaps 60,000 people gathered to protest in favour of parliamentary reform. The local Manchester magistrates had summoned the assistance of the local mounted militia (this was before the invention of the Police). In order to arrest the leader of the protest, the militia cavalry charged the peaceful demonstration with sabres drawn. The massed crowd could not escape. 11 people died from trampling and sabre wounds. Perhaps 500 were wounded. The magistrates had clearly acted unwisely, but Lord Liverpool's government, afraid of a loss of public order, backed them to the hilt. The incident lived long in the public consciousness. It led to the founding of the Manchester Guardian (now the Guardian newspaper), and indirectly to the parliamentary reforms of 1832 that finally abolished the rotten boroughs

TIM CHARLESWORTH

Constantly bolstered by magistrates like the one I saw, did the Police begin to believe they were above the law?

It was a time when 'the establishment' did everything it could to support the Police, a time when northern working class people, like miners, were seen as a problem, maybe even as the enemy. It was a time when it was possible for a Police force to negligently oversee the deaths of 96 northern football fans, then to cover up their mistakes and blame the northern working class people for causing the disaster. It was a time when the establishment would believe the story and felt it had a duty to do everything it could to support the Police.

In my one little case at Marylebone magistrates, I saw several things that seemed to resurface in the way that the Police handled the Hillsborough disaster. The slapdash attitude to recording evidence; the acceptability of altering the notes of individual officers to support a particular version of events; the lack of interest in accurately and dispassionately recording events; the vilification of a young working class man and the implication that sober officers should always be believed over people who had consumed alcohol.

It seems to me that we can learn a number of priceless lessons from the Hillsborough enquiry, which have a wide application:

- The Police are not always right
- Police officers, regardless of seniority, are not always to be trusted. Unfortunately, I suspect that this is still partly true today
- It will never be acceptable to treat human beings like animals, at any place, at any time, for any reason
- It is not acceptable for any institution to vilify people who are vulnerable. Being a 'scouser' is no more acceptable as a basis for discrimination than race, religion, way of speaking, social class, wealth, gender, sexuality or age
- The vast majority of football fans in the late 1980s were not violent thugs

IT'S HAPPENED AGAIN

I hope that everyone involved in our policing and legal system will take note and strive to ensure that the hideous mistakes made in the aftermath of this disaster will never be repeated.

In the words of the Arsenal Independent Supporters Association (AISA) *'congratulations to the Hillsborough Family Support Group who, after 27 years of campaigning, have finally achieved some measure of justice for 'the 96''*. In the words of Trevor Hicks (father of Vicki and Sarah, killed in the crush) *'I think if anyone is a winner today it's society at large in that, no matter who you are, how big you are, or where you are in your organization, the public will come after you if you do anything wrong'*.

From me, thank you, you have made the world a better place for my children to grow up in. Not only is all the effort, expense and anguish that has gone into the Hillsborough inquest 'worth it', it's worth it ten times over. A blow has been struck for justice. My personal hope is that the story is not quite finished yet. Tampering with evidence is a criminal offence, and I would like to see Police officers who tampered with the evidence after Hillsborough prosecuted for it.

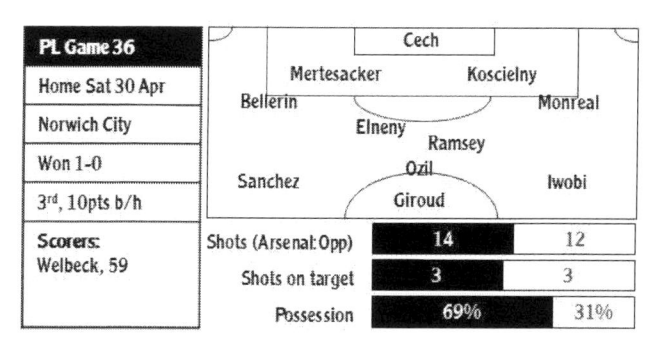

PL Game 36	
Home Sat 30 Apr	
Norwich City	
Won 1-0	
3rd, 10pts b/h	
Scorers: Welbeck, 59	

Lineup: Cech; Bellerin, Mertesacker, Koscielny, Monreal; Elneny, Ramsey; Sanchez, Özil, Iwobi; Giroud

	Arsenal	Opp
Shots	14	12
Shots on target	3	3
Possession	69%	31%

This was a match remarkable for politics rather than football. Two supporters groups, REDAction and The Black Scarf Movement, organised a protest against Wenger and the Board.

TIM CHARLESWORTH

They asked people to hold up pieces of paper that said: 'Time for change, Arsenal is stale, Fresh approach needed' after 12 minutes, signifying the number of years since we have won the League title. This is a peculiarly English idea of a protest. Arsène is a Frenchman and in France people man the barricades, set fire to things and conduct mass beheadings when they are mildly irritated. In the 1990s, I remember French farmers blockading Calais and setting fire to lorry loads of (live) sheep in protest at the low price of lamb. I imagine Arsène wasn't overly petrified by the prospect of having some bits of paper adorned with a firm, but essentially polite message, waved in his general direction.

His press conference the day before the match however, suggested he was rattled. He started talking about how difficult it is to perform at home in front of a hostile crowd (true, but was this really the moment to make the point?). He continued with the observation that Arsenal had done well enough away from home to win the League, but home form had let us down. This was as close as you might reasonably get to blaming your fans for your failures, and didn't seem like a hugely wise comment.

As it happened, the protest rather backfired. The AKB faction retaliated to a small number of protest papers, with a rather rousing rendition of 'There's only one Arsène Wenger', a tune not heard in the Emirates for many a long year. It is my favourite Arsenal song and bought a tear to my eye. My eldest daughter was born shortly after the Invincibles season, and I used to sing 'there's only one Arsène Wenger' to her as a lullaby when she was a baby. She is ten now, and has no interest in Arsenal or football, but she still occasionally demands that I sing her 'one Arsène Wenger' at bedtime. Happy days. I should point out that a quick search on social networking site, LinkedIn, reveals there to be not one, but at least twelve, Arsène Wengers.

Overall, the protest was a bit of a triumph for AKBs like me. It actually demonstrated how much affection for Wenger remains and it all fell a bit flat for the WOB protesters. Overall I was reminded of the 70s and 80s, when football was riddled with

IT'S HAPPENED AGAIN

hooligans. Arsenal fans weren't very good at being hooligans. In times of stress, adrenalin rises in anticipation of the 'fight or flight' moment. Arsenal fans (me included) generally chose flight in this situation and were not very widely feared. Happily, modern fans have all but abandoned hooliganism, but can still be fairly frightening when in protest mode. Being protested at by Arsenal fans however, is a bit like being savaged by a Panda. One Man U wag summed up the mood beautifully on Twitter: "Kicking off in the stands at Arsenal. Brioche and mini vol-au-vents flying everywhere."

On the pitch, this was a game with low billing. Most eyes were elsewhere, with Leicester at Man U and Tottenham at Chelsea. Another exciting conclusion to a League season in which we were not involved! The Arsenal players looked suitably disinterested. It is not often that we see professional footballers jumping out of tackles, but we saw it here for the second game in succession (Koscielny of all people). Norwich were fighting for their Premier League lives and had the better of the chances. We won thanks to a well taken Welbeck goal; fears of finishing outside the top four easing a little. The win flattered us, but this is poor compensation for the many matches we have dominated but lost this season.

The team was unchanged again, amidst general incredulity that Giroud was once more starting ahead of Welbeck. Gabriel came on for Mertesacker after a hamstring strain. Iwobi looked tired and was replaced early by Welbeck.

LEICESTER ARE CHAMPIONS!!!
11th May 2016

What a genuinely fantastical outcome this is. I remarked at the beginning of this book that each season was an incredible story. And this Leicester tale is one that will be told and retold for decades to come. This is genuinely heart-warming, unless of course you realise that you have spent a year of your life writing a book about the right season, but the wrong team! Odds of 5,000:1 were widely available at the start of the season, with Leicester's newly appointed Manager, Claudio Ranieri, the favourite to be first Manager sacked.

Arsenal fans rather enjoyed the final instalment. Tottenham were away to Chelsea, needing a win to keep their mathematical chances of the title alive. After going 2-0 up, Spurs disintegrated. They set a Premier League record with nine booked players. It is a miracle that none of them were sent off. (In the end only Moussa Dembele really suffered, with a six game retrospective ban for eye gouging). Chelsea equalised in the last ten minutes and Spurs generally looked like they might cry. The truth is, however, that (whisper it) Tottenham are a good team and will likely challenge again next season.

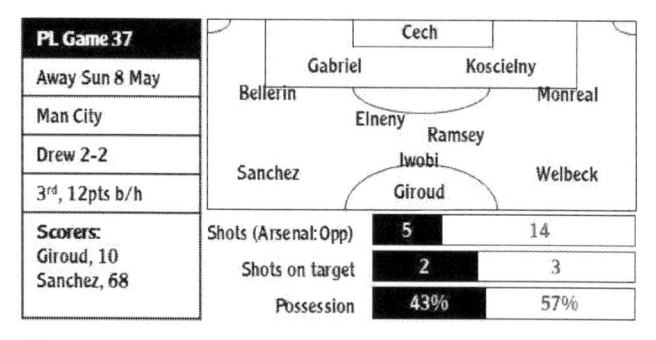

PL Game 37		
Away Sun 8 May		
Man City		
Drew 2-2		
3rd, 12pts b/h		
Scorers: Giroud, 10 Sanchez, 68		

Formation: Cech; Bellerin, Gabriel, Koscielny, Monreal; Elneny, Ramsey; Sanchez, Iwobi, Welbeck; Giroud

	Arsenal	Opp
Shots	5	14
Shots on target	2	3
Possession	43%	57%

This was remarkable as a proper game of football amidst the 'end-of-season' dross that has been served up in recent weeks. Both teams looked lively and competitive. Man City were coming off a narrow defeat to Real Madrid in the Champions League Semi Final the previous Wednesday. The fixture had, for a long time, looked like a potential title decider, but in the event was effectively a third place play off. The added spice was that if Man City failed to win, Man U would have a chance to take their place in the top four. It was Manuel Pellegrini's final home game as Man City Manager. Arsenal needed a point to keep their destiny

IT'S HAPPENED AGAIN

in their own hands and a win to draw level on points with Tottenham (Spurs having vastly superior goal difference).

Man City came out of the blocks like a team angered by its loss to Real Madrid. Arsenal looked in difficulty from the kick-off and Aguero duly scored after eight minutes. Man City had the better of the game overall, but Arsenal twice came from behind, showing a lot of character and resolve.

Ozil was out with a minor injury so Iwobi played at no. 10 and Welbeck moved to the right wing with Alexis on the left. Welbeck pulled out of a fairly innocuous challenge with a limp and it looks like a knee injury that may keep him out of Euro 16. If so, it's a cruel injury to a player who has recently missed a year of football.[*] He was a likely starter for England. Jack Wilshere came on to replace him and reminded us all of what we have been missing from this prodigiously talented 24 year old. Iwobi moved to the left to accommodate Wilshere in the middle and Sanchez moved to the right.

The result means that Arsenal could still finish fifth, but only if we lose the final game. A draw will be enough to secure third place and avoid the dreaded Champions League play-off fixture.

---

[*] It turned out that this was a serious injury that is likely to keep him out for most of the following season too

CHAPTER FORTY ONE
AND SO IT ENDS

FOOTBALL AS OPERA, TEARS ALL ROUND
May 11th 2016

Last weekend provided us with the moment that posterity might deem to be the iconic one of the season. Leicester's triumph is remarkable in so many ways, but it's not easy to pick an on-pitch moment that sums it all up. There have been a few last minute dramatic goals and some lovely moments of skill.

The most memorable goal however, is probably Eden Hazard's strike against Tottenham that sealed the title for Leicester. Given that no Leicester players were on the pitch, this probably won't cut it as posterity's special moment in the season. Leicester's win was a special achievement in a special season. It needs a magic moment to define the spirit of it all, something like Michael Thomas' goal or Sergio Aguero's goal for City in 2012.

On Saturday, Leicester gave us that defining moment. It was Leicester's final home game of the season. The flag-waving crowd was in party mood. The stadium was packed long before kick-off, on a perfect sunny day, the like of which only an English spring can produce. Football is characterised by disappointment and failure. Most fans don't win the League, or indeed any other trophy. In most seasons, three (maximum) sets of fans will experience the joy of a trophy, and three more will experience the crushing pain of relegation. For the rest, it's the purgatory of midtabledom. We all understand disappointment and we can all relate to teams like Leicester, whose fans are doomed to mostly expect disappointment with very little prospect of the joy side of the equation.

The Leicester fans' happiness was all the greater for its unexpected nature and it would be churlish not to share a little

IT'S HAPPENED AGAIN

of it. Not only had they won, but they had been spared the nerve-shredding experience of a close finish. The heroism of it all was personified by 64 year-old Claudio Ranieri, the man who openly wept on the day that Leicester qualified for the Champions League.

It's worth pausing a little to reflect on Claudio's story. A second rate player, he started to make his mark on the game managing lower league teams in Italy in the late 80s, 30 years ago. He has managed in Spain, Italy, France and England, but never won a league title. And it's not as if he has never managed teams with a chance of winning league titles. The clubs he has managed include post-Abramovich Chelsea; Valencia; Roma; Inter Milan; Juventus and Monaco (during its silly money phase). After being sacked by Monaco in the summer of 2014, he entered the 'semi-retirement lounge' of international football with lowly Greece. They sacked him a few months later, after losing to the Faroe Islands! It was at this moment that Leicester, having had to sack their Manager amidst a minor scandal, turned to Ranieri. It was clearly a temporary 'safe hands' appointment, but it attracted widespread ridicule (mainly thanks to the Faroe Islands incident).

Expectations were low back in August, when Ranieri began the season as bookies' favourite to be the first Manager sacked, with his team 5,000-1 outsiders for the title. It is worth stepping back a moment and considering what 5,000-1 means. Arsenal were 32-1 to beat Liverpool by two goals in 1989. That victory was roughly 156 times more likely than Leicester's. Greece were 150-1 to win Euro 2004 and Buster Douglas was 42-1 to beat Mike Tyson in 1990.

Ever since Jose Mourinho took over from Ranieri at Chelsea, Mourinho has levelled a barrage of insults in Ranieri's direction, apparently designed to ensure that Ranieri got no credit for the title Chelsea won in 2004-5, less than a year after he left. The situation was worsened when Ranieri made a bit of a hash of taking over Mourinho's European Champion team at Inter.

TIM CHARLESWORTH

Mourinho laid in again. His verbal assaults have been characterised by the kind of bullying, hectoring tone that only Mourinho can really perfect. Ranieri has maintained a dignified silence in response. In the 2015-16 season, it was Mourinho who got the sack: he was succeeded as champion Manager by Ranieri. Some people are not sad at this twist of fate.

Ranieri behaved in a remarkably un-football-like, gentlemanly manner all season. He refused to criticise referees, even under the severest of provocation and never had an unpleasant word to say about any of his rivals (even Mourinho). He also steadfastly refused to consider the possibility of winning the Premier League, long after such a denial became absurd. He finally relented after Leicester had qualified for the Champions League; accepting that they were aiming to win. He didn't really have any choice. Because Leicester had already qualified for the Champions League, there was no point even playing their final fixtures unless they were trying to top the League!

On Saturday he stood beaming and besuited, silver hair glinting in the sunshine, hailed by his adoring crowd. Who could begrudge him this day? Next to him stood his friend, opera star Andrea Bocelli, bedecked in a Leicester shirt. Ranieri gently raised one hand and the fomenting masses fell silent. Bocelli proceeded to belt out the Puccini aria - and football anthem - Nessun Dorma. I defy you to watch this scene without hairs raising on the back of your neck.

Of course, those of us of a certain vintage can never forget Nessun Dorma as the theme for the operatic World Cup, Italia '90. It is the scenery for Paul Gascoigne's tears, sadly prescient of the way that his talent would be frittered away from that moment on. It summons the sadness on Stuart Pearce's face after he missed his penalty. Pearce, a dead shot from the penalty spot, looked like a twelve year old boy ready to burst into tears, but desperately hanging on to his daddy's advice that 'big boys don't cry'. Diego Maradona, the ultimate flawed genius, sobbed openly. Through injury, he had dragged his team almost single-

IT'S HAPPENED AGAIN

handedly into the final, only to be defeated by a German penalty (something we can all relate to). Maradona's star would never shine again.

1990 represents a magical moment. Gazza's tears caught the attention of women and children. Football was bounding back into the mainstream after the dark violence-ridden 70s and 80s. The tragedies of Hillsborough and Valley Parade were behind us. The past was full of hooligans and quagmire pitches, the future full of all-seater stadia and the shiny Premier League era. It was the new spring, which led to the summertime in which English football is now basking. Initially, the choice of Nessun Dorma as a theme tune had seemed to be a crass attempt to overlay football with a touch of culture. As the tournament unfolded, it seemed the like perfect backdrop to the beautiful game.

But even if you are too young to remember Italia 90, the pure elegance of the music is undeniable. Nessun Dorma (None Shall Sleep) is a triumphant and defiant love aria from the Puccini Opera, Turandot. It is sung by the love-struck Prince who believes his love will conquer all, including the outright hostility of his heart's desire, Princess Turandot. It is a curiously good analogy for Leicester's season.

And all this reminded me of a truism. Football is opera. It's full of drama and triumph, rags to riches, triumphs against the odds and fallen giants. This season has even reminded us of Hillsborough, a genuine tragedy. It's a game of rich prima donnas, preening peacocks, Olivier Giroud's beard and Carlos Valderama's hair. The ever changing costumes are full of vibrancy and colour, designed to accentuate the elegant physiques of the 'players'. Only in football could the 1991-3 Arsenal away strip be revered for its artistic merit. Above all it's a game of song.

The sport's unofficial anthem, *'Abide With Me'*, celebrates the working class origins of the professional game. Up and down the land, football fans sing their hearts out, remembering fallen heroes like Rocky, the 96 and the victims of the Munch air disaster. We sing with wit; of Freddie's red hair; of 'boring Arsenal' and Patrick Vieira's country of birth. Above all, clubs throughout the nation proclaim their side as 'the greatest team the world has ever seen' when only one of them, at best, can be right. Football is truly operatic. Many thanks to Leicester and Ranieri for reminding us all of that fact.

My own abiding memory of the season will be our home game against Leicester. This was a cruel game for our opponents. It was game 26, and people were just beginning to wonder if top of the table Leicester really could do the impossible. Third placed Arsenal were the bookies' favourites for the title and so the biggest threat to the Leicester dream. We were emerging from a mid-season trough, caused largely by a string of injuries. If we could beat Leicester, we would close to within just two points and Leicester would clearly crumble.

I watched the game on a big screen, in a local pub with my seven year old twins. We sat next to a young couple in Leicester shirts. The whole thing was an emotional roller coaster. Leicester led through a dubious goal, and seemed to be closing the match out in the professional and efficient manner of champions, when they were the victims of a harsh red card. We grabbed the bull by the horns and inexorably pulled ourselves back into it.

Just when it looked like time would run out, Danny Welbeck scored that fabulous last-gasp winner. The pub (mostly Arsenal fans) erupted in joy. It was clearly the turning point. We were on the way to our first league title in 12 years. Oh the joy of it! Only it wasn't joy for everyone. My daughter, who is a far superior human being to me, grabbed hold of her leaping father and pointed towards the crestfallen young woman in the Leicester shirt whom she had befriended during the match. 'Why is she sad Daddy?' she asked.

The look on the Leicester fan's face told me everything. I had seen Michael Thomas and Alan Sunderland score their goals. I had watched Liam Brady, Mesut Ozil, Dennis Bergkamp and

IT'S HAPPENED AGAIN

Rocky play. I had seen Arsène Wenger's teams in their pomp; I had seen the Invincibles. I really wanted Arsenal to be champions, but I didn't need to see Arsenal win the title in 2015-16. She deserved to see Leicester win. She had the grace to smile at my daughter and to resist the urge to punch me in the face in return for my insincere commiserations, before she trudged forlornly away from the scene of raucous celebrations.

It has been a terrible season for us in many ways, with the frustration of the last decade threatening to bubble over, but I can't help smiling when I think how Leicester's triumph will have banished the inconsolable look she wore that day.

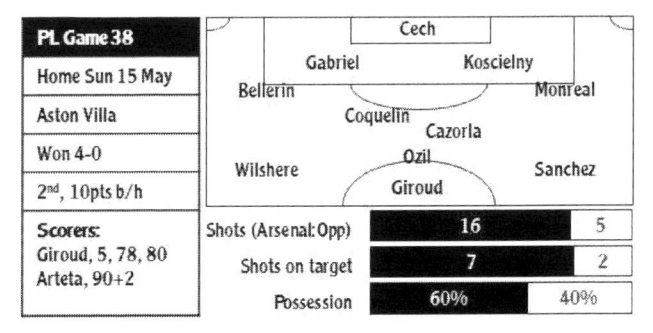

PL Game 38		
Home Sun 15 May		
Aston Villa		
Won 4-0		
2nd, 10pts b/h		
Scorers: Giroud, 5, 78, 80 Arteta, 90+2	Shots (Arsenal:Opp)	16 / 5
	Shots on target	7 / 2
	Possession	60% / 40%

Formation: Cech; Bellerín, Gabriel, Koscielny, Monreal; Coquelin, Cazorla; Wilshere, Özil, Sánchez; Giroud

We awoke with heavy hearts this morning. For 20 years in succession we had celebrated St Totteringham's Day, and it had been a lovely run, but all good things must come to an end. We suspected that Spurs-ribbing would never be quite as good again. By golly, Tottenham deserved their day though; their long-suffering supporters certainly did.

Tottenham only needed a draw against relegated Newcastle United in order to finish second and above Arsenal for the first time in 21 seasons. Surely even Spurs couldn't mess this one up!

The only real issue at stake was whether we would finish third or fourth. It is important to finish third, because then you qualify automatically for the Champions League group stage. If you finish fourth, you have two extra games to play right at the start of the following season, in order to qualify. These are high pressure games, which are a problem for teams like Arsenal who do not rotate well. Even worse, there is the possibility that you could lose, costing the club something like £30m in lost Champions League revenue.

We only needed a point to guarantee third, so we were pretty confident. Of course there was also an outside possibility that we could beat Spurs. Such an eventuality had seemed totally impossible a few weeks ago, but Spurs had worked hard to get in this position by scoring only one point from their previous three matches. Optimistic Arsenal fans couldn't quite forget the myriad of imaginative and absurd ways in which Spurs have conspired to be beaten by Arsenal in recent years. Even so, we could only beat them if they failed to even get a point at relegated Newcastle. Even Spurs couldn't mess this one up.

Aston Villa are comfortably the worst team in the league and so a home game against them is really the easiest fixture of the season. We all expected a comfortable victory, and there was no real prospect of us failing to get the point we needed. The team news was quite surprising. In the centre of midfield the Coquelin-Cazorla partnership was finally restored for the first time since November. This pairing had been so important to us over the last 18 months and we had really felt its loss. Nonetheless, it was a bit surprising to start these two. Coquelin had been dropped due to poor form, Elneny had done well and Cazorla had done nothing to prove his fitness.

Was this a signal for next season? Was it a last chance for the pair, particularly Cazorla, to prove their fitness for the upcoming European Championships? Wilshere starting on the right was also an odd decision, with Sanchez reverting to the left despite the success of his switch to the right. It seemed harsh on Ramsey and Iwobi to be dropped to the bench after good performances in a crucial match against Man City. Wilshere did well in that match, but if this wasn't the last game of the season,

IT'S HAPPENED AGAIN

I doubt he would have started. Was Wenger trying to help him get into the England squad for Euro 16? It all rather added to the air that Arsenal were not taking this match very seriously.

I have avoided giving blow by blow accounts of matches in this book, but now in the final match, I am going to break my own rule. This one is worth remembering. We scored early, through Giroud, and looked quite comfortable.

At 19 minutes, Wijnaldum scored for Newcastle. Suddenly we were interested. Newcastle is a funny place, with a raucous crowd, where odd things happen (a few years ago we drew 4-4 there, after leading 4-0). Spurs had plenty of time to come back, but you never know.

39 minutes into the game, Mitrovic scored again for Newcastle. Now we were really interested. Spurs only needed a draw, but they now had to score two goals away from home. That is not straightforward, even for a very good team (which Spurs undoubtedly are).

As the second half crept on, we were starting to get nervous. At the start of the day we had been relaxed because we knew we wouldn't catch Tottenham, but now the possibility was real. We started chewing our fingernails and suddenly we needed to win as well. Our one goal lead was looking a bit precarious. However dominant you are, it only takes one good shot to fell a team with a one goal lead and we had recently been the victim of just such an ambush at the hands of Crystal Palace in Premier League game 33.

At 60 minutes Lamela pulled one back for Tottenham and our hearts were really in our mouths. Now Tottenham had the momentum. And then on 67 minutes, Mitrovic was sent off for Newcastle. We all had a sinking feeling. In Premier League game 29 Tottenham had scored two goals within minutes of us being reduced to ten men. Now they had plenty of time to get the one goal they needed. It had been a nice little daydream, but now it was being snatched from us. Somehow, it's harder to have something taken away than never to have had it at all*.

And then something nice happened. Not many nice things have happened this season, so it's best to really enjoy them when they do:

1. 73 mins - Newcastle get a penalty - Wijnaldum scores (3-1). It's back on isn't it?
2. 78 mins - Giroud scores, 2-0 to Arsenal - Surely we are going to win now, so now it's just down to Newcastle and Spurs
3. 80 mins - Giroud scores, 3-0 to Arsenal - Now we really have won, and this is starting to become fun - a nice hat-trick for Giroud, a hard working lad who has been given a hard time recently
4. 84 mins - Aarons scores for Newcastle (4-1) - Surely Newcastle will win now? Surely it's in the bag?
5. 86 mins - Janmaat scores for Newcastle (5-1) - Oh happy day! St Totteringham is unexpectedly at the door. This is the ultimate humiliation for Spurs
6. 90 mins - Arteta scores for Arsenal[†] (4-0) - what a perfect end. A goal in his final appearance for Arsenal and his final

---

*'Loss aversion' is a scientifically observed phenomenon, first studied by Israeli-American psychologists, Daniel Kanheman and Amos Tversky. Their work resulted in a Nobel Prize being awarded to Kanheman in 2002. Unfortunately Tversky had died in the meantime, and Nobel prizes are only awarded to the living. In order to get one, you have to be clever and stay healthy for long enough for the impact of your work to be widely recognized. Kanheman and Tversky's work demonstrated that human beings really are irrationally programmed to excessively dislike losses. We prefer to avoid losses than to acquire gains (by a margin of approximately 2:1). Think about whether you would make more effort to get a £5 discount or to avoid a £5 fine

[†] I have stuck with official Premier League statistics throughout this book, but now, in the spirit of 'end-of term' carefree recklessness, I am making my own decision. Arteta scored this goal with a high finish over the keeper's head. The keeper got a fingertip to it and deflected the ball onto the underside of the bar. The ball came back off the bar, hit the falling keeper and went in. By some strange nonsense, this is classed as an own goal by the Premier League. Rubbish. If the keeper hadn't touched it, it would have gone in. He did well to get his

IT'S HAPPENED AGAIN

professional game. He has been a good, loyal captain and is widely respected. What a lovely end to a difficult season for him. This is serious icing on the cake! (we've already 'had it' and 'eaten it', in defiance of the old proverb)

7. Final whistles blow. Amazingly, unbelievably, wondrously, improbably, teasingly, exhaustingly, joyfully, absurdly, comically, beautifully, in the summer sun: IT'S HAPPENED AGAIN!

HAPPY ST TOTTERINGHAM'S DAY EVERYONE!!!

Thus endeth the season.

---

fingers to it, but he didn't prevent a goal by doing so. This goal was a lovely moment, and I won't have it blotted out by some bureaucrat following a silly set of rules. Arteta scored

TIM CHARLESWORTH

The final table

	Team	P	W	D	L	GF	GA	GD	PTS
1	Leicester City	38	23	12	3	68	36	32	81
2	**Arsenal**	**38**	**20**	**11**	**7**	**65**	**36**	**29**	**71**
3	Tottenham	38	19	13	6	69	35	34	70
4	Manchester City	38	19	9	10	71	41	30	66
5	Man United	38	19	9	10	49	35	14	66
6	Southampton	38	18	9	11	59	41	18	63
7	West Ham	38	16	14	8	65	51	14	62
8	Liverpool	38	16	12	10	63	50	13	60
9	Stoke City	38	14	9	15	41	55	-14	51
10	Chelsea	38	12	14	12	59	53	6	50
11	Everton	38	11	14	13	59	55	4	47
12	Swansea City	38	12	11	15	42	52	-10	47
13	Watford	38	12	9	17	40	50	-10	45
14	WBA	38	10	13	15	34	48	-14	43
15	Crystal Palace	38	11	9	18	39	51	-12	42
16	Bournemouth	38	11	9	18	45	67	-22	42
17	Sunderland	38	9	12	17	48	62	-14	39
18	Newcastle United	38	9	10	19	44	65	-21	37
19	Norwich City	38	9	7	22	39	67	-28	34
20	Aston Villa	38	3	8	27	27	76	-49	17

IT'S HAPPENED AGAIN

CHAPTER FORTY TWO
PATHETIC ARSENAL FANS!

May 18th 2016

What a day. The joy, the sunshine, the happiness, a fond farewell to loyal players; it was almost perfect. Nobody will put this season down as a great success, but at least it has given us one very happy memory and will now always have a little place in our hearts. It is another legendarily improbable way of extending the run of St Totteringham's Days. The fact this one gets us to 21 is extra special.

Robbie Savage described our joy as 'pathetic'. This was an interesting comment, because it rather missed the point and in doing so highlighted a difference between professional footballers and fans. If you look at it objectively, our joy was indeed 'pathetic'. The rivalry with Tottenham is a bit silly and in our hearts we all know that. However, football supporting is a leisure activity, the rivalry with Tottenham is a bit of fun and is part of our identity as Arsenal fans. Pochettino made the point before the Newcastle game that Tottenham's ambitions should be higher than just beating Arsenal. Apart from being very funny in hindsight, this is also true. Similarly, St Totteringham's Day is not a suitable target for the professionals who are employed by Arsenal FC to win football matches, but that doesn't mean us supporters can't enjoy it.

Part of the joy of being an Arsenal fan is that wherever I go in the world, I can strike up a conversation with an Arsenal fan I have never met before. The reason we can do so is that we have shared experiences, whether it's Michael Thomas' goal, the Invincibles or Lasagnegate. We are part of a community. It's a worldwide community and I love it. If that's pathetic, then so be it.

TIM CHARLESWORTH

We have been treated to a number of special 'last day' St Totteringhams in the past 21 years and this was one of the very best. What made it truly wonderful is that our differences were forgotten. It has been a difficult season in many ways. One of the most distressing things for me has been the discord amongst the Arsenal fan community. Our collective happiness gives me an excuse to write a piece that I have wanted to write all season, but until now have lacked the opportunity to do so.

This has felt like the most divided season I can remember amongst Arsenal supporters. It has perhaps lacked some of the bitterness of recent years, the 'spend some fucking money' chant of August 2013, or the shock of the Wenger confrontation at Stoke station in December 2014. What this season has had though, is a depth of division that I haven't seen before. In the second half of 2015-16, particularly following the Man U defeat, we split into two apparently irreconcilable factions - the Arsène Knows Best (AKB) and the Wenger Out Brigade (WOB) - and fans are really starting to identify strongly as one or another (I should declare myself an AKB in the interests of integrity). As attitudes hardened, it began to feel a bit like the Montagues and the Capulets.

I'd like to make an observation about the WOB, which I know may cause offence, so I will try to do it politely. I think it is generally true that the WOB tend to be younger and perhaps more recent fans, whilst the AKB tend to be older fans who remember the pre-Arsène period. This is not universally true; some very long-standing fans are in the WOB and some younger fans are AKBs, but as a generalisation, I believe it is valid. This has led to some fairly unpleasant accusations that the WOB are 'plastic fans'. This is obviously highly offensive, as many in the WOB camp are devoted fans who believe their position is in the best interests of our great club.

We would do well to remember that we were all new fans at some point. If you became a fan because your father was a fan, of course he would have been a new fan at some point (or

IT'S HAPPENED AGAIN

perhaps his father was). I don't think we can claim any special status if we support Arsenal because we were, or are, Islington residents. The club was originally based in Woolwich and the fans from south of the river may have had negative feelings about the Jonny-come-lately Islington people who started following the club after the 1913 move. Personally speaking, I am a first generation fan, converted when I watched Alan Sunderland score the winner in the 1979 Cup Final as a six-year-old (see Before We Get Started). My father was not a supporter and I have never lived in north London. Many will have joined us during other successes, such as the double team of 71. Probably the largest section of our support descends from people who started following Arsenal during the astonishingly successful 1930's era.

The truth is that success attracts supporters. That is why we have more supporters than Barnet, or Tottenham. We were all 'glory hunters' at some point and it is unfair to criticise people for this. I have lost count of the number of current professionals who say they want to play for Arsenal. The main reason for this is that people who are professional footballers tend to be in their mid-20s and therefore grew up watching Arsenal teams with Vieira, Bergkamp, Pires and Henry in them. Children, in particular, are influenced by success. Lots of the children of 15 years ago are, not surprisingly, now adult Arsenal supporters.

The arguments and insinuations about who is a 'proper fan' remind me of the immigration debate in Britain. I always think that prejudice against immigrants is particularly daft, because we are all immigrants. 10,000 years ago, no humans lived in Britain, so we are all descended from immigrants. Britain has been populated and repopulated in successive waves. Below is a list of those waves, highlighting only the most significant:

- The original **hunter gatherer immigrants** who populated Britain 10,000 years ago (Britain was populated and then abandoned by a series of such immigrants over a period of 40,000 years)

- Around 4,500 BC, **farmers** came to Britain and the population increased substantially. The resulting Neolithic population built Stonehenge, amongst other things
- The **Beaker people** arrived around 2,500 BC, bringing metalworking with them
- The **Celts**. This mysterious language group seems to have arrived in Britain about 800 BC, bringing skill with iron
- The **Romans** (43 AD). Very few actual Romans came to Britain. But Britain became part of the Roman Empire and - much like other Roman provinces - people became more mobile than ever before. This 'mobility' was probably not replicated until the twentieth century. People came to Britain from all over the Roman world in this period. Some even stayed.
- The **Anglo-Saxons**. The details of this immigration (c. 410-550 AD) are murky, but it was obviously significant as our language, English - a corruption of 'Angle-ish' - is the descendant of the languages spoken by these people from northern Germany and Denmark
- The **Vikings**. The legendary warriors from Scandinavia settled mostly in Northern England in the late Anglo-Saxon period
- The **Normans**. These warrior people were descended from Viking invaders of Normandy (Normandy means 'land of the North Man'). They only came in small numbers, but their descendants were the aristocracy that ruled Britain for most of the 1000 years after 1066
- The **Huguenots**. These were French Protestants, prosecuted in France and finally expelled by Catholic Louis XIV in 1685. Most of those that weren't killed in France came to England.
- The **Jews**. Britain's Jewish community came with the Normans, but was expelled in 1290, gradually coming back from 1650 onwards. Most modern British Jews are descended from the early 20th Century immigrants that came to Britain fleeing persecution and genocide in Eastern and Central Europe

IT'S HAPPENED AGAIN

- **People of the Empire.** In the 19th Century, Britain became part of a global empire again. People came in from all over the empire, particularly at the time of its dissolution after World War II. The largest groups came from India, Pakistan, Bangladesh and the Caribbean. They mostly fled persecution, came because of family ties, or were economic migrants.
- **Eastern Europeans**: the new millennium has seen major immigration from Eastern Europe; seeking work, taking advantage of the freedom of movement offered by the European Union, with Poles forming the largest single group

People from all of these groups (and many who have mixed heritages from two or more) are Arsenal supporters. I can guarantee you that however 'British' you may feel, you are not exclusively descended from the very small group of hunter gatherers who originally populated Britain 10,000 years ago; and indeed were not even the first humans to do so.

In the same way, I don't believe any Arsenal fan is descended from a line of people who attended the first Dial Square match in Woolwich in 1883 and haven't missed a game since. So whilst some of us have longer Arsenal heritages than others, let's please not use this as a weapon to fight each other with. We are all immigrants, and we are all 'newcomer' Arsenal fans; just at different stages of our journeys.

In particular we should note that the Invincibles era will have attracted a lot of new fans. These fans are experiencing an Arsenal fallow period for the first time and are finding it hard to take. It is a particularly cruel time because it has been characterised by a lot of false hope and misinformation. 2012-13 and 2007-8 were both defined by long periods of leading the Premier League; the incredible achievement of staying in the top four has also misled fans about the ability of the club to compete. On top of this, Arsenal was quite dishonest with us about the financial restrictions that it was working under between 2005 and 2013. It is only in the last three years or so, with the restrictions easing, that the club has started talking openly about its problems. At the time, with large cash surpluses in the accounts, it was not at all clear that the club was struggling financially. Now, just when the fallow period looked like it may be coming to an end, we have had another disappointing season. People are naturally frustrated.

The fact that we have all these relatively new fans is a great thing. It is a result of our success. We have an unusually high number of these fans in the stadium as well. The opening of the Emirates allowed an extra 20,000 people to become regular matchgoers. Most of them will turn out to be lifelong fans. Even the tiny number that really do tear up their season tickets in protest will continue to be fans and may return to the stadium at some point in the future. They will probably have children who will also be fans. And it is the depth of the fan base, more than anything else, which will determine our long-term success. So let's welcome all our fans, whoever they are and however they came to us. We can have legitimate disagreements about whether or not Arsenal needs a new Manager, but when we are tempted to lapse into insults about who is a 'real' fan, let's try to remember the spirit of St Totteringham's Day 2016

CHAPTER FORTY THREE
WHAT WENT WRONG?

A SERIES OF GAMBLES?
May 23rd & 31st 2016

All Managers have to take risks with the way that they put their squads together. It is not possible to have two or three world class players for every position. As well as being prohibitively expensive, world class players will not tolerate long periods on the bench. So Managers try to provide a squad large enough to cover for rotation and injuries.

Rotation is reasonably predictable because we know roughly how many games Arsenal will play. Injuries are, of course, unpredictable. Particular problems come when a player and their backup both become injured. This happens more often that you might think. Often the backup is suddenly thrown into playing a lot of games after a long period of inactivity, which is a great recipe for injury. In such cases the Manager must go to the third choice, or play someone out of position and this starts to weaken the team considerably.

If we look at the season as a whole, Wenger took two big gambles. Neither came off. He gambled on Coquelin being an effective Defensive Midfielder and he gambled that Walcott could be an effective Striker. The result of these failed gambles was that our Central Midfield was weak and we didn't score enough of the chances we created. That was enough to cost us the title. Of course there are other issues that have affected the season (Sanchez's form and injuries, The Ox disappointing again, Ramsey disappointing), but these two are the big ones. In the end, Walcott was only effective for a couple of months; and the heart was ripped out of our midfield.

TIM CHARLESWORTH

Cazorla's disappointment

One of my lasting memories of the season is watching Santi Cazorla warming up against Manchester City in the penultimate game of the season. It was sad because it reminded us of what we missed. It was also sad because, after Sanchez's equalizer, Wenger changed his mind and bought Coquelin on instead to try and cement the point. Santi looked crestfallen and who can blame him. The bemused look on Santi's face reminded me of Robert Pires being substituted in the 2006 Champions League Final. Pires' substitution appeared to be entirely sensible to us (following Jens Lehmann's red card), but Pires could never reconcile himself to it. He left the club and despite having a basically good relationship with Wenger, he still can't accept the decision to this day.

This reminds us that footballers are individual sportsmen at heart. Although they play a team game, they can only focus on being the best that they can be. Pires and Santi are great team players, but they cannot control what everyone else does and they necessarily see the world through their own narrow lens. And it's not difficult to sympathise with Santi. He had waited nearly six months to return to the first team. He had the European Championships coming up. He is 31 and has always been slightly on the fringes of the Spanish team. He is unlikely to get another chance to go to a major tournament. He desperately needed to prove his ability to play at the top level before the end of the season, and it was torn away from him by a Sanchez goal. Of course he should have been pleased about this; the bemused look on his face suggested the internal struggle between the happiness at our goal and the personal disappointment of staying on the bench.

Predictably, the one start against Villa in the final game of the season was not enough to get Santi one of the highly competitive midfield spots in the Spanish squad. In reality, an additional substitute appearance at the Etihad probably wouldn't

IT'S HAPPENED AGAIN

have made any difference, yet I can't help but sympathize with Santi being denied his opportunity.

Ripping the heart out of our midfield

Amidst another midfield injury crisis, around New Year 2015, Santi moved to a deeper Midfield role alongside Francis Coquelin. The experiment was an instant hit and the two stayed together during a very successful period which included a strong run in the League and a triumphant FA Cup campaign. We all hoped the partnership (and the success it brought) would stay together in the new season; and it did. Their run in the team coincided with Arsenal comfortably scoring more points than any other team during calendar year 2015 (81 points in 38 games in 2015 is champions' form - Leicester won with 81). Cazorla's career had a new lease of life and he was arguably playing better than at any time previously (and he has been pretty good at other times).

Coquelin was injured in a horrible away defeat at WBA on 21st November 2015. Arteta replaced Coquelin, played poorly and also got injured. It was effectively the end of Arteta's Arsenal career. Coquelin returned in the New Year, but was not the same player, which can sometimes happen. We have seen something similar with last year's player of the season, Chelsea's Eden Hazard, who seemed to struggle to overcome the after-effects of his injuries. Coquelin, like Hazard, is a player who relies on athleticism and for whatever reason he seemed to have only recovered 95% of his full potential. Although he returned in February, our initial euphoria was misplaced and he was dropped again as the season wore on.

The following weekend, 29th November 2015, we drew 1-1 away with Norwich. This didn't look like a difficult fixture and a win would have taken us to the top of the League. Instead we got injuries to Koscielny and then Sanchez. As a result, we had no substitutes left when Cazorla injured his knee, so he stayed on the pitch. Did Santi make the injury worse by playing on? Probably. Either way, his season was over too.

So a horrible series of misfortunes within seven days of one another denied us our two starting Central Midfielders and one of their reserves. Although we didn't know it at the time, we had effectively lost Santi, Coquelin and Arteta for the rest of the season (having already lost Wilshere). In Arteta and Cazorla we had also lost the only players in our squad really capable of playing the 'second playmaker' role. Hereafter, the creative burden fell too heavily on Ozil and it was too easy for opposition teams to stifle our flair by heavily marking him. In the second half of the season we seemed to lack imagination; this was very much a result of Cazorla's absence. Can any team be reasonably expected to survive this?

On the one hand, this is an unfortunate series of events. On the other hand, statistically speaking, you can expect a run of bad luck to occur, at least once, in a long season. We seem to have had many consecutive seasons where we suffer bad luck in a crucial position. If something keeps happening, you have to conclude that it is not unusual. Although we have been unlucky in Central Midfield we have had a 'fortunate' season in other respects:

- Mesut Ozil has been pretty much fit all season
- Our starting centre backs have all been fit for the majority of the season
- Bellerin has been largely available all season, which was particularly important in the context that Debuchy went AWOL

So the question we have to ask is whether or not Arsenal should have been prepared for this kind of eventuality and so have had a better 'Plan B' in place.

IT'S HAPPENED AGAIN

Coquelin was an obvious risk

Certainly Coquelin was an obvious weak point in the team. He had never completed a full season as a first team regular. Despite his brilliant displays in the early months of 2015, it was not clear that he could sustain this for a whole season, or that his body would hold up to the challenge. Right from the start we looked vulnerable to any major injury he might pick up. I suspect that Wenger seriously toyed with buying another Midfielder in the summer. The rumour mill suggested that he was flirting with Morgan Schneiderlin, amongst others. In the end, Wenger decided it was silly to spend a lot of money on an expensive reserve (or the players decided to go elsewhere?).

His back up was Arteta, but Arteta has been next to useless this season. A combination of age and injury have robbed him of both game time and effectiveness on the occasions he has been on the pitch. With the benefit of hindsight, it was obviously a mistake not to acquire a backup for Coquelin in the summer. The purchase of Elneny in January implicitly recognised the error. But should we blame Wenger for the initial decision, or was it an 'understandable error', only detectable with hindsight.

When I examined the question myself pre-season, without the benefit of hindsight, I basically concluded that the lack of cover for Coquelin was a risk, indeed the greatest risk in the squad, but that it wasn't really practical to sign a top class replacement:

Firstly, that would be a very expensive solution to a relatively small problem (it looked small at the time anyway)

Secondly, a player like Schneiderlin would not join Arsenal on the basis that he would be a reserve for Coquelin. Signing a lesser player was pointless when you already had Arteta and Flamini (and maybe Wilshere)

Thirdly, Arteta was a faithful servant of the club and a reasonable (if not convincing) backup. It was not realistic to sign a replacement that would effectively consign Arteta, our club captain, to the rubbish heap

Fourthly, we had further backup in the form of Flamini (and possibly Wilshere as well). Had I known that Flamini would get about as much game time as Coquelin, I might have concluded differently, but Wenger couldn't be expected to know this before the season started

Was the ageing of Arteta predictable?

Mikel Arteta was 33 at the start of the season. Before the emergence of Coquelin, he was a vital cog in our team and we visibly suffered in his absence. 33 is an age when some players seem to lose the ability to play at the top level, but others are more than able to continue. It was not ridiculous to assume that, with a lower playing workload, Arteta would thrive. We have seen this effect with many players, like Teddy Sheringham, Ryan Giggs and Lee Dixon, who could continue to perform well into their late thirties if playing less games. Wenger obviously thought that Arteta fell into this category.

In reality Arteta's season was ruined as much by injury as age and this might simply have been bad luck. It is all too easy to assume that a player gets injured because he is old, but this is not necessarily the case. He may just have suffered an unfortunate series of injuries like Hazard. However, we might observe it appeared to fans that Arteta was losing pace and agility as early as the second half of 2013-14, 18 months before the start of the 15-16 season.

Of course, I don't see Arteta on a daily basis. I don't have access to his fitness performance stats (and wouldn't know how to interpret them if I did). Wenger had this advantage over me and still made the wrong call. We could criticise Wenger on this basis, but I think that this sort of thing is more an art than a science and I don't believe Wenger really had a lot more useful information than me when making this judgement. So certainly

IT'S HAPPENED AGAIN

Wenger took risks in midfield when finalising his squad in the summer of 2015. We don't know whether he tried to cover these risks by signing a new player, or he simply decided these were risks worth taking. We can certainly question whether or not an emotional affection for Mikel Arteta coloured his judgement about the captain's usefulness as a back up to Coquelin. Overall, risks have to be taken and it seems to me that Wenger probably took a sensible risk, but got caught out.

The Second gamble of summer 2015: strikers

The second gamble was in the no. 9 position. We went into the season with Giroud and Walcott as our main options. It's not clear to me which one of the two (if either) was intended to be 'first choice'. Welbeck was also part of the picture, but injured at the start of the season with an uncertain return date.

Has Wenger ever intended Giroud to be lead striker?

Olivier Giroud gets a lot of unfair criticism. He is not the best striker in the League, but he is one of them and he does his job for Arsenal to the best of his ability. A lot of supporters think he is not quite good enough for a title winning team; they are probably right. However I think this point is overstated. Football is a team game and people often over-estimate the importance of a single player. This is particularly true of Strikers, who are both important and very prominent players. France won the World Cup in 1998 without a prolific Striker, as did Spain in 2010.

In most cases, a successful team has a successful Striker. However, there is a causality problem with this observation. A Striker playing for a very good team is almost bound to score a lot of goals because he will be given a lot of high quality chances by his team mates against a stretched defence. Similarly, his opponents will have to pay attention to other members of his team and will thus be prevented from marking the Striker out of the game.

Giroud is often used as a stick to beat Wenger with: the Manager's faith in Giroud is used as an example of his poor/declining judgement. Whenever I hear this analysis, I am always struck with the thought that it might be plain wrong. It is not clear to me that Wenger has the faith in Giroud that is usually assumed. The assumption is based on the fact that Giroud has been our principal Striker for the last four seasons. However, I am not sure that Arsène has intended it to be this way.

It is always a bit difficult to discern Arsenal's real intentions in the transfer market, because they are very secretive about it. However, the following observations seem to be credible:

- Giroud joined in the summer of 2012, when Van Persie was still at the club. It is not clear that Wenger expected Van Persie to leave. Wenger can be very optimistic in these circumstances and it seems he only really gave up on persuading Van Persie to stay a few days before RVP left. It may be that Giroud was really signed to replace Chamakh - to compete with and complement Van Persie, rather than to replace him
- The following summer (2013) we know that Arsenal bid £40m for Luis Suarez. It is reasonable to assume that Suarez was intended to supplant Giroud as the main Striker. Arsenal also appeared to be confident for most of the summer that they would get their man eventually, so perhaps didn't really develop an alternative plan in the case that the Suarez acquisition failed
- The summer of 2014 is particularly difficult to read. We signed Sanchez. Wenger used him as a Striker early on: is it possible that he was intended to supplant Giroud? Wenger talks a lot about how he thinks the best Strikers come from South America at the moment. Wenger was also linked with a number of other strikers (although it's not clear how reliable these links were). He also signed Welbeck at the end

IT'S HAPPENED AGAIN

of the transfer window; using him a lot as a no. 9 in the early matches of the season. As Giroud returned from injury in the autumn of 2014, Welbeck lost his place. However, this may have been due to Welbeck's slow scoring rate, rather than because Wenger always intended to bring Giroud back
- In the summer of 2015, there were plenty of rumours that Wenger was trying to sign both Higuain and Benzema. Maybe he was priced out of this option by Napoli's demands? Maybe Benzema decided to stay put? His Plan B was to use Walcott and Giroud. His early season selections suggest that he intended Walcott to be the main Striker, with Giroud in a supporting or rotating role. This is difficult to imagine now, given Walcott's hideous loss of form, but if you look back to Wenger's choices in September 2015, he appeared to favour Walcott. As the season wore on and Walcott's form faded, Giroud lost his starting place again, this time to the returning Welbeck

It seems from all this that it is perfectly possible Wenger has never intended Giroud to be his leading striker. Perhaps Giroud has simply been the beneficiary of a series of form failures, injuries and failed bids for other players.

If this is the case; and I suspect that my analysis is - at least partly - true, then we could make the following observations about Giroud:
- He has played for us during one of the less glamorous periods in the club's history, but has still given his all
- He has worked incredibly hard on his positioning, particularly his near post runs and has really made the most of the talent he has
- His main problem is that he lacks pace and agility. He is a very heavily built guy (that's why he is so dominant in the air). I think the level of agility he has achieved suggests good commitment to training and conditioning

- Pace can also be 'trained', but is limited by natural leg cadence. It looks to me that he has achieved pretty much the maximum pace someone limited by his natural leg speed could achieve
- Despite some severe provocation, I have never once heard him criticise the fans, the Manager or the club
- He makes a valuable and often underestimated contribution in defence, especially at set pieces. You don't often see a goal headed by the man he was marking! This has been particularly important during a period when the team was very vulnerable to set pieces
- If you exclude penalties, Giroud (15) scored five League goals less than Kane and Aguero (20) last season and four less than Vardy (19). I think he is a better link player and a better Defender than any of these three, so is his overall contribution to the team really a lot less than them? Remember he also only made 26 of 38 starts in the League.
- Whatever you feel about him, he has made an important contribution to our team over four seasons. Without him, I doubt that all the FA Cups, top four finishes and St Totts Days would have happened. I know we wanted more, but let's not forget what he *has* helped us to achieve

So when I hear our fans singe na-na-na etc. Giroud (to the tune of 'Hey Jude'), I believe it is sung with genuine affection and appreciation for what he has done. He may not be Thierry Henry, but that's a pretty high bar to judge anyone by. After all, I am no Charles Dickens, but if you have got this far, you seem to think it is worth reading what I write...

Walcott

And so I come to our other main striker, Theo Walcott. I really hold my head in my hands when I even think about writing this piece. I had such high hopes for Theo at the start of the season. I think Wenger did too. He sanctioned a big salary and he gave him the Striker's slot in the squad that Theo had cherished for so

IT'S HAPPENED AGAIN

long. There were hiccups early in the season and some bad misses, but Walcott slowly established himself as our main Striker. He won the starting berth from Giroud, and seemed set to finally fulfil his destiny. He looked dangerous in behind (as ever) and managed to add some ability to hold the ball up when receiving it with his back to goal. Opposition defences looked uncomfortable defending against him. This was the kind of footballing alchemy that only Wenger can pull off.

I was feeling quite smug at this point, referring fellow Gooners to my summer articles suggesting that this is exactly what would happen. I had even tipped that they should back Walcott to win the Premier League golden boot (I know!). You will be glad to know that I put my money where my mouth was.

I don't understand what happened next, or why. Let's start with the chronology of events:

- Walcott was on the bench for a fairly meaningless League Cup third round match against Sheffield Wednesday in late October. He came on, after just five minutes, for the injured Alex Oxlade-Chamberlain. A few minutes later, he went off again with a hamstring injury. The general assumption is that because he came on so early, he wasn't properly warmed up. Certainly a hamstring injury can result from minimal warming-up
- He came back into the team in early December. He initially played on the left of the front three, effectively covering for the injured Sanchez. This was a little odd, as I don't remember Theo ever playing in this position before. The team went on quite a good run, including the away win at Olympiacos and the home win against Man City. Wenger is often reluctant to change a winning team, so Theo ended up with a long run on the left wing. He played OK during this period, but was not particularly impressive and didn't score many goals.
- I was mystified during this run. I kept expecting Theo to get a game at Striker. In hindsight, I remain confused. Giroud

played every game in this spell and ended up losing form through sheer exhaustion. He played 15 games in succession during the physically toughest period of the season (December to February). This is an average of a game every 4.9 days. Why didn't Walcott get a game at Striker?
- Part of the answer must be that Theo's form was poor. Perhaps Wenger could see problems in training or his physical data that suggested he shouldn't play at no. 9. Even so, this seems odd
- Walcott did get some substitute appearances as a Striker. Was Wenger drawing conclusions from these unimpressive cameos? Surely Walcott merited a couple of starts at no. 9, simply on the basis of the form he showed in the same position earlier in the season. Strikers, more than any other position, need confidence. Wenger is good at putting his confidence in people, yet in this instance he failed to do so
- Walcott finally got a couple of starts in the Striker position late in February; in the FA Cup fifth round vs. Hull and then again away to Man U. This seemed mostly to rotate the out-of-form Giroud, who came back for the Barcelona game in-between. Neither were great performances and after them Welbeck seemed to be preferred as the alternative to Giroud. The Man U game was his last start of the season

It almost seems like a dream to imagine that Theo was ever an efficient and effective no. 9 for us, let alone that it happened just six months ago. In researching this piece, I had to go back and watch quite a few early season videos to convince myself that I was not going mad. And when you watch them, there he is, only he doesn't look like the same player that we saw in the second half of the season. If you get a chance, have a look at the Bayern victory, where Walcott was superb, or the Man U win.

IT'S HAPPENED AGAIN

So what's next?

I suspect there is some untold story behind Walcott's dramatic loss of form in the second half of the season. Whatever that story is, I don't think it's viable for Wenger to allocate him one of the primary Striker slots in the squad. If we aim to enter next season with two main Strikers, it seems likely that Giroud will be one of them, while it's possible that Wenger had Welbeck slated for the other slot.

My feeling is that Welbeck's scoring rate doesn't quite justify that inclusion, but either way it is academic because, following a serious knee injury, Welbeck will not be available next season. I don't think Wenger can gamble on the Walcott-Giroud pairing again (and fans may become mutinous if he does). To me, it was an understandable gamble for 15-16, but it didn't work out well, and I don't believe it's a credible way to go into the 16-17 season. It seems to me that, if Walcott is to have a future in the Striker position, he is going to have to work his way past two men who will start the season ahead of him. I don't think that Akpom or Sanogo are ready to fill this gap, so we will need to turn to the transfer market.

The perils of buying a striker

It is worth remembering how rare it is for a Striker acquisition to be successful. Have a look at the following list of top scorers in the 2015-16 Premier League:

	Goals	Pens	Non-Pen goals
Harry Kane	25	5	20
Jamie Vardy	24	5	19
Sergio Aguero	24	4	20
Romelu Lukaku	18	1	17
Riyad Mahrez	17	4	13
Olivier Giroud	16	1	15
Odion Ighalo	15	0	15
Jermain Defoe	15	1	14
Alexis Sanchez	13	0	13
Troy Deeney	13	6	7

Not a single one of these players signed for their team in the summer of 2015. The top ten signings in the summer of 2015 were:

Purchaser	Player	Selling Club	Fee (£m)
Man City	Kevin De Bruyne	Wolfsburg	54.5
Man City	Raheem Sterling	Liverpool	49.0
Man Utd	Anthony Martial	Monaco	36.0
Man City	Nicolas Otamendi	Valencia	33.0
Liverpool	Christian Benteke	Aston Villa	32.5
Liverpool	Roberto Firmino	Hoffenheim	29.0
Man Utd	Memphis Depay	PSV Eindhoven	27.9
Man Utd	Morgan Schneiderlin	Southampton	25.0
Chelsea	Pedro	Barcelona	21.4
Tottenham	Heung-Min Son	Bayer Leverkusen	18.0

Obviously not all of these are Strikers, but most of them are Forwards, so this is quite a sobering list for someone who is setting out to acquire a top scoring Striker. It strongly suggests that you could easily spend a lot of money and fail to acquire someone who will score more goals than Olivier Giroud.

In fact, it is very rare for a new Striker to make a big impression in their first season at a new club. In recent years,

IT'S HAPPENED AGAIN

Diego Costa was very good for Chelsea in the first half of the 2014-15 season, following his move from Atletico, but he has been quite average since. Sergio Aguero was effective in his first season in the Premier League (23 goals). Giroud got 11 in his first season, and Van Persie was temporarily successful after moving to Man U. Expensive failures in recent years are legion - Falcoa to Man Utd, Torres to Chelsea, Benteke to Liverpool, Carroll to Liverpool, Bony to City.

Conclusions

So, I suspect Arsenal will look to buy another striker for next season, because Wenger will not wish to repeat the Walcott-Giroud gamble. However, the chances of acquiring someone who will score a lot of goals in the Premier League are (I'm sorry to say) small. I suspect that this position will continue to be a problem next season.

CHAPTER FORTY FOUR
THE OZIL ENIGMA

I can't write a book about Arsenal without talking about their greatest enigma - and my favourite player - Mesut Ozil. I have agonised over this piece all season, writing it and rewriting it, but never getting it to the point that it was ready for publication. The main problem is what I have to say is essentially critical and this is very difficult for me because I have a major man-crush on this guy. To me, he is the most beautiful boy to pull on the famous shirt since our beloved Rocky. The long-suffering Mrs C. (and, in fact, pretty much everyone else) gives me a mystified, yet tolerant look when I express this opinion (which is often), but I stand by it. The look my wife gave me when I returned from a football tournament in which my son was playing, with a framed portrait of Mesut was a little less indulgent and a bit more hostile.

Putting aside questions about Ozil's looks, on which opinions are divided (essentially between me and everyone else - how can people fail to see the beauty in those defence penetrating eyes?), let's have a look at what he contributed. I wrote early in the season listing the factors that would determine whether or not we had a successful year. They were: can Coquelin keep it up; will Walcott score lots of goals; will Gabriel have a great season; will Wenger rotate well; and will Ozil have a great season. I stand by these questions. Of course there were other factors which turned out to be important, such as the Cazorla injury, the failure of Arteta and the mid-season loss of form from both Sanchez and Giroud, but these problems were really consequences of the main issues.

None of the answers to these questions were very positive: Coquelin did well until injured in November and never regained his form; Walcott and Gabriel were essentially disappointing, Walcott in particular; and rotation went poorly - mainly due to

IT'S HAPPENED AGAIN

injuries and poor performances from squad players. Perhaps this tale of woe is not surprising, given the outcome of the season was essentially poor.

That just leaves the Ozil question. He is the most sumptuously talented player I have seen in an Arsenal shirt (with all due respect to Henry, Fabregas, Bergkamp and Brady). This player has the potential to lead Arsenal to great things in Europe as well as in England. By these standards, I think he was disappointing. So reluctantly, I find myself asking the question: what went wrong with Ozil?

Ozil is a lazy player?

A comment often made in the commentatorsphere is that Ozil is lazy or 'gets lost in the game'. This view doesn't really bear close scrutiny. It seems to arise from something a bit odd about Mesut's demeanour on the pitch. On the rare occasions that he loses the ball, he turns his eyes to heaven in exasperation. His face is a picture of pure amazement and desolation. He completely loses interest in what happens for the next few seconds and makes no attempt to get the ball back or otherwise assist his team. Contrast that with Alexis Sanchez when he loses the ball. Sanchez turns instantly and fiercely in the direction of the impertinent upstart who is responsible for this outrage; adopting the general body language of a starving Rottweiler who has just had his bone taken away and is intent on substituting the offender's testicles. Most sensible players are just glad to get away with their testicles intact and lose interest in retaining the ball. We all enjoy watching Alexis do this, but it just isn't the way that Mesut plays.

I'm not a great fan of statistics in football, but their use is becoming more and more common and they can tell us some interesting things. One statistic that is widely quoted and seems quite revealing to me, is the distance that players cover in the game. Modern football is a physically intense business. It is common for players to be covering distances in excess of 10km every match. If you consider that this distance is covered in a series of backwards and sideways movements, interspersed with jogging and sprinting, you can understand that this is a major athletic achievement, often repeated twice a week.

In defending Ozil against his detractors, people often cite statistics showing that Ozil covers more ground than most Arsenal players; in fact he is often top of the team in this statistic. This really surprises me and I think it tells us something about what Ozil is doing on the pitch.

Football is about overloads

Most goals in football are the result of temporary 'overloads' - situations in which a team creates a temporary numerical advantage over the opposition in a particular area of the pitch (set pieces and long-range shots are the exception). This idea is described most eloquently by the world's most widely admired coach, Pep Guardiola: *"In all team sports, the secret is to overload one side of the pitch so that the opponent must tilt its own defence to cope. You overload on one side and draw them in so that they leave the other side weak. And when we've done all that, we attack and score from the other side."*

Guardiola perhaps slightly overstates the point - the exploitation of overloads takes a lot of skill and if you watch Sunday afternoon park football, it may not be so obvious that 'overload exploitation' is the key to victory. However, for professional level team sports, his point becomes incredibly incisive. The point is most obvious in rugby, but can also be observed in hockey, basketball, American football, netball and even cycling. The best example of an overload goal I saw this season was Barcelona's first against us at the Emirates. A very brief overload was ruthlessly exploited by Messi, Neymar and Suarez. Before we knew what had hit us, they had passed it into the net!

IT'S HAPPENED AGAIN

When you think in terms of overloads, you suddenly see the importance of the 'distance covered' statistic. If you think of football players as chess pieces that are constantly moved around the pitch, probing for an overload situation, you can see the dynamic. If you want to create an overload in attack you need to commit players forward, and if you want to avoid being overloaded in defence, those players need to get back more quickly than your opponents get forward. If one team covers more distance than the other, it will have a considerable advantage in the creation of overload opportunities, which is why it is so important for football players to cover a lot of ground. Spurs and Southampton looked like they were working particularly hard to try and exploit this insight.

Ozil the dummy runner

When I watch the world's greatest team, my eye often follows Ozil rather than the ball. (This can be slightly irritating when watching on television, as the cameraman does not always reflect my personal preferences.) I see Ozil making a lot of runs, pulling the opposition defence out of shape and making space for his teammates; this is exactly how you create overloads. The statistics suggest that he is doing a lot of this, but is it really the right way to use his sumptuous talent?

In my opinion, Ozil is the best passer and assist-maker in the world. Should be we using him as a dummy runner? Wouldn't it make more sense if everybody else acted as a dummy runner in order to create space for Ozil, who kept his movement down to the minimum necessary for him to get into space? This would ensure that Ozil got more of the ball and that when he received it he was fresher and able to do more damage.

TIM CHARLESWORTH

Ozil the success

So there is no serious doubt that Ozil made a good contribution to Arsenal last season. He was available to play virtually all games, he created space for his teammates, covered a lot of ground, scored six goals and made 19 league assists (best in the division). He also created an all-time league record 181 chances; he overwhelmingly won the vote as Arsenal's player of the season and rightly so. Ozil also narrowly missed out on equalising the all-time Premier League record for assists provided in a single season, currently held by Thierry Henry (20). The interesting thing is that Ozil produced his 15th assist in Premier League game 17 on 21st December and seemed well on target to break the record. For the last 19 Premier League games of the season, he produced just four assists: this is the period of time during which Arsenal went from leaders to also-rans. Lots of factors led to Arsenal's demise, but in my opinion the most important of these was Ozil's loss of form.

There is some debate about this drop in form. Ozil's chance creation rate didn't particularly decline in the second half of the season and some commentators have argued that it wasn't Ozil that performed poorly in the second half of the season, but our Strikers - Giroud in particular - who started to miss the chances that Mesut created. I have to say, I don't quite buy this argument. Ozil's performances looked weaker to me in the second half of the season. He didn't seize control of games as he did earlier in 15-16; and I think that at least part of the reason the chances were missed is that they were of a lower quality.

Overall however, when I watched Ozil play, whether in the first or second half of the season, I felt I was looking at a great player rather than a leader. When you look at the truly great players: Ronaldo; Van Basten; Pele; Maradona, they don't just execute their skills well, they seem to demand the ball and demand responsibility. In the bigger games and tighter situations these players seem to impose their personality on the game even more; almost able to win games on their own. We saw this

IT'S HAPPENED AGAIN

characteristic with Vieira and Henry at Arsenal and even to some extent from Van Persie. I think the reason that Ozil fails to dominate games is nothing to do with work rate (as we can see from the distance statistics) and everything to do with the amount of ball he gets.

Messi and Ronaldo are the two most dominant current players in the game and you can't help noticing that they see a lot of the ball. This is partly why they score so many goals and assists. Basically, their team mates are getting the ball to them as much as possible. This is just a variation on the oldest schoolboy tactic in the book - give the ball to your best player and let him do his worst; and this is exactly what is not happening with Ozil.

Why is Ozil running too much?

So it seems to me that the reason Ozil is failing to dominate is that he is doing too much running and not seeing enough of the ball. In considering why this might be, there are two factors about Ozil that are worth considering:

1. **Ozil the Mourinhista.** In times gone by, we would see players who would contribute little to the game other than goals or the odd defence splitting pass. Such a player would often be described as a 'passenger', or it would be said the rest of team was 'carrying' them. This is the type of player that commentators have in mind when they describe Ozil as lazy.

    In reality, these players are becoming increasingly hard to find. Modern technology can tell us (and more importantly, coaches) how far a player has run in a game, leaving the old 'flair players' nowhere to hide.

    The master of getting the best, physically, out of flair players is Mourinho. We have seen this most recently with Eden Hazard, but he can also count Ronaldo, Drogba and Di Maria amongst his successes. We often forget that Ozil is a player who was signed and managed by Mourinho at Madrid. There is no doubt that Mourinho is a major influence on his career and Mourinho almost certainly helped turn Ozil into the hard-running athlete that he is today.

2. **Ozil the little boy.** In a strange way, Mesut Ozil reminds me of Ian Wright. Wright was a genuinely great, single-minded goal scorer. He had a good instinct for where to be, a good eye for a shot, pace to get in behind and tenacity to gamble. Ozil is similar in his single minded determination to get assists. He uses all of his attributes (great control, ability to put his body in the right place, good pace over five yards, incredible vision, imagination) in order to create goal scoring chances. When presented with a goal scoring opportunity himself, he will tend to pass to another player if there is a chance of an assist and only shoots if there is really no other sensible option. His goals are scored almost reluctantly and his celebratory smile always seems to have a hint of embarrassment or apology to it.

And this brings us to an interesting point about Ozil's character. He really doesn't come across as the 'Alpha Male' type. This is probably why he got on so well with Ronaldo at Real Madrid, who is the ultimate example of an Alpha footballer. Ozil grew up playing 'cage football' on small, urban, five-a-side, fenced pitches. He played with his elder brother Mutlu and his friends. His brother (now his agent) is five years older than him. This environment seems to have been an important part of Mesut's development in two ways. Firstly, it helped him focus on his touch and elusiveness. He obviously couldn't compete with these boys physically and so had to find other ways of protecting the ball. Secondly, he seems to have developed a predilection for the assist.

It's not hard to imagine the little Mesut was 'tolerated' by these older boys as long as he did what they wanted him to do.

IT'S HAPPENED AGAIN

In particular, boys like to score goals; perhaps the young Mesut ingratiated himself with these older boys by going to great lengths to set them up with goal scoring opportunities. Instead of being reluctant to pass the ball to the 'weak' boy, they learnt that if they passed it to him, he would try to set them up to score. Thus the 'king of the assist' was born.

It is difficult for all of us to escape the instincts and habits of our childhood. When I watch Ozil play, I see the little boy anxious to please his team mates, to work hard for them and to create assists.

Where next for Mesut?

So let's not tolerate any talk about Ozil being a 'waste of money' or a 'lazy player'. This was Mesut's best season in an Arsenal shirt and probably the best season of his career. He is still improving and developing. He was a bit disappointing to me, especially in the second half of the season, but only because I have such high expectations of him.

If Ozil is going to dominate games, he needs to do less dummy running and get the ball in to his feet a lot more. Now clearly this is not something he can do alone; it requires the cooperation of his teammates. Wenger is a sophisticated Manager who believes in trusting his players and allowing them to work out problems themselves. I can't imagine anything more 'unWenger' than him telling the team to 'just give the ball to Mesut', so I think we can count this possibility out.

Ozil is naturally a shy chap, but Wenger is a good man for dealing with shy players because he trusts players more than most Managers. (Mourinho, is also good for shy players, because he distracts attention from them with his antics). I think we often underestimate the level of personal confidence that is necessary for a player to demand the ball in front of 60,000 noisy, often fickle, football supporters. We forget that these are sensitive young men, who have left education early and are often playing in a foreign country amidst a foreign culture.

Mesut is simply not going to have a Damascene change of character and turn into a Ronaldo demanding the ball. It is more likely that his teammates will demand that he take the ball more often. And this is not such an unlikely scenario as it might first seem. Mesut has established himself as our best player, the team is hungry for success and they have a Manager who lets them work out problems for themselves. Ronaldo sees so much of the ball because he demands it and his talent allows his teammates and Managers to forgive his outrageous demands; Messi sees so much of the ball because his pure talent demands it. Ozil is, like Messi, a naturally quiet character who likes his football to do the talking. This is not a barrier to greatness.

This is also, potentially, one of the rare cases where the fans can make a difference. I'm not sure we are doing enough to make him feel loved. Where are the Ozil songs? I like the 'We've got Ozil' song which emerged in the second half of the season, but I don't hear it enough. Let's get behind this guy and give him our confidence. We should certainly stop calling him lazy. Not only is this clearly factually wrong, but it actually encourages the wrong behaviour (i.e. making more dummy runs). Perhaps we should stop praising him for the distance that he covers and concentrate on the things that really matter, like goals and assists.

Ozil is now 27, the peak age for a footballer. He is fully familiar with the English league and with his team.

Familiarisation with his teammates is a particularly important issue because his play is so unusual, with passes coming from places and angles that you are simply not used to unless you have played with him before. He didn't quite do it last season, but he wasn't far away. It would probably help if Wenger could use Ozil more sparingly, especially in the first half of the season. The emergence of Iwobi as a genuine alternative no. 10 may help here.

IT'S HAPPENED AGAIN

Personally speaking, my faith is undimmed. Mrs C. has very generously allowed me to put the framed picture of Mesut up in our bedroom (albeit in a spot where only I can see it). She says that this is slightly unseemly in a 43 year old accountant, but nonetheless tolerates the eccentricity. I still feel that Mesut will lead us to the Promised Land. Maybe next season...

CHAPTER FORTY FIVE
SO ARSENAL WON REALLY DIDN'T THEY?

After a season like that, we need to clutch at straws a bit, so here are some to grasp:

Lucky Leicester

The first point to make is that we finished second and lost to a team we beat twice - 7-3 on aggregate - and who had all the luck. I don't find this a particularly outrageous statement. Luck is part of football. We should remember that Leicester were 5,000-1 to win the Premier League. In order for them to win, an awful lot of stars had to line up. They had to make successful signings, have a Manager who could handle the pressure, avoid major injuries in certain positions and to crucial players; and of course they had to be lucky with refereeing decisions. So it's not really surprising to discover that Leicester had an unusual number of penalties awarded in their favour, or that crucial refereeing decisions fell their way more often than not.

Sometimes commentators and football pundits say that 'it all evens out in the end'. This is patently untrue. In a season of 1,000 matches it might work, but with only 38, we need luck on our side. The Premier League is a great test. Luck is clearly not the most important factor and it can't give us as much help as it can in knockout competitions like the FA Cup. But that doesn't mean it isn't a factor.

Top of the table for penalties in 2015-16 was Leicester. They were awarded 13 penalties during the season, of which they scored 10. Arsenal were awarded two and scored one (Cazorla slipped whilst taking the other). So, you could argue that refereeing decisions 'gifted' Leicester 9 goals more than Arsenal. If we added nine goals to Arsenal's goal difference last season, it would have been 38, 6 better than Leicester. Of course it's

IT'S HAPPENED AGAIN

difficult to say how many more points this would have earnt Arsenal. A penalty goal can give you two points (turning a draw into a win), one point (turning a loss into a draw) or no points (because you were already winning anyway, or you lost by more than one goal). If each penalty was worth a point on average, then this would have closed the nine point gap between Arsenal and Leicester.

Now this analysis is a little dubious. It seems unfair not to recognise that Leicester 'earnt' their penalties. Certainly they had fast Forwards running at Defenders and this is likely to lead to penalties. However, can it really be right that a team like Leicester, who had less possession than Arsenal, really earnt 13 penalties to Arsenal's two? It seems that good fortune, in the form of refereeing decisions, must have played some part in the outcome.

The money table

Arsenal earnt more money from the Premier League than any other team. Money breeds success in football and so Arsenal had the most successful season of any team. Payments are based on a number of factors such as finishing position and how many matches were televised:

1	Arsenal	£101.0m
2	Manchester City	£96.8m
3	Manchester United	£96.3m
4	Tottenham Hotspur	£95.0m
5	Leicester City	£93.0m
6	Liverpool	£90.4m
7	Chelsea	£87.1m
8	West Ham United	£85.6m
9	Southampton	£84.5m
10	Everton	£82.9m
11	Stoke City	£79.0m
12	Swansea City	£75.3m
13	Watford	£74.1m
14	West Bromwich Albion	£73.0m
15	Newcastle United	£72.7m
16	Crystal Palace	£72.4m
17	Sunderland	£71.7m
18	Bournemouth	£70.4m
19	Norwich City	£66.7m
20	Aston Villa	£66.2m

The really interesting thing about this is that, due to the new Premier League contract, the team that finishes last in the League next season will almost certainly receive a higher payment than Arsenal.

IT'S HAPPENED AGAIN

This is not unambiguously great news for Arsenal. We generate more match day income than any other team in global football. The Emirates is not football's biggest stadium, but the combination of high ticket prices in London and the extensive corporate hospitality available there means it generates more money than any other in the world.

If match day revenue becomes relatively less important as a source of income, then Arsenal's advantage against other English teams will be eroded. Already we are seeing that the extra cash generated from participation in the Champions League is delivering less of an advantage to teams. When added to the obligation to have a larger squad in order to cover the extra games, it is not clear that Champions League participation is giving teams a decisive advantage. The Champions League qualifying teams from last season finished second (Arsenal), fourth (Man City), fifth (Man U) and tenth (Chelsea) this season.

English teams are the best in Europe, aren't they?

The new Premier League contract was signed in February 2015 and comes into effect for the 2016-17 season. It represents a 71% increase on the previous deal (£5.136bn, 168 games per season, £10.19m per game). The shocking fact is that next season, all 20 of the Premier League clubs will be in the top 30 wealthiest clubs in the world as a result of these payments. Newly promoted Hull, who finished fourth in the Championship, will earn a minimum of £100,000,000 (£100m) in Premier League television rights and will almost certainly have a higher income next season than stellar names including Inter Milan, Benfica, Porto, Napoli, Marseille, Lyons, Deportiva La Coruna, Villarreal, Anderlecht and Ajax of Amsterdam. There are many claims in the commentatorsphere that the English League is the best in the world. It is certainly the most marketable.

And many of the big clubs around Europe are worried about this. Over the last season, directors of clubs including Barcelona and Bayern Munich have publicly expressed fears that they will not be able to keep pace financially with the English teams. However, it is conspicuous that English teams are not dominating Europe in the way that their income levels suggest they should. Already, 15 of the top 30 income earners are English teams, yet this season in the Champions League Man City lost in the Semi Finals; Arsenal and Chelsea lost in the last 16; and Manchester United failed to progress from the Group stages. German teams, with considerably less income, did just as well; and Spanish teams massively outperformed them.

The 2016 Champions League Final was contested by two Spanish teams for the second time in three years; and a Spanish team won for the third consecutive year. There were three Spanish teams in the Semi Finals and, as if to ram home the superiority of the Spanish league, Sevilla beat Liverpool in the Europa Cup Final.

If there is a 'dominant league' at the moment in Europe, it seems to be Spanish, not English. It is interesting to consider why this might be:

1. The English league is more competitive, with relatively narrow gaps between the top and bottom teams: there are no easy games for English teams in which they can rest players. Therefore the Spanish teams arrive for European games with relatively fresh legs, whereas the English teams arrive tired. The most successful time for English teams in Europe was the late 2000s, culminating in the 2007-8 Champions League. In this competition no English team was defeated by a foreign team - Arsenal lost to Liverpool in the quarter-finals, Chelsea beat Liverpool in the semi-finals and lost to Manchester United in the final. This was also a period in which English teams were dominant domestically. In 2007-8 the top three teams all scored more points that Leicester did in 2015-16 and there was an 11 point gap between fourth placed Liverpool (76 points) and fifth placed Everton (65 points). Domestic confidence allows teams to

IT'S HAPPENED AGAIN

turn their attention to European competition. Today's English teams are a lot less confident than they were ten years ago
2. The top English teams have also performed poorly in recent years. Money is important in football, but it is not everything. Man U have struggled to adapt post-Ferguson, Chelsea failed to replace their successful team as they aged, Manchester City have similarly failed to renew a maturing team and Arsenal have been becalmed for a decade. English teams are not doing well in Europe because England lacks genuinely excellent teams at the moment
3. Real Madrid and Barcelona are experiencing golden ages, personified in the magic of Messi and Ronaldo. Both clubs have been very well managed and led over the last decade and are reaping the rewards. Unlike the English teams, they are making the most of the resources available to them and performing at a very high level. If you ignore these two teams, the performance of Spanish clubs is not particularly good
4. Bayern Munich and Paris St. Germain are also comically dominant in their own leagues at the moment and are similarly able to devote their attention to European competition
5. The English League has a 'blood and thunder' style of play. This is particularly unrelenting and exhausting for the players and prevents them from performing well in Europe. I list this idea here because it is widely held, although personally I do not accept this theory. The same thing was true in the late 70s/early 80s and the late 2000s, both of which were periods of dominance for English teams in Europe. If the blood and thunder did not stop them from succeeding in these periods, I do not see why it should be true now
6. The Spanish league is the 'Goldilocks league' - not too hot and not too cold. The English league is too hot - leading to exhaustion, whereas the French league is too cold - not

enough competitive games to keep the PSG players in peak competitive condition. The Spanish league provides enough competition to keep the top teams sharp, but not enough to exhaust them
7. In recent years the richest two teams in the world have been Real Madrid and Barcelona. In this respect, their success is not surprising. English teams may be dominating the money leagues, but the Spanish clubs are still hanging on to the two top spots

So English teams are not dominating in Europe. However, the financial power of the English League will soon become overwhelming. Other factors are also likely to start moving our way. The English Premier League was absurdly competitive in 2015-16, yet it is likely to start moving the other way as the top teams re-establish their poise. The golden ages of Barcelona and Real Madrid will not last forever: Barcelona's top players are getting past their best and Real's superstar Ronaldo will surely not stay at the top much longer. The Spanish league is likely to become more competitive and the English less so. The Goldilocks halo may well move back to England over the next few years. If it does, Arsenal are well placed to take advantage (unless of course they are in a post-Wenger adjustment phase?).

CHAPTER FORTY SIX
STREAKY WENGER

A rarely observed feature of Arsène Wenger's period at Arsenal is the unlikely series of 'runs' or 'streaks' that he has put together. The most famous of these is of course the series of 49 unbeaten league matches from 7th May 2003 to 16th October 2004.

The great Invincibles run is, however, merely the greatest of quite a collection of records set by Arsène's teams. These remarkable runs begun to appear quite early in Arsène's time as Arsenal Manager. At the end of the 1997-8 season, we won ten consecutive games, a very unusual sequence that delivered the League title that year.

At the end of the 2001-2 season something similar happened, with 13 consecutive victories delivering another title. This second run continued one game into the following season, ending with 14 consecutive victories, still an all-time record in English League football.

Between 19th May 2001 and 30th November 2002, a run of 55 league games, Arsenal scored at least once in every single game. Even for a strong attacking team, this a remarkable sequence and an English League record. This run included every game of the 2001-2 season - the only time any team has completed a season scoring in every game.

In 2001-2002 Arsenal also went an entire season unbeaten away from home. This was an amazing run of games and represented a feat not achieved in the 20th Century, Arsenal becoming the first team since Preston North End in 1889-90 to do it. Preston were playing in the inaugural season of the Football League and played only 11 away games compared to Arsenal's 19. This incredible record has been totally overshadowed by the fact that Arsenal repeated the feat two seasons later, remaining unbeaten at home as well in 2002-3. However, Arsenal remains the only modern team to have done this and our achievement shouldn't be underestimated.

Lest you think these records are all quite old, Arsenal won a league record of 12 consecutive away victories between March 3rd and October 26th 2013. In fact, some of the remarkable runs are still in progress. It is notable that two of these runs were maintained in rather improbable fashion this season:

1. At the start of the season we had qualified for the Champions League knockout stage for 15 consecutive seasons, truly an epic run for a team that has been on the fringes of the European elite during this period. After defeat in our first two group games, it seemed highly improbable that we would qualify, but we did thanks to a home win over a very strong Bayern Munich side, and an amazing 3-0 victory away to Olympiacos that was a really exceptional effort
2. For the last two months of the season we barely dared to utter the words 'St Totteringham'. It was pretty clear that our run of 20 seasons finishing above Spurs had come to an end. I don't need to tell you what happened (again), but suffice to say: 'oway the 'toon' and thanks to 'Pochettino's army' for making our day

It is also worth noting that this season was our 20th consecutive Champions League qualification. Perhaps this achievement never seemed as improbable as the other two, but we might note that super-rich Chelsea and Manchester United both failed in this quest in 2015-16 and Man City only did it by goal difference. We might also note that there have been a number of occasions in this 20 season run where we have qualified on the final day of the season, and often in some surprising ways (many thanks are again due to Spurs and their Lasagne chef here).

Is there a pattern? Of course, if you do anything for long enough, you are bound to set records, and Wenger has been with us for nearly 20 seasons now. We have also had some pretty good teams in that time and - again - good teams are likely to set records. However even taking these factors into account, there does seem to be an awful lot of records and 'runs' being set here. Alex Ferguson was Manager of Manchester United for 26 years and his teams were even more successful on average than Wenger's have been. Some records were set during this period, but on nothing like the scale Wenger has achieved. After such a long time, this starts to look like more than a coincidence.

It seems that Wenger likes these records and even perhaps works extra hard to maintain them. He is a man conscious of his place in Arsenal history; maybe he senses that some of these records are unlikely to be broken and will be spoken of long after his death. He seems especially proud of the Invincibles season, and rightly so. Certainly, Arsenal seemed to expend a lot of mental and physical energy in qualifying from the Champions League group in 2015-16. After the first two defeats in the group, Wenger could have pragmatically conceded defeat and rotated the team to conserve energy for the League challenge. But he didn't do so; he put every effort into recovering the situation. Did this take too much out of the team, did they pay for it later in the season?

And what about the record of top four finishes? Arsenal have not been the best team in England over that 20 years, but no other team can match our record. Teams with greater financial resources and more celebrated Managers have all failed. This record and many others that have been set during Arsène's time are characterised by consistency. And this highlights something interesting about Wenger. In my view, he is good at getting the best out of the players available to him.

A lot of nonsense is talked about the game, but actually it is not that complicated:
1. You need to get good players together
2. Those players need pace skill agility and a good attitude. They need to think about what they are doing and

occasionally a Manager needs to give them advice and instructions

3. Then they need to work well together. This is not magic either. 90% of it is about partnerships:
   - Centre Backs need to be aware of each other's positions.
   - Full Backs and wide Midfielders need to be aware of each other's positions so that they don't over-expose their flanks, but also maintain width in attack
   - Central Midfielders need to work together to ensure that at least one of them is protecting the back four as the team moves forward
   - The no.9 and no.10 need to work together and be aware of each other's movement and runs

This analysis is a little over-simplistic, but it describes 90% of what makes football teams work. It is easy to get distracted by other factors, but Wenger does not often fall into this trap. And that is why his teams perform so consistently. He is not one of the game's great innovators, but few are.

Occasionally Managers come along who fundamentally change the game, and of course these are Managers who think beyond the basics. Herbert Chapman was one of these, as were Jimmy Hogan and John Reynolds who we met earlier in this book. Bill Shanky was an innovator, as were Rinus Michels, Johann Cruyff and Pep Guardiola. We might, at a stretch, add Matt Busby and Brian Clough to this list, but probably not other top Managers such as Paisley, Mourinho or Ferguson, who were great leaders, but not really innovators.

Most good football Managers, simply manage the basics well; it seems to me that Arsène does this more consistently than any Manager I have ever seen.

CHAPTER FORTY SEVEN
IT'S HAPPENED AGAIN

So there it is, the story of a football season. Not the one I set out to write; of glory and victory, but a story none the less. Arsenal played 27 games at home, selling over 1.5 million tickets at about £50 each to watch the game. I'm hoping that a few of you might pay £10 or so to read a nice review of our story. If you've read this far, then I hope you liked it.

It turns out that my wife was right to suggest I write a book about Arsenal after all. I published articles regularly on Untold Arsenal all season. I enjoyed writing them, I got useful feedback, and those articles are mostly reproduced as chapters in this book. Whilst I was writing, it appears that my family continued to eat cash at an alarming rate, but I had less time to spend any myself. Maybe I can plug some of the holes by selling some of these books. Even if I don't, I feel the journey was worth the effort. I am quite impressed with myself (and actually surprised) that I managed to get to the end. Thanks for coming with me. I now need a short sleep. Six months ought to do it!

After Mikel Arteta's final goal of the season, I took my head out of the metaphorical football clouds and noticed that some remarkable things were going on in the rest of the world:

- Wars in Iraq, Syria and Afghanistan don't seem to be any nearer to conclusion. However, lots more people have died. This seems far more important than Arsenal, but somehow so far away
- Donald Trump was, rather extraordinarily, still in the race to be US President. This was now less funny than it had been last summer, and more disturbing
- Gun massacres continued in the US and Barack Obama continued to look bemused at his compatriots' hostility to gun controls

- Britain voted to exit the EU!!! How did this happen? I was busy watching the football!
- For those of us who grew up in the Thatcher years, it was rather reassuring to have another female prime minister, Theresa May. It felt like the natural order was restored!
- England still weren't very good at football, exiting the Euro 16 championship at the hands of mighty Iceland
- Cristiano Ronaldo was in tears of pain when a knee injury forced him off the pitch in the final of Euro 16, turning to tears of joy when Portugal won in extra time. Ronaldo is much maligned - and indisputably egocentric - but I rather respect him. He is incredibly hard working and has an indomitable spirit - you will do well to catch him ever giving less than 100% effort, on or off the field. He may be arrogant, but he has earnt his success through hard work and persistence. His shirt-removal habit may be narcissistic, but it's a torso worth looking at!
- After the tragedy of losing the Euro 16 final to Portugal in Paris, France suffered real tragedy when 85 people, including ten children, were murdered by a supporter of the dying "Islamic State". Sadly France, the birthplace of modern liberty, seems to be the target of choice for these people. I cried in my heart for France; for liberté, egalité, fraternité; for the beautiful religion of Islam that has given so much to the world; and whose good name is being besmirched by misguided terrorists. Vive la France
- The European refugee crisis continued. The stories of lost people and broken homes continue to tear at our consciences and our sympathies
- Alexis Sanchez won the Copa America with Chile for the second summer in succession. Victory was sealed in a penalty shootout in which Lionel Messi missed his penalty, dragging it horribly wide (I can do that!). Messi promptly retired from international football following his fourth defeat in a major final

IT'S HAPPENED AGAIN

My bet is that this will be remembered as the 'It's happened again season'. Never before has a season been quite so similar to those which preceded it (if you'll forgive The Oxymoron). The last day of 2015-16 was perhaps its finest moment. There were some good results: the home victory over Manchester United; the defeat of an exceptional Bayern Munich team; the home win over Manchester City that promised so much; the away win over Olympiacos that completed a great escape. But ultimately none of these wins really delivered anything worthwhile - these games are unlikely to be spoken of in hushed terms by future generations. By way of contrast, the 21st consecutive celebration of St Totteringham's Day was special. I observed, when discussing Matthieu Flamini's legacy, that it matters not only what happens, but what happens after. If there is a 22nd consecutive St Totteringham's Day then the magic of the 21st will be diluted, and perhaps this book's last claim to fame will melt into the ether of history. However much I want to sell books, I can't quite bring myself to hope that Spurs beat us next year.

In a much wider sense, it really did all happen again. For the 129th season, 11 men ran around a field kicking a ball, while others cheered them on. Each home match was attended by roughly sixty thousand souls. As always, we both decayed and renewed during the season. As Nick Hornby predicted at our beginning, some of our community didn't make it to the end. The stones outside the North Bank still state their quiet messages insistently to the world, but a few more of them now are messages from beyond the grave. Farewell to our departed; I hope they died with Arsenal top of the League. We also welcomed many new members to the Goonersphere, attending their first match, falling in love with the artistry of Mesut Ozil, or just following their parents down the road of supporting the reds. For the vast majority of us who were there at the start and the finish, we are a year older, a year wiser, slightly greyer and a little more sanguine (a lot greyer if you were writing a book as you went along). Babies were born, parents were lost, wars were fought and prime ministers fell and rose.

TIM CHARLESWORTH

For the WOB, the discontented and the cynical, this season was déjà vu all over again. We fell short in the league through an inexplicable run of poor results; injuries plagued us, Wenger promised jam tomorrow and told us what a 'good spirit' there was in the squad. We finished in the top four without ever really threatening to be champions, we qualified from the Group stage of the Champions League, but lost in the first knock-out round. We were not bold in the transfer market, nor did we throw money around in a desperate attempt to win trophies. Wenger was measured, consistent; ungracious in defeat, generous in victory.

Above all, Arsène Wenger's Arsenal are incredibly consistent. This is a rare sporting achievement, but it is almost as if fans have become tired of the purgatory of lukewarm success. Some people seem to crave the rollercoaster ride that we have been denied for so long. Wizened old fans suggest that if we sack Wenger and splash some wild cash on players who may or may not turn out to be any good, the likely result is that we will finish outside the top four. And I think the discontented probably accept that this is true. Football is a game of emotions, highs and lows, good and bad. The young hotheads are yearning for those extremes, even if the lows are more likely than the highs. The one thing that they don't want is for the same thing to happen again.

To be continued (until death do us part)…

THANKS

My long-suffering, genius editor, Emma Marlow

Claire Smith Photography (cover photo) of **www.clairesmithphotography.co.uk**

Tony Attwood (Arsenal historian and publisher of Untold Arsenal). Also all-round good chap who has always been very supportive and kind to me

The Arsenal Independent Supporters Association (AISA)

Sally Davis (biographer of Henry Norris)

Trevor Hicks for making the world a better place. I am so sorry for your loss. I never met them, but I will never forget your girls

Dave Cutcliffe (final edit and the man who taught me to love Arsenal). He was the man who shared the 1979 Arsenal vs. Man U FA Cup Final with my father and six-year-old me. I suspect I will recall that afternoon on my deathbed

My wife, for everything including putting up with my quasi-amusing jokes about her in this book

My mother, for teaching me to really understand literature

The staff of the British Library (who tolerated a lot of stupid questions!)

ACKNOWLEDGEMENTS

WEBSITES

Untold Arsenal (**www.untold-arsenal.com**). Run by Arsenal historian and all round good-egg, Tony Attwood; publishing articles by a variety of authors, including me! The site the best place on the web for intelligent discussion about matters Arsenal

The Gooner magazine. The original Arsenal fanzine, now online as the Online Gooner (**www.onlinegooner.com**)

Angry of Islington (**www.angryofislington.com**). Produced by a slightly bad tempered Gooner, Phil Wall, who publishes infrequently, but is always worth reading

7am Kick off (**7amkickoff.com**)

Arseblog (**www.arseblog.com**). The best written of the blogs and certainly the most professionally produced. Andrew Mangan also produces the 'Arsecast Extra', the best podcast on the web

A Cultured Left Foot. (**www.aclfarsenal.co.uk**)

The Arsenal History (**www.thearsenalhistory.com**)

www.wrightanddavis.co.uk/norris (a remarkable biographical website about Arsenal's first hero, Henry Norris)

Most of the statistics in this book are sourced from **www.arsenal.com** and **www.bbc.co.uk**

www.wikipedia.com (general source for everything)

www.theswissramble.com. By far the most intelligent analysis of football finance available anywhere. In fact some of the best football writing full stop is on this site

The Fink Tank by Danny (now Lord) Finkelstein is not really a website, but more of a column published in The Times. It is probably the most intelligent and well thought out statistical analysis of football in existence

BOOKS

"Arsènal, the making of a modern superclub", Alex Fynn and Kevin Witcher

"Arsène Wenger: The Inside Story of Arsenal Under Wenger", John Cross

"The Crowd at Woolwich Arsenal", Mark Andrews

"Woolwich Arsenal FC: 1893-1915 The club that changed football", Tony Attwood, Andy Kelly and Mark Andrews

"The End: 80 Years of Life on the Terraces: 80 Years of Life on Arsenal's North Bank", Tom Watt

"Invincible: Inside Arsenal's Unbeaten 2003-2004 Season", Amy Lawrence

"So Paddy got up - an Arsenal anthology", edited by Andrew Mangan

"Addicted", Tony Adams and Ian Ridley

"How Not to Be a Professional Footballer", Paul Merson

"We All Live in a Perry Groves World", Perry Groves and John McShane

"Arsène & Arsenal", Alex Fynn and Kevin Whitcher

"Fever Pitch", Nick Hornby

"Winning", Clive Woodward

"Bounce: The Myth of Talent and the Power of Practice", Matthew Syed

"Black Box Thinking: Marginal Gains and the Secrets of High Performance", Matthew Syed

Tim is a 44 year old father of three who lives in Berkshire. The institutions responsible for his education are Dolphin School, St. Paul's School, the University of Bristol and Cranfield School of Management. He enjoyed every minute of them all.

In his quieter moments (when not watching Arsenal) Tim is an accountant, economist, water company manager, dog owner, friend, son, grandson, uncle, brother, godfather, squash player, runner, tennis player, swimmer, footballer, school governor, former local councillor and Parliamentary candidate; and most importantly, a dad and husband.

He is also the inventor of the world's finest socks, but that's another story entirely...

15536231R00241

Printed in Poland
by Amazon Fulfillment
Poland Sp. z o.o., Wrocław